Prince Ibrahim's Favorite

A Novel

© Nancy Hartwell Enonchong, 2013

Cover illustration by
Kitty McNaughton

Tammy Simmons has just been emancipated after more than five years as a harem and brothel slave on the Persian Gulf. She has become the very happy and grateful fourth wife of the man who rescued her, the newly appointed Minister of Foreign Affairs of Cameroon.

She is suddenly faced with overwhelming adjustments: recovering from years of degradation and close confinement and reinserting herself into a confusing and intimidating world, being the lowest-ranking wife in a polygamous household, learning how to live in exciting and proudly African Cameroon, and the very public life of a wife of a prominent personality. She thought she could push a button and return to her pre-enslavement persona, but being back in the real world is a lot more difficult than she had expected.

At first, Prince Ibrahim, her most recent master, is a very good sport about losing his favorite slave. As time goes on, however, he realizes that none of his other girls can hold a candle to his beloved Mukhmala, and he decides that he wants her back…

Become better acquainted with the harem girls you will meet in this book in the companion volume, *Voices from the Harem,* where they each tell their own story of abduction, betrayal, and enslavement.

This book is dedicated to all the girls locked away in a
harem,
far from their homelands,
wrenched away from their families and loved ones,
unable to communicate with the outside world,
and whose very survival now depends on the whims of
the men who bought them.

You are not forgotten.

This book continues the story from *Harem Slave Girl: One Thousand, Nine Hundred and Four Days of Hell on the Persian Gulf.*
However, it may be enjoyed independently.

Its companion volume, *Voices from the Harem,* relates the stories of all 111 girls in Prince Ibrahim's Il Giardino Posteriore Harem (the Rear Garden): how they came to be there, how they have adjusted to slavery, what they think of the harem and their master. It is not a conventional novel. It has no plot, but the individual stories are fascinating and poignant.

Pronunciation notes:

Yerima – YEH ree mah
Aïssatou – Ah YEES a too
Amsaou – AHM sa oo
Yaounde – this is the French spelling of the German distortion of the word
    Ewondo (the major ethnic group in the area). Yah WUN day
Douala – DWA lah
Maroua – MAR oo wah

Many Muslim names in Cameroon are in the nominative case of Arabic, so it's Mohammadou rather than Mohammad, Aïssatou rather than Ayeshah, Ismaëlou rather than Ishmael, Ahmadou rather than Ahmad, etc. The h (*taa marbuta*, or "tied t") at the end of many feminine names in Arabic becomes a t when declined, e.g., Fatimah becomes Fatimatou.

Also, since unexpected syllables are stressed in certain names, they have been written with accents, even though normally they are spelled without, for example, Atángana. French names have been written with accents as correct in French, e.g., Gérard.

Many African names begin with one-letter syllables, M or N, such as Mveng or Nsom. Most non-Africans find this puzzling, and wind up overcomplicating things. It's actually easy. Just say the sound Mm or Nn (not em, not um, not meh), just M, then the rest of the word. After a few tries you'll be able to do it with no problem.

CHAPTER ONE

Tammy Simmons, now Sudari Abdoulaye, was feeling very intimidated, very foreign, and clutched the arm of her handsome new husband Yerima with both hands as he led her into the dining room. She managed a tentative smile as she was introduced to his senior wife Aïssatou, his second wife Amsaou, and his third wife JoAnn. Aïssatou kissed her warmly on both cheeks. Amsaou rose and gave her a big hug. JoAnn looked pointedly out the window.

"This is Sudari, as I'm sure you've guessed. JoAnn, it means jewel, by the way. I'm asking for all of you to be understanding and helpful to her. I've told you her story, how she spent more than five years in the most horrible type of bondage, and was very nearly tortured to death for getting revenge on a man who had constantly tormented her. She's been through extremely traumatic experiences and it may take her a while to adjust to normal life."

"As if this household is anything resembling normal," Aïssatou remarked, rolling her eyes.

"Well, as close to normal as we have around here," he said with a chuckle.

"I'm very happy to finally be here in Cameroon," Tammy said, "and want so hard to do things right. I know I'll screw up, but I promise to try my best."

"I'm sure you'll do just fine," Aïssatou said.

"We're delighted to meet you and promise that we'll do whatever we can to help you," said Amsaou.

"Hmpf," said JoAnn.

Yerima's eyes narrowed, and he adjusted the folds of his ice-blue gandoura with annoyance. "All right, let's get down to business. Madame Prime Minister, what's going on with the servants' quarters?"

"I'm in the process of reviewing four bids. I've eliminated one because I was offered a kick-back. Allah! Don't people know me by now?" Aïssatou shook her head in exasperation. "And, Mr. President, I'd like to give an update on the pilferage case. I interviewed all the kitchen staff and reviewed the feed from the security cameras and it became clear that the guilty party was Oumarou. I have fired him and am considering legal action."

"What's the value of the missing supplies?" Yerima asked.

"At least 700,000 cfa."

"Excuse me, please, sir," said Tammy, "how much is that, please?"

"Around fourteen hundred dollars. Give him thirty days. Restitution or prosecution. That's substantial. Anything else? Finance?"

"We're considerably over budget, as a result of Alizée's excesses," reported Amsaou. "We're still recovering from her vacation to the Seychelles and that party she threw."

"Great party, though," remarked Yerima, "but in any case, she's history and we'll do the best we can to get back on track. By the way, I got an email from her the other day and she sends her regards. She plans to remarry. Owner of a jewelry store there in Grenoble."

Appreciative laughter. "Perfect," said Amsaou, "If he also owns a shoe store and a dress boutique, it'll be even better."

"And a travel agency," added Aïssatou. "Please extend our warmest congratulations and our wishes for every happiness."

"Arrogant bitch is finally out of our hair," snapped JoAnn, "and I notice that it took our esteemed husband no time whatsoever to find a replacement. Only this time, instead of a countess and sculptor, our co-wife is a professional whore."

Tammy stiffened.

Yerima turned to JoAnn. "I asked for your understanding and support, if I'm not mistaken. Do you wish to apologize?"

"I said nothing that isn't absolutely true and see no reason why I should offer an apology." She raised her chin and met his gaze.

"I was a slave, and my master leased me to work in a men's club," Tammy said evenly. "That's a long shot from making a voluntary career choice."

"A woman who gives sex to men she doesn't know is a whore to me," countered JoAnn.

A sigh. "She was a *slave*, JoAnn. It wasn't her idea at all, and it's a miracle that she survived."

"I thought slavery had been outlawed."

"Of course, just about everywhere, but there are more slaves on earth right now than at any time in human history. Passing a law is one thing. Eradicating the

9

practice is something else altogether." Yerima decided to get back to business. "So, Madame Minister of Agriculture, what's going on?"

"Wait a minute, please, Mr. President, I haven't finished," protested Amsaou. "Shall I transfer the remaining budget from the now-defunct Ministry of Cultural Affairs to the new Ministry of Education? How should we handle that?"

"Sorry. Yes, sure, normally that would be the way to go, but it would mean that Sudari starts with a deficit. Do we have a surplus anywhere that we can tap into until she can get her new undertaking up and running?"

"Yes, sir, Agriculture is running a nice surplus."

"Then please adjust the budget accordingly."

"May I please point out," said JoAnn hotly, "that our surplus is due to extremely careful management, and because we haven't yet purchased all the plant material we need for landscaping the perimeter fence. So basically you're punishing me, and I must strongly object, Mr. President, sir."

"We're not punishing you at all; we're just trying to get Education going. What else do you suggest?"

"You're taking resources away that we had already programmed for the benefit of this entire compound. Already approved."

"We're all aware of that, and commend you for your excellent management. But money has to come from somewhere, and it's going to come from Agriculture. That's my decision and if you have a problem with it you will talk to me after the meeting. Am I clear?"

"Yes sir." She eyed him defiantly.

"And, finally, our new Minister of Education. Welcome to the household business meeting. What do you have in mind?"

Tammy smiled nervously. "I haven't even met the children yet, but I know I'll need books and supplies. I'd like to get to know them, figure out what pushes their buttons, and use that as a launching pad for improving their academic skills. I plan to emphasize reading, writing, and vocabulary, which are fundamental to everything."

"We meet every Tuesday right after lunch and we try to keep it to fifteen minutes. Anything else? All right then, thanks, everybody. You're all doing a terrific, terrific job."

Tammy stared adoringly at Yerima. She was actually his wife, and was in Yaounde with him, and it was amazing. Amazing.

"Yerima, I need to talk to you," said JoAnn, with fire in her voice.

"Sudari, my dear, let me give you a tour of the *saré*," said Aïssatou, "unless you're busy with something else?"

"No ma'am, not at all, ma'am. And thank you, ma'am. First, though, may I ask a dumb question? I've never before seen a tablecloth embroidered with spiders."

Aïssatou laughed. "That throws a lot of Europeans." She caught herself. "Here, anybody who isn't African is called European. Even if you're Japanese or Mexican, we call you European. The tablecloth is from Yerima's

11

home town. Maroua is an extremely rich center of African handicrafts, especially textiles and leather. Hand-spun, hand-woven, and hand-embroidered cotton, grown right there. And, my dear, we like spiders. We admire them for their resourcefulness, their ability to make something out of nothing, and we think that their webs are architectural marvels.

"But back to our tour. The *saré* is more like a small village. Right now we have 74 people living here, and we feed another fifty or so every day. There's Yerima, the four of us, the nine children, assorted cousins and nephews and abused wives and other relatives, twelve staff, and nine emancipated slaves who used to belong to Yerima's father. This is the family dining room, of course. Over here is the state dining room – that's getting a lot of use with his new job – and here's the butler's pantry, the fully equipped commercial-style kitchen, the staff dining room, and the supply room. Oh, Chef Emmanuel, please meet Madame Sudari, His Excellency's newest wife. She's originally from right outside Washington. Chef Emmanuel is amazing. Every single thing he makes is delicious, and he even makes his own pâté."

"Wow! I'm so happy to meet you, Chef. Do you know how to make catfish creole, by any chance?" Tammy asked.

The chef bowed. "Yes indeed, Madame Sudari. Welcome to Cameroon. Is that what you'd like for dinner tonight?"

The chef had bowed. To her! Tammy turned to Aïssatou. "You mean, ma'am, I'm allowed to choose?"

"Within reason, my dear."

"Oh, Chef Emmanuel, you have no idea how happy that would make me. I haven't had catfish creole in ages. Thank you so much."

"My pleasure, madame. And again, welcome."

What a strange but wonderful new world, people bowing to her. And letting her pick out what to eat.

The tour continued. "Upstairs are eight guest suites – right now two of Yerima's brothers are visiting – and this wing down here is Yerima's: his office, his bedroom, his gym. It's kept locked because of all the confidential documents he deals with. This new job is already eating him alive, you know. Meetings all day, receptions every night. And it's wearing me out too, because I attend official events with him, and now there's one practically every evening. I used to write my judgments at night, and I'm getting behind."

"By the way, ma'am, I just want to tell you how much I admire you. Yerima told me how your father tried to force you into marriage and how you ran away and managed to finish your education. I admire that so much. You understand how tough things can be when everything, and I mean everything, is stacked against you, and I just admire you so much."

The senior wife took her hands. "Thank you, Sudari, that's very nice of you. And you don't need to call me ma'am." She smiled. "Although, I must confess, I like it. I distinctly remember the first time someone called me ma'am. Here in Africa, we're taught to defer to men, obey men, depend completely on men, and it's painfully hard to break that cycle. So when I was appointed to the bench, and people – even men! – started calling me ma'am, it was quite a thrill. Yerima told us your story, and you've really got guts.

13

Sometime, I'd like to sit down and chat with you. I'm very interested in the institution of slavery and it'd be fascinating to hear it from someone who's actually experienced it."

"With pleasure, ma'am. And I don't mind calling you ma'am one bit. I said yes sir and yes master so many times that I just about wore out the words, but it feels downright good to say yes ma'am to a woman. And about being a slave, I can tell you how it is in one word: horrible. The Office was the worst. I spent sixteen or seventeen hours a day providing the most revolting services you can imagine to disgusting men. Even though they were generals and oil tycoons, most of them were horrible, and treated me like dirt. If it hadn't been for Yerima, who was always so much fun, I would've gone stark raving insane. When we had a big fight I got so depressed I wanted to commit suicide, but they control you so minutely, it just wasn't possible."

"But you did manage to commit murder."

"We didn't think of it as murder, ma'am, it was revenge. Sweet, sweet revenge. For years, that man tormented us, betrayed us, lied to us, humiliated us, ground us under his foot. Nenzima and I finally had our chance, and we grabbed it."

"Nenzima? That's a Mangbetu name. A noblewoman's name. My sister-in-law is named Nenzima. From Kinshasa."

"Yes ma'am, Zima was from the Congo. My best friend." Tammy stifled sobs. "She committed suicide before they found us; I was stupid and thought it over too long. If Yerima hadn't rescued me, they would have boiled me in oil. They aren't very nice to slaves who

14

murder Arabs, ma'am, especially Chairman of the Board."

"It's all right, my dear, don't cry. All that's behind you now. Yerima adores you, and he's a very good person. He has his moments – the man has a whopping temper, as I'm sure you know – but for the most part he's easy to get along with, and tries very hard to treat all four of us even-handedly. Amsaou and I grew up in polygamous households, but I must say, he hasn't had much luck with his white wives. Alizée got fed up and went back to Grenoble. I frankly don't understand how they stayed married for sixteen years, because I don't think they ever agreed on anything except when their clothes were off. And now things seem to be rapidly falling apart with JoAnn. Have you ever lived in a polygamous household, my dear?"

"Does being a slave in a polygamous household count?" Tammy made a face.

Aïssatou laughed. "Perhaps. By the way, my dear, do you plan to convert to Islam?"

"One of my owners forced me to convert, which I really resented, so I'd prefer to stay Christian, if that's all right, ma'am."

"Of course. That's a decision of the heart. Catholic?"

"No ma'am, Protestant."

"There's a Presbyterian theological seminary here in town, and they conduct services in English."

"Oh, wow. I'm Methodist, ma'am, but that's close enough."

"Methodists are in the Congo and Presbyterians are here. From what I understand, they decided not to compete. JoAnn's raising Cathy and Michael as Catholics. Yerima's very open-minded about religion; my father would've had a heart attack at the very idea. But this is a Muslim household, and your husband is a Muslim, and you must accept that. He's not a very strict one, but a reasonably devout, practicing Muslim."

"Of course, ma'am. I have no problem with that."

"Plus, as Minister of Foreign Affairs, he's a public figure, which means that overnight, all of us have become public figures as well. We must always dress fashionably but modestly, and comport ourselves in such a manner that there is never any question about our integrity, our fidelity, or our honor. And since he's a member of Government, we must never make any comment that can be construed as being the least bit critical of Antoine. People will try to trick you, and let's face it, Yerima has plenty of enemies, so always be on your guard. If you're ever in doubt, just smile graciously and keep walking. This is an order, my dear: be courteous to everyone, especially the people who deserve it the least."

"That's a very good policy, ma'am. Right now I don't plan to go anywhere, I just want to sit in my apartment and hug Cleo and Titi and thank my lucky stars that Yerima rescued me."

"We do not use pagan expressions in this household, my dear."

"Lucky stars? I never thought about that before, ma'am. Well, then, let me thank Almighty God that Yerima rescued me."

"That's much better. Now, over here is the servants'quarters. Right now it can accommodate 36, but we're expanding it to 60, and that's what we were talking about at the meeting. We say servants, but this is where the cousins and everybody else stays, including my niece who fled from her abusive husband and several girls who ran away rather than be forced into marriage. My son Ismaëlou has turned fourteen and is too big to stay in the women's house, but isn't really mature enough to move to the main house, so when the addition is complete, he'll have his own room here too. The men's bathroom is at the far end, and the women's is over here. Here, let me unlock this room and show you. Not bad, huh? And very clean.

"If you don't keep your room inspection-clean, you risk losing it, and these rooms are in hot demand. If you have a job, you pay 25 percent rent; if you don't, you contribute 20 hours a week to the compound, pulling weeds, peeling plantains, or doing other chores. Over there is the VIP guest house. It has four suites, a salon, a dining room, and a small warming kitchen."

"Marble?" Tammy asked, eyes open wide.

"Yes. Right now, Amsaou's parents are there. You must invite your family to come visit us too. I think they'll be relieved to see that you're not living in a grass hut with lions and hyenas roaming the back yard. Over there is the chicken coop, and there's the vegetable garden, and back there is the flower garden."

"They're gorgeous, absolutely gorgeous, ma'am. And by the way, my dad used to be with the State Department – a specialist in North African affairs – and he spent several weeks with us in the ambassador's residence after Yerima rescued me, so I'm pretty sure they know I'll be living comfortably."

"JoAnn does a beautiful job with the gardens. She's a botany professor at the agricultural school, you know. A good person, a very sweet person, and she loves Yerima profoundly, but she really has issues with being one of four. She was supremely glad when Alizée left – they never got along at all. Unfortunately you two will be sharing a car and driver, but be as understanding as you can. She's number three and you're number four, so you'll need to defer to her. It's the only way we can keep peace."

"I'm not used to going places, ma'am. I'm still getting used to eating real food instead of wolfing something down between assignments, wearing clothes and shoes, walking around without guards, and feeling the sunshine on my skin. I'm just so grateful to be alive that if Yerima told me I'd never be allowed to set foot outside my apartment, I wouldn't mind a bit."

"Speaking of which, that's where you receive your female guests, that's where you sleep except when you are in Yerima's bed. This is the Fulani way. If you ever have a male guest – and you need permission from me or Yerima to do so and there'd better be a damn good reason for it – you will receive him in one of the parlors in the main house and there will always be a third person present. Once again, bear in mind that you are a public figure whose behavior must always be above reproach.

"And remind me to show you the secret entrance to the tunnel and the entry code for the underground bunker. We never know when there might be a *coup,* or some other public disorder. Oh, my dear, I just remembered, I need to put you on Yerima's schedule. We try to work things around female cycles and such. When are you due?"

"I have no idea, ma'am. At the Rainbow Harem I was dyed green, and even though I left there more than three years ago, the toxins are still screwing up my system. And at The Office, they gave us shots that stopped our periods altogether so we could work every single day. I have no idea how long it will take before I'll be a normal female again."

"Did you say, dyed green?" Tammy nodded. "*Ça, alors!* My gracious! Whatever for?"

"Sheikh Fahd thought it looked pretty, ma'am. There were six of us, all different colors."

Aïssatou shook her head. "So, for the time being, at least, we can ignore that? Thursday night, all right? The schedule is posted in the kitchen of the women's house. When it's your turn you report to his room at nine o'clock. First, you completely disrobe. Fold your clothes neatly and place them on a chair. Get in bed and assume the position of absolute surrender. Has he taught you that?"

Tammy nodded.

"Then you wait for his instructions. This is your primary responsibility as a wife and here, we never tell our husbands no. There's no such thing as the 'doghouse' where you American wives send your husbands. When JoAnn told us about that, we positively went into shock. Anyway, here, the husband is in control. When you agreed to marry him, you agreed to submit to him, and as you know, Yerima has enormous

19

needs. Even if you're tired, have a ferocious headache, are so furious with him that you're not speaking to him, you report on time and submit to him. I want to underscore that point. Are we clear here?"

"Yes ma'am. Even if we're not speaking, though?"

"If he sends you away, that is his prerogative. But you must make yourself available."

Tammy sighed. "That's pretty extreme, ma'am, if you don't mind my saying so."

"Did you marry him of your own free will?"

"Yes ma'am."

"What does the word *yérima* mean?"

"It means prince, ma'am."

"You agreed to marry a prince of the proud Fulani people, and that is how we do things. A wife embraces her husband's culture, especially if he is a royal prince."

"Yes ma'am. I love him so much that I even offered to be his servant, out of gratitude for saving my life, so I'm prepared to do just about anything."

"Really? His *servant*?" She stared at Tammy.

"Yes ma'am. I couldn't imagine, simply couldn't imagine, living without him, even if it meant scrubbing pots and mopping floors. In any case, believe me, it would've been a huge, huge step up from being a slave in a brothel."

"You certainly are cut from different cloth than Alizée. She loved Yerima, but she hated everything about his life, everything. Outright culture rejection. Then, when he left for two years to serve as ambassador overseas, it was the last straw. She lived only for her nights with him, and when he was posted far away, she gave up.

"Let me tell you a story, Sudari. My marriage to Yerima got off to a very rocky start. He was a lot more domineering than I'd figured, and we were at each other's throats. We'd been married seven or eight months, and I was preparing for a big exam, and he wanted me to drop everything and do something huge for him. I told him he was out of his mind. He beat me up, and I mean, he really beat me up. I was furious. I reminded Yerima that his *saré* had a back gate just like the one I'd used when I ran away from my father.

"He was floored, because his own mother was beaten every few months and considered it an expression of love. Anyway, four or five days later, I was still so sore I could barely move, I hadn't gotten any studying done because my eyes were almost swollen shut, I regretted like mad having married the man, and he had the nerve, the unmitigated nerve, to summon me.

"Listen, my dear, Fulani women are constituted exactly the same as Americans; the only difference is what our cultures demand of us. I went to his room, but refused to acknowledge him, and he got madder and madder. He took me anyway. Rough. Something broke in me, and I did the unthinkable and rebelled against my husband. To my amazement, that excited him beyond belief, and, let me tell you, Sudari, I've never forgotten that night. You know how manly he is even under normal circumstances, but you get that man super-excited, and you're in for quite a ride.

21

"That night, our marriage turned around. We both remembered how much we loved each other, even when things were tough. He made a commitment to be less demanding, and I promised to be more accommodating, and nineteen years later, we're still here. If I had told him no, which I desperately wanted to do, our marriage might very well have fallen apart."

"He once told me that marrying you was the best decision he ever made, ma'am. And he's exceedingly proud that you're a judge."

"He never said that to me. How do you like that?"

They laughed.

"Well, *pour revenir à nos moutons*, back to the topic at hand. The schedule used to work pretty well, but with this new job, things aren't always predictable. He's more often than not carrying out some official responsibility that preempts marital appointments. And even when they hold, he spends half his time on the phone with Antoine. If things are running late, if he's not too tired, he'll send for you when he gets home. On Sundays we all have dinner together at one, and when that's over, if it's your turn, you accompany him to his room."

"Yes ma'am, I understand. I'm going to try with all my heart to make this work. Yerima saved my life, and I gladly gave that life to him. I desperately want all of you to be proud of me." She rubbed her forehead. "I'm feeling overwhelmed, and I'm still really jet-lagged, and if it's okay with you, ma'am, I'd like to go back to my apartment and lie down."

"Speaking of jet-lagged, how was your visit to Washington?"

"Surreal, ma'am. My dad is great, and my brother is doing fine – he's in college now, and wants to work for the FBI in their human trafficking section – but when I was kidnapped my mom had a nervous breakdown. She's attempted suicide several times, she's been in and out of the hospital, and she's aged at least twenty years. She used to be a hot interior decorator, always elegant and perfectly groomed, but now her hair's scraggly and her complexion is awful and her eyes have this other-worldly look about them and she hasn't been able to work, and I barely recognized her. So it was a big deal for her that I was rescued, and I showed her pictures from the wedding, and we're hoping that she'll be able to turn things around."

Aïssatou almost fell over laughing. Tammy spoke excellent French, but occasionally made mistakes, and she had just delivered a beaut. "My dear, you translated 'nervous breakdown' literally, but we don't say *'panne nerveuse,'* we say *'crise de nerfs.' Panne* does mean breakdown, but only for mechanical items such as automobiles."

Tammy smiled apologetically. "It felt really strange, ma'am, going back to my old room. It hadn't changed, but I have. I was only eighteen then. It was like being in a foreign country. I spent three weeks at home, and then went to Marseilles for a week with Pierre and Clotilde. They'd felt terrible, so it was good to let them know that I was okay and didn't blame them for what happened."

"That's where you were abducted?"

"Yes ma'am. I'm feeling woozy and I really need to lie down, though, ma'am, if that's all right."

"Of course, my dear, you are free to do so."

Tammy smiled. "I like that word. I like that word a lot, ma'am. Thank you for the beautiful tour and your sage advice."

"My warmest welcome to this family. We're already proud of you, Sudari, for having lived through hell, and *alhamdulillah*, praise God, you're still able to smile. I think you'll do just fine."

"*Jam ná?*" Tammy said as she slipped into her chair at the breakfast table and reached for the carafe of coffee. It felt so good, waking up when she felt like it – or more accurately, when the raucous parrots perching in the huge mango tree outside the bedroom window felt like it – actually sitting down for a meal, and wearing her favorite jeans and comfy sweatshirt and fuzzy blue slippers. And she absolutely loved the Arabica coffee, grown and roasted just a few mountains over to the west.

"*Jam,*" everyone chorused.

"JoAnn, did you take the last *pain au chocolat* again?" Tammy asked. "You're always doing that."

JoAnn made a face.

"Sudari, my dear, please go get dressed."

"Ma'am?"

"No lipstick? A baggy sweatshirt and blue jeans? And those blue porcupines on your feet? Who is your husband, please?"

Tammy had to smile. "Minister of Foreign Affairs, ma'am."

"Listen, my dear, you promised to honor him. I'm asking you to honor him with your appearance. Now, go get properly dressed."

"Ma'am, I'm not going anywhere."

"Oh, look at that slob over there. She's the wife of the Minister of Foreign Affairs, can you believe? It's his image we're trying to protect. I'm not going to tell you again. Go get properly dressed. And I don't want to see that sweatshirt and those jeans outside of your apartment again. Or those porcupines."

"Yes ma'am."

JoAnn continued feeding Michael in his high chair and made a snotty face at her.

A few minutes later Tammy returned wearing a navy skirt and yellow blouse.

"My dear? I thought I told you to get dressed."

"I'm sorry, ma'am. I brought a few things back from Washington with me, but they're what I wore in high school. My last job, um, I mean, um, I don't know what else to put on."

Aïssatou stared at her. "Of course. I didn't think of that, my dear. We need to get you a proper wardrobe."

The following Saturday, the senior wife called Tammy to her apartment. "I took the liberty of picking out some *pagnes* that I thought you might like. We'll start you off with ten outfits and gradually build from there, all right? You need to look good."

"Ten? I don't really need more than two or three, ma'am."

"Yes, you do. Your husband is a highly prominent personality and you must always be mindful of your appearance. Tell me which cloth you like."

Tammy went through the stack of traditional cotton prints. Most of her choices were blues and purples, but she liked a red-and-yellow pattern as well as a brown-and-gold one.

Aïssatou showed her a deep green palm frond print, and another with bright green swirls. "I thought this color would look really good on you."

Tammy laughed. "I'm sure it would, ma'am. They're very pretty, but I'm afraid I overdosed on green when I was in the Rainbow Harem. I was dyed green, I wore green gowns and jewels, I ate off green plates, I slept in a green room on green sheets…I just can't bring myself to wear green anymore. At least, not yet. If that's all right with you, ma'am," she added hastily.

"Of course, that's understandable. Now let's get you over to Jacques so he can make you some good-looking clothes, and on the way back we're going to stop and buy you some shoes. High-heeled shoes. I've also chosen a few designs. Which ones do you like?" Tammy made her choices. "All right. What else do you need, my dear?"

"Would it be okay if I bought some perfume? And I need cat food for Cleo and Nefertiti. And a cartridge for my printer. And, um, maybe a chocolate bar?"

"Of course, Sudari." Tammy wiped away a tear. "What brought that on?"

"It's been so long, ma'am, I've almost forgotten what it's like to go shopping."

"Are you afraid?"

"Oh, no, ma'am, I'm just trying to absorb the fact that I need clothes. It's a big change for me. One that I like – very much – but I need to get used to it all over again."

"In Pidgin we say, softly softly, catch monkey. In other words, one small step at a time. We keep a list on the white board in the women's kitchen, and if you need something, just write it down and we can usually get it to you by the next day. The cost will be deducted from your allowance. And listen, on Monday I'll send you my car and I want you to get your hair and your nails done. All right?"

"You're being so good to me. It's actually fun, ma'am, I'm just a little overwhelmed. And thank you so much. The world seems so big and so scary; I never could have done it on my own."

"Yerima wouldn't stand for anything less."

"And I've never been to sub-Saharan Africa before. I like Yaounde, gloriously and proudly African, but I still have to get used to that too."

Late the following afternoon, Fatimatou knocked on Tammy's door, carrying a package neatly wrapped in brown paper. "Madame Aïssatou asked me to bring this to you."

Jacques had already finished sewing all ten outfits. She stared at them. Ran her fingers over the smooth cloth. She tried one on. He hadn't even measured her, but it fit perfectly. Stared at them some more. Smiled. Not the ill-fitting stained hand-me-down at Sheikh Khalid's.

Not the boring uniform at The House. Not the frilly fairy princess ball gowns at the Rainbow. Clothes. Real clothes. That belonged to *her*. It was good to be free.

Thursday evening at three minutes to nine, Tammy knocked on Yerima's bedroom door. A buzzer sounded, and she opened it.

He was sitting up in bed. He moved a stack of files to one side, grinned impishly, and said, "Welcome, welcome, little wifey."

Tammy saluted. "Reporting for duty, dear sir." She took off her clothes, folded them neatly as instructed, and climbed into bed.

"Let me get rid of these stupid dossiers. This job is the most fun I've had in years, but it's relentless. How are you, babe?"

"Aïssatou tells me that I must submit to you no matter how I feel, so I dragged myself over here and suppose that you'll figure out something to do with me." She smiled wickedly.

"Ah," he said, "Chances are, I'll think of something. But don't forget, babe, you're in my bed, so rules apply."

Tammy groaned. "We're married now. Please don't tell me I still have to call you master, because bless your generous heart, you emancipated me."

"You only have to call me master when we're in bed. But I insist on that."

She slumped. "Actually, Yerima, I was hoping I'd never have to say that word again. I don't even want to hear about anybody with a master's degree, or mastering a language. Forgive me if I'm being a little sensitive, dear sir. Are you sure about this?"

"Damn sure. All my systems revolve around the fact that when you're in my bed, I'm your loving master and you're my devoted slave. And you know that my systems work, um, very well." He looked at her sideways, eyebrows dancing.

She sighed. "They do, they do, I admit. Can we compromise? Can I call you *jaumu?* I know it means the same thing, but my brain doesn't seem to object to it so much."

"Yes, babe, you may. I just want to say, welcome. Welcome to Cameroon. Welcome to my household. Welcome, most especially, to my bed. I'm sorry we didn't have a chance to take a honeymoon, and I know that you really needed to go see your family, but here we are, married six weeks, and this is the first time that you've actually been in this bed. That month you were visiting your folks, I missed you so much. Don't you leave me like that ever again, you hear? I married you because I couldn't live without you, and then I had to spend a whole month without you anyway." He gave her a long kiss. "Do you remember how to give cat baths?"

"Of course, *jaumu.*" She set happily to work, starting with his broad, muscular shoulders. Not a disgusting hairy member of The Office. Her husband. Her extremely gorgeous husband. Oh, what delicious fun!

"I want to hear all about your trip. Later, though. Holy shit, you're good at that."

29

And holy shit, how it was turning her on.

The phone rang.

"I don't care if it's the President himself," she said, "I'm not going to miss one single second of private time with my darling *jaumu*." By this time she was making little circles with her tongue on his abdomen, getting closer and closer to Grand Central.

"Well, guess what, it just so happens to be the President himself. Hey, cuz, what's up? Yes, it went reasonably well. A frosty start, but toward the end there were a few smiles. If this is going to happen, it'll be behind the scenes, not at the table. Of course, of course, I'm on it. Yow! Holy shit! No, um, there's a very wicked blonde here doing some very wicked things to me and I'm not going to be coherent much longer. Okay, I sure will. Antoine says hi."

"Does he call you at this hour of the night very often, *jaumu*?"

"I'm afraid he does. But he's my boss, so I try to live with it. Can you show the little prince how much you love him?"

Tammy knew what that meant from their succulent encounters at The Office. Expert fingers. Clever tongue. The little prince was feeling very cocky indeed, and the big one started moaning and clutching her.

The phone rang.

"Shit! Hey, cuz. It's all right, don't worry. Oh, you heard about that already? Yes, I fired him for *faute lourde* – grave misconduct. Signed the papers just this afternoon. He was mad as hell, says he's going to haul my ass into Labor Court. No, not in the least, we've got an iron-clad case. No, Antoine, I can't transfer him to the boonies because of course Foreign Affairs doesn't have offices in the boonies. I just plain fired him, as he richly deserved. Tony, my dear cuz, excuse me for being blunt, but I could care less whose brother he is. You pay way too much attention to that crap. If this country is ever going to move forward, we need to hold people accountable for their own actions and not let them perpetually hide behind someone else. Huh? Which joint commission? To tell the truth, that hasn't even crossed my radar screen. Okay, I'll add that to my list." He turned to Tammy. "Antoine apologizes."

"He apologizes, but he still interrupts." She sighed.

"Hello?"

"All right, dammit. *Jaumu*."

"I don't approve of the way you said that. He's my boss, the President himself, and if he calls me, I answer."

She smirked. "Just like Ibrahim required of me: immediately, fully, and willingly. Darling, he's your *boss*, not your master."

He stared at her strangely for a moment, absorbing what she said. Then his high-voltage smile sent her heart racing and the interruption was forgotten. "My sexy little slave is now going to suck her master's toes. Slowly. Luxuriously. Sumptuously."

"*Jaumu*, you have the longest, most beautiful toes I ever saw in my life. I don't think I ever said those words in the same sentence before, but it's true."

"Stop wasting time and get to work." He grinned. After a few minutes he straddled her and covered her face, her shoulders, her chest, with kisses made of molten gold. She began to whimper. "Oh," he said, "your jewel has grown nice and fat. Ready for a visit."

Forty-five minutes later, she lay contentedly in his arms, heart pounding fiercely, her body filled from one end to the other with golden light.

"Whoever'd imagine that this cool, classy lady would turn out to be such a ball of fire? Hey, babe, what's wrong?" he asked, wiping a tear from her eye.

"Nothing, nothing at all. I just can't believe this. Here I am, rescued from a psycho, the wife of the Minister of Foreign Affairs, and I'm in his own bed, and he's a prince, and a person I respect in so many ways, and an incredible lover, and I just can't hold it all in."

"I love you with all my heart, Sudari, and believe me, we are going to have one fantastic marriage. By the way, babe, how long do you think it'll take you to learn to speak Fulfulde?"

"Oh, to get along, probably five or six months. Really well, two years. *Jaumu*," she added quickly.

"Because I want to take you up to Maroua, and show you my horse ranch, and introduce you to all the family, including my brother Daoudou, the *lamido,* or sultan. But you need to speak decent Fulfulde first. A lot of people up there don't speak French."

The phone rang.

This time, it was the Minister of Finance. "Yes, Seydou, he just called me about that too. I hadn't even given it a passing thought, but he wants it racheted up on the list of priorities. Can we please chat about this tomorrow? I'm, um, I'm with my bride." Chuckles. "*Mañana*, then." He turned to Tammy, who was glaring at him. "Where were we?"

"We were going up-country to see relatives and horses. *Jaumu*." She was getting sarcastic.

He looked at her disapprovingly but let it pass. "Turn over," he said. "Round two." Blessedly, the phone stopped ringing, and two hours later, they finally fell asleep, snuggled into each other's arms.

In the middle of the night, Tammy woke up screaming.

"Babe, babe, it's all right, I'm here. What happened?"

"I'm sorry," she blubbered. "I was back at the Rodeo, hanging from that meat hook, hearing the screams of the people they were torturing, and I knew that in a few days that would be me."

He held her tightly and covered her face with kisses. "That's all behind you, babe. You're safe now."

"I'm sorry," she said, gathering herself.

"You went through hell, that's for sure. But I'm here for you, remember? You think you can get back to sleep now?"

She nodded. "Thanks, darling. Thank you thank you thank you."

"It's why I'm here. Now, babe, go back to sleep. I'm here. I won't let anything happen to you."

When the alarm went off at six-fifteen they reluctantly untangled themselves. "Seven-thirty breakfast meeting with a South African delegation," he said. "Isn't it fun waking up in each other's arms? We never got to do that at The Office."

She smiled. At The Office, he'd always turn off his phone so they could spend hours together in uninterrupted bliss. But now he was Minister of Foreign Affairs, and his cousin was the President, and she was his wife instead of his favorite slave at the gentlemen's club. Life had most assuredly changed. And most of it – almost all of it – was much for the better.

Tammy picked up the house phone. "Yes, darling?"

"Can you come over here, please? I need you to help me with a project. I think you'll like it."

"Okay, is thirty minutes okay? I need to–"

"No, sorry, babe, I need you now."

She sighed. She wanted to finish matching up the *al-hijra* and Gregorian dates for her manuscript. Another sigh. She'd given him her life, and now he needed a little piece of it. Inconvenient, but not the end of the world. "All right, darling, I'll be right there." She brushed her hair, put on fresh lipstick, and walked over to the main house.

It was a beautiful day. An early morning rain had made everything smell fresh and clean, and monkeys were chattering excitedly from the woods at the northwest corner of the property. A long line wound up the front porch, down the sidewalk, almost all the way to the gate. Dixon, the major-domo, was taking everyone's name, joking, working the good-natured crowd.

Yerima was in the elegant blue-and-silver main parlor, looking every inch the prince in a pale yellow gandoura. He gave her a thousand-watt smile and patted the couch next to him. She swallowed and sucked in her breath. Sometimes she forgot just how magnificent her husband was. She felt overwhelmed with love and humility, overcome by the need to thank him in a very public way for freeing her from slavery and giving her such a beautiful life.

"May I sit at your feet, dear sir? To show everybody how much I respect you?"

"No, madame, you may not. I want you to sit right here next to me, so I can show everybody how much I respect *you*." He handed her his laptop. "This is petition day," he explained. "All these people need something. Some of them just need a few francs for a prescription. Others need help getting a messy situation sorted out. Some are merrily trying to wangle something for nothing. A few of them are so annoying, you want to strangle them. You help with one thing, then they turn right around and demand – demand! – something else. Just like the Arab saying, You give someone cloth, and then he asks for lining.

"Anyway, things were getting out of hand, so Amsi created this database. Dixon will give you the name on a slip of paper. What I need you to do is to check it. If you see something questionable, show me, and I'll know what to do. And then enter whatever I give them so we have a record of it for next time."

"There must be close to a hundred people waiting to see you."

"I do this once a month, and sometimes there are a lot more than that. When school starts, everybody needs help with fees and books and uniforms. And when the holidays hit, of course. Most of them are relatives, but some come because they can see the word *sucker* written across my forehead in flashing red lights. Dixon? All right, please, we can get going."

The first petitioner bowed deeply before the prince. His roof had been damaged by a recent storm and he needed help to pay for the repairs. He showed Yerima two different bids. Tammy checked; he hadn't requested help in nearly two years. Yerima gave him the money he needed, and the man bowed his way out. *"Úsoko, úsoko."* Thank you, thank you.

The second was a woman whose four children needed shoes. Her husband was in prison and she made so little selling beans and rice by the side of the road that she couldn't afford them. It had been more than six months since she'd requested help, so Yerima gave her money.

And so it went. New eyeglasses, help with a motorbike repair, pleas for jobs, vouchers for visits to the compound infirmary, a toolkit for a young mechanic, a sewing machine repair, a new lens for a photographer. One man tried to get money for a prescription that was more than two years old; Yerima yelled at him and sent him away. "He thought we'd never notice. But don't worry," he said, "he'll soon be back. Once he bandaged his left foot but forgot and limped with the right one. He thinks he's really clever. Be sure to put down what he attempted to do."

One woman wore an extremely revealing décolleté and made no bones about coming onto him. "You do a favor for me," she said, "and I'll do a favor for you, Your Highness, that you'll never forget."

"You're quite beautiful, and I appreciate the offer, but I'm well served in that respect by my lovely wife here." She said her boss at the garment factory gave her a poor review because she refused to sleep with him. Yerima said he'd be happy to look into the matter. "Happens more than you'd like to know," he told Tammy. "Sexual harassment at work is still pretty common. We need more women executives, more women in responsible positions. And continue to educate men that just because women report to them at work, it doesn't confer other, uh, benefits. She's probably telling the truth."

Two teen-age nephews had come together, and all they wanted was pocket money. Yerima gently lectured them about getting an education so they could make something of themselves. He cited several examples from the family, including himself, hoping to inspire them.

They listened politely, and then stared at him in confusion. "But Uncle, why should we go to all that trouble, when we have you?"

Yerima leapt to his feet, looking far taller than six-feet-one, his legendary temper suddenly and terrifyingly on full display. Tammy shrank to as small as possible, and Dixon ducked. They exchanged uneasy glances. "With that attitude, you two leave this compound right this second and don't come back until you both get jobs or are both back in school. Dixon, alert the gate not to admit them any longer, even to eat. I said, get going! What the hell are you two waiting for?"

They slunk off, casting black looks behind them.

Dixon called the gendarme on the spot, while Tammy nervously made notes in the database. Yerima sat back down, so maybe it was safe to look up again. Whew. The raging storm had passed as quickly as it had formed.

He gave her a big grin. "The principal downside to petition day, shameless leeches. Okay, Dixon, let's continue."

Dozens more of the same. At length Dixon said, "It's three o'clock, so I've cut off the line, Excellency. "Eighty-two today."

Yerima nodded. "Since we started keeping good records, the numbers have dropped off substantially. Funny thing about that. How many people did you turn away?"

"About fifteen, Your Excellency."

"So, you told them to come earlier next time?"

"Of course, Your Excellency." He sounded just a touch annoyed.

Yerima chuckled. "Sorry, Dixon. I ask you that every month, don't I? I mean no disrespect. This is the last time I ask that. I promise. And I apologize."

"No problem, Your Excellency, I understand."

"This database is amazing," said Tammy. "Amsi's an absolute genius, and somebody should write a study about all the people you help. Today you have profoundly affected the lives of all these people, and you act like it's the most normal thing in the world."

"It is. It's called the African extended family, and there's nothing, and I mean nothing, more important than that. Almighty God has blessed me richly, and now it's my responsibility to pass the blessings along. This is the main reason I get up in the morning, Sudari, to be able to help people who deserve it so much. What's the total so far, babe?"

It was more than most people made in an entire year. "Yerima, my love, my hero, my darling, what I like is the way you talk to them. You don't look down on them. You say it was a pleasure to help, and the way you smile, they know it really was."

"I told you you'd like this project," he said. "See? The fellow you married isn't such a bad sort after all. Alizée hated this; she just saw it as a drain of money."

Tammy gave him a huge kiss, right in front of Dixon, right in front of the next petitioner. "Not at all. It's stimulating the economy. It's helping people cope with what life throws their way. The fellow I married amazes me more every day. I'm so proud to be your wife right now I could positively explode."

"Wait until tomorrow night for that," he whispered, eyebrows dancing with mischief.

Next day, Amsaou rapped her signature *doc-doc doc doc-doc* on Tammy's door and let herself in. "You free for lunch tomorrow, darling?"

Tammy shifted Nefertiti to the other shoulder and made a big deal about checking her calendar. "Let me see. If I move things around, I think I can squeeze you in. I read a book at ten, sit on the balcony at eleven, play with the kittens at twelve..."

Amsaou smiled. "I'll ask Isidore to pick you up at twelve-thirty. You sure do like those cats, don't you?"

"I adore them. They always have their priorities in perfect order and help keep mine straight, too. Books and cats are what I missed the most. And chocolate."

"I had no idea that slavery was still so prevalent."

"You'd be amazed, Amsaou. Hundreds of girls are shipped to the Gulf every year, and experts estimate that there are between 25 and 30 million slaves worldwide. I'm extremely, extremely lucky that Yerima rescued me."

Amsaou was general manager of a large hotel, and she gave Tammy the grand tour. It took a while, because they were stopped every few feet by an employee, a guest, or a vendor. Tammy couldn't help but be impressed by her co-wife's patience, good nature, amazing ability to multi-task, and how she quietly oozed competence. It's when they finally seated themselves on the covered terrace in a light rain that Amsaou allowed herself the luxury of rolling her eyes and saying, "Allah! Am I the only person who works in this place?" She chuckled and sighed.

Over a beautiful salade niçoise, Tammy took a bite of albacore and said, "Yerima tells me that you're a singer."

Amsaou laughed. "Oh, I used to sing a little, but it's been years. He plays jazz saxophone, you know, and he's darn good."

"He played *Danny Boy* at our wedding, and it got him a standing ovation."

"Oh yes. *When the Saints, Over the Rainbow, Si Tu T'Appelles Mélancolie, Zangálawah* … Plus, his own compositions. My favorite is *La Lune de Minuit sur Maroua*, Midnight Moon over Maroua. He's not in the same league as Manu Dibango, but he's darn good. When we were in the band, he'd have all the girls with their tongues hanging out, absolutely at his feet. I couldn't stand him at first – too arrogant – but then I noticed he was overflowing with good-natured mischief, had the courage to stand up for what he believed in, and a very generous heart. And I gradually realized that the cockiness was just self-assurance. He knew exactly who he was and where he was going. Fifteen years ago – fifteen years – he told me he was going to be Minister of Foreign Affairs before the age of fifty, and guess what. He's forty-eight. Time to spare."

"Is it true that Michael Jackson paid Manu Dibango for the African part of *You Gotta Be Starting Something?*"

"Yes, we were all so proud, Cameroonian music in a Michael Jackson hit!"

"Yerima tells me he might run for President one day."

"Yes, he might, but not as long as Antoine is in office, and he's up for reelection late next year. Yerima'd be a wonderful President. He's been all over the world dozens of times, is unbelievably disciplined, could charm a starving crocodile, and genuinely wants to help everybody he comes across."

What a bang-on accurate description, Tammy thought. "What's your favorite part of being married to him?"

She laughed. "Our nights. The days are great – he's a good, good person, and I'm very proud to be his wife – but the nights are beyond belief, as I'm sure you know."

A knowing chuckle. "And your least favorite?"

She sighed. "Alizée was a real challenge. She outranked me, of course, and we hardly ever saw eye-to-eye. She kept treating herself to expensive clothes and vacations whether we could afford them or not, and treated JoAnn and me like maids. We were nervous when Yerima told us that he was bringing home another white wife. Maybe my first impressions are mistaken, but you don't seem to be that way at all."

Tammy laughed. "Amsaou, I'm just getting used to wearing *clothes* again. My last job didn't need them at all." Her co-wife smiled. "Tell me about JoAnn. I haven't exactly been overwhelmed by her friendliness."

"Yerima met her when he was with the UN in New York. She's complicated. She's very, very American. After eight years here, she still only speaks a few words of Fulfulde, she rarely wears African clothes, and she's not the least bit interested in improving her rotten French. But she's an excellent botany professor, she loves Yerima – I can't tell begin to tell you how much she loves the man – she's a devoted mother, and she's done wonders with the landscaping and gardening in the *saré*. We're not buddies, but we respect each other. She's thrilled that she finally outranks another wife, because she was number four for a long time. She'll probably want to rub your nose in it, at least for a while."

"It's human nature," Tammy observed. "And believe me, I've gotten good at putting up with crap. All I did for five years, two months, and eighteen days. Not that I was keeping track, or anything. Question: if her French is so lousy, how does she teach?"

"In English. Bilingual country, bilingual university system."

"Amsi. Question, please. I see women in the compound with bottles and it looks like they're pounding seeds. What exactly are they doing?"

Amsaou laughed. "Those are dried melon seeds. They're peeling them to extract the meat."

Tammy stared at her.

"Then they take the meat and make something like a cake from it. It's absolutely delicious, but of course, it takes forever."

"Peeling melon seeds. You've got to be kidding!"

"No, not at all. It takes about a week a couple of hours a day to get enough to make a cake, and you give it to your husband, and he says, 'Good. Now go make another one.' African cuisine is very long and labor-intensive for the reason that women's time used to mean absolutely nothing. That's changing, but cooking still takes inordinate amounts of time."

"Peeling melon seeds. Wow."

"Chocolate mousse, Dari?"

"Oh, my! Two of my favorite words, especially in that order. You know, during my recent check-up, I was diagnosed with a severe, severe chocolate deficiency. A life-threatening condition."

Amsaou smiled. "So, it's an essential part of your therapy, correct? Then I'll get you two."

"Oh yes. *Medicinal* value."

"Books, cats, and chocolate."

"It's actually a pretty long list, but those would be the top three."

"Clothes?"

"Maybe somewhere around tenth. If it were up to me, I'd live in jeans and t-shirts. What I missed the most was books. Not one in more than three years, the whole time I was at The Office. Luckily, Sheikh Fahd at the Rainbow Harem had a huge library, and I went absolutely nuts, devouring more than five hundred during the year I was there. As far as cats are concerned, I didn't even *see* one in five years, much less get to hug one. And for me, chocolate is a major food group, but I'd only get a piece or two every few months. I had less chocolate in five years than I used to have in a week.

"Another thing that I missed a lot was keeping up on current events. I'd go weeks on end without seeing a newscast. Every now and then an executive would have on CNN or BBC or Al-Jazeerah, and I'd hear snatches of this or that, and there was one guy who'd almost always fall asleep and I'd get to listen until he woke up. But that was it." She scraped out the last possible bit of mousse from the bottom of the second bowl. "If I weren't married to Yerima, I'd shamelessly lick this bowl right here in front of everybody. I hope you appreciate my herculean efforts at self-control."

Amsaou threw her head back and laughed. "How you lived through all that and you're still able to joke around is beyond me," she said.

"We got into all kinds of trouble if we cried, so the only thing left to do was laugh. And Yerima kept me sane. Then we had a big fight, and he stopped coming, and..." Tammy's voice broke. "And another man who was real nice to me, even wanted to marry me, gave up because Prince Ibrahim made it clear that I wasn't for sale, so Taymoor stopped coming too. Then Heineken, a lovable eunuch who liberated an occasional chocolate for me, was finally able to buy his dream cabin in Colorado, and there was nobody left. I was so depressed, and the job was so horrible, I wanted to commit suicide."

She was sobbing now. "All I had left was my master Ibrahim, who owned me for three years. He was wonderful in bed, but he was mentally unstable, had a huge drinking problem that made him violent and vindictive, and I feared every day for my life. I don't even know how many girls he's had put to death – most of them, deliberately, for breaking his thousands of rules – but he's also killed them accidentally, when he was drunk. I knew he'd kill me too, sooner or later, so one day I told him as gently as possible that his drinking had gotten out of control. He exploded – that was the mushroom cloud you saw to the north a few months back. I was in sooo much trouble.

"One day, on top of the jail time and paddlings and probations and everything else he'd already ordered, he summoned me and issued additional measures. Amsi, have you ever played Yerima's game of contrition?" Amsaou gave Tammy a telling smile. "Well, he had me lying prostrate on the rug, and my body thought it was

45

that game, and it really turned me on, and Ibrahim demanded to know why his punishment was having entirely the wrong effect, so I told him about the game, and that really turned *him* on, and before you know it, we'd both passed out."

Amsaou's hands flew to her forehead and she laughed until she could scarcely sit up. "Hmm. Now I understand why a particular ambassador wanted so desperately to marry a particular American."

"Amsi, it was the smartest thing and the stupidest thing I ever did in my life. The good news is, Ibrahim was so ecstatic that he cancelled all twenty thousand disciplinary measures that he'd sentenced me to for like, the next five hundred years. And it made Yerima so jealous that when he found out I was supposed to be executed, he bought me and emancipated me. But it also made me Ibrahim's all-time favorite slave. He called me Mukhmala – it means velvet – and I can't believe that he's being such a good sport. I try not to think about what he might do."

"But, Dari, darling, you're *married* now."

"He knows. He gave me a diamond necklace for the wedding and gave Yerima a gorgeous Arabian stallion. We were surprised. Shocked, in fact. The man is totally, totally, totally into control, and totally, totally, totally into getting what he wants. The fact that I'm married wouldn't slow him down one bit. He's got unlimited amounts of money and an ego that wouldn't fit into the Milky Way."

"You're still afraid of him, aren't you? Relax, darling. It's natural. It's a part of your return to normalcy. He owned you for three terrifying years, but all that's behind you now. It'll take you time to recover."

46

A loud clap of thunder made both of them jump.

"You're right, Amsi, I shouldn't be worried at all." Tammy forced a grin. But even Amsaou's dazzling smile couldn't get rid of the nervous knot in the pit of her stomach.

CHAPTER TWO

All one hundred and eleven women of Prince Ibrahim's fabled harem – with the exception of the ones in detention, in the infirmary, or on death row – were gathered in the spacious courtyard. He had invested intense passion, not to mention a fortune, to assemble the most beautiful female *derrières* anywhere on earth. Il Giardino Posteriore. The Rear Garden.

"Good afternoon, my beloved beauties," he began. "I trust that all of you are having a pleasant day. Unfortunately, I'm already late for a board meeting, so I've asked Mr. Faisal to announce a few policy changes." He waved a cheery goodbye.

Groans. Rolled eyes. Impatient sighs.

Annoyed, Mr. Faisal took the microphone. "I haven't even told you what they are, and you're already complaining. Yes, Six Beta?"

"When they're good changes, sir, His Highness tells us himself, sir. When they're not so good, sir, he dumps the job on you."

This observation was met with a wave of knowing giggles. Even Mr. Faisal, not known for his joviality, couldn't suppress a smile.

"They're nothing to get upset about, believe me. His Highness is a rare master who understands that life in a harem isn't always exciting. First, he has asked me to see what electives you'd like in addition to your daily training and aerobics classes. I'm passing out these forms with a few ideas, like karaoke and English and French and belly dancing. If you want something else, write it down. As long as at least six ladies are interested in an activity, we will offer it. One proviso: no competitive sports or games, which are unbecoming to the gentle sex. You may sign up for two of these activities each day but there is absolutely no obligation to do so, you won't be scored on your participation, and they will have no effect whatsoever on your monthly evaluations. Now, see, is that so bad?"

Smiles. Nods. Even a couple Thank you, sirs.

"Maybe there's hope for the id– I mean, our esteemed lord and master, after all. That actually sounds like a good idea," whispered Eight Epsilon.

"Don't jump to any conclusions," replied Four Gamma. With Prince Ibrahim, you never know. You just never know."

"Now. A number of you have expressed the desire to be as alluring from the front as from the back, and His Highness is graciously accommodating these requests. Starting on Sunday, you will each be fitted with a device that will, over the next few months, give you a figure that will be the envy of any woman. It is non-surgical, non-invasive, and extremely effective. You will wear it until you have become an F; thereafter, you will wear it two days a month to remain beautifully toned."

"Did you ever say anything like that?" whispered Two Nu, the striking platinum blonde with the orange-bordered tunic.

"Not me."

"Me neither."

49

"I've, like, heard of those things. They're, like, horrible. They give you like, electric shocks, like, every five seconds."

"What the hell *for*? We're not whores, we're harem girls."

"Oh, really? We're just whores for one man, that's all."

"This is just another one of his *fichu* ego trips. I'd like to open a shrine dedicated to the man's *fichu* ego, but there's no *fichu* place in the solar system big enough."

"What the hell's an F?"

Mr. Faisal held up his hand and they fell silent. "You *will* comply. May I remind you, these orders are from His Highness himself. Several of you have expressed confusion about the size, since different countries use different conventions. F is the EU standard; in the U.S., it's DD, in the U.K., E. Three ladies here will not be obliged to participate in the program because they are already of appropriate dimensions. Five Beta, Three Iota, and Zero Theta, please step forward and remove your tunics."

Admiring gasps.

"Next item. His Highness has been disappointed in the performance of many of you in his bedchamber and finds it necessary to upgrade your skills. Also, starting on Sunday, you will each receive an additional hour of instruction each day under the supervision of Mr. Abdulaziz, the former Director of Training at The Office, the elite gentlemen's club known for its highly professional staff. This will be interactive training and you will be evaluated on your technical skill, ability to deliver maximum sensation, eagerness, and respectfulness. These scores will feed into your monthly performance ratings, so I advise you to take the classes seriously.

"All right, one last thing, sort of like a little game. His Highness has become concerned – especially since the recent brawl – that you ladies get so caught up in your petty squabbles that you forget that you have a kind and benevolent master to whom you owe your very existence. Starting tomorrow, each day, right after inspection, you will draw a token that represents a privilege to be surrendered that day. Perhaps it will be sight, or wearing your tunic, eating, or speech.

"Each day you will draw a new token and surrender a different privilege. You will do so out of devotion to your master, out of your strictest obligation to obey his orders, and out of the duty of submissiveness incumbent upon all women. Hand in your survey forms, and you are dismissed. Oh, by the way, if you show any reluctance, you will draw a second token and surrender a second, or even a third, privilege for the day. You are dismissed."

"What the hell will this sicko think up next?"

"He's always been a control freak, but this is ridiculous."

"If he really wanted our lives to be interesting, he'd let us out of this godforsaken place."

"Or at least let us watch Oprah. Or the news. Or something besides those raunchy DVDs."

"I've had it. I'm not going to put up with this nonsense another minute."

"Oh? And just what do you plan to do? Scale the three-meter wall? Take down the Prince, and his four bodyguards, and all six eunuchs, and Mr. Faisal and Mr. Abdul and Mr. Sayeed with your bare hands? I mean, they even make it impossible to commit suicide. I know; I've tried. You think you're the first girl who wants to get out of this place? Calm down, babe. I don't much like the changes either, but at least they're not life-threatening."

"They can only mean one thing: he's hitting the sauce again. He was better, but it looks like he's relapsed. For a while he was showing signs of being almost somewhat nearabout approximately normal."

"He *is* drinking, and I heard that the reason why is because there was a girl at The Office who was so good she made him pass out. Then another man bought her and took her to Africa. Ever since, he's been depressed."

"Pass out? Jesus! What did she *do*?"

"Wow. I think I'm doing okay with him if he doesn't haul off and slap me."

"These new policies are horrible. Horrible."

"So? No matter what we think, we're stuck with them."

"At the Ranch," interjected Six Zeta, "you were kept in restraints around the clock, and weren't allowed to say anything, ever. Either you had a pacifier in orifice one or a bridle bit. The only exception was at the branding parties, when the screams were part of the entertainment. So believe me, this is no big deal."

"Oh, for heaven's sake, y'all," said Five Iota. "Y'all are complaining about nothing, as usual. Prince Ibrahim owns us. He can do whatever he damn well pleases with us. And if it pleases him to have us blindfolded for a few hours to demonstrate our so-called devotion, what real difference does it make?"

"Oh, shut up, you suck-up, you."

"Bless your heart, sugar, I'm a suck-up who learned the hard way. Advice from someone who's been stuck here for eight years, sugar: if your sweet little patootie means anything to y'all, for heaven's sake, shut up, smile, keep those rabble-rousing opinions to yourself, and be ready to say at any time, *bil-khidma ya agati*." How may I serve you, master?

"I *hate* being cooped up in this place. And I *hate* saying yes master, how can I degrade myself again to flatter your incredibly overblown ego, master. So demeaning!"

"Y'all are here, and y'all aren't going anywhere, sugar, so deal with it."

"No sir," Five Gamma said a few days later. "May I respectfully ask permission to please draw another token, please, sir? I'm very sorry, sir, but when can I please get something to eat in this place, sir? I just got out of eleven days' detention and hardly had anything to eat the entire time, sir, then day before yesterday I drew the damned silence token that meant I couldn't eat, and yesterday it was the no food token, sir, and now today again, sir, it's the silence token. Yesterday I passed out twice, sir, and I'm so weak from lack of food, I'm about ready to pass out right now."

"You do not question your master's orders," said Mr. Sayeed, eyes blazing.

"I'm not questioning them in the least, sir; I simply want to be alive tomorrow to be able to obey him again. Sir, excuse me, sir, but this is ridiculous."

"Five demerits, fifty strokes, and you will draw two more tokens today. Trevino? Firenze? All right, since you won't, I'll draw them for you. In addition, you will surrender the privilege of sight and the privilege of walking."

The eunuchs took care of the preliminaries, bent her over the padded leather cylinder, and strapped her in place. The courtyard was filled with screams and sobs as they methodically carried out the correction, one stroke a minute, for nearly an hour. Then they blindfolded her, silenced her, bound her ankles, and left her lying in the courtyard.

She died the next day.

Prince Ibrahim was holding court, surrounded by his four bodyguards, both daytime managers, and all six eunuchs. All the girls had prostrated, he'd put his feet on their heads, and they'd all recited the affirmation of submission.

"Now, my beloved beauties, I have a wonderful surprise for you," he said. "My personal chefs have prepared a feast: chicken marsala, risi bisi, caprese salad, and tiramisù." He clapped, and maidservants appeared with glorious plates of food.

Everyone applauded.

"There's only one catch," he added. "If you are among the lowest ten performers, you will be served a meal, but you will not be allowed to eat it. Instead, you will kneel and personally feed it to one of the top ten. If you take one forbidden bite, you will be sternly disciplined."

Two Gamma sighed. The goddam control freak strikes again, she said to herself. She knelt and served her meal to snooty-ass Six Alpha, hating every last molecule of her master. This was the last straw. A couple of the other girls had approached her about killing him. Before, she'd hesitated, but now, she was in. This was absolutely, positively, the last straw.

Prince Ibrahim smiled fondly as his beloved girls knelt before him, the tens to the right, zeros to the left. Every last one just as beautiful as beautiful could be. A stunning collection of the most superior female posteriors in the world. Zero Beta had drawn the privilege of serving as his foot-rest, and she was doing an excellent job.

"Sabah al-khayr, morning of abundance, my beloved beauties."

"Sabah an-nour, morning of light, master," they responded.

"Have you had an exciting morning so far?" he teased, black eyes twinkling. A few chuckles, a few groans. He grew serious. "Betas, please rise and step forward."

Ten Beta, Nine Beta, et cetera, all rose and took two steps forward, becoming more and more nervous as they looked into his eyes. The twinkles had been replaced by an unsettling steeliness.

"One of you will die today. Do I have a volunteer?"

He had to be kidding.

To everyone's consternation, Four Beta tentatively raised her hand.

"Come. You are prepared to die for your master?"

She knelt. "Nothing would make me happier, master."

"Why do you say that?"

"Because, master, it shows my utter devotion to you. I love being your slave, master. I love the control you have over me. Dying for you would simply be my ultimate surrender."

The other girls were rolling their eyes.

"How would you like to die?"

"That's not for me to say, master."

"Even if I were to command you to be tortured?"

There was scarcely a moment's hesitation. "If that is your pleasure, master. I have many times promised to obey you immediately, fully, and willingly. If you wish to have me tortured, I must accept that it is your command."

Prince Ibrahim smiled proudly. "You are a very, very good slave. Rise and remove your tunic. I am sparing you today, because of your exceptional level of devotion. You will live to serve your master another day. Betas, come and kiss her ass. And I strongly suggest that you show fervor as you do so, because she has saved your lives today."

They exchanged nervous glances, gulped, and kissed Four Beta's ass. And if Prince Ibrahim had cared to notice, he would have seen hatred in their eyes.

"At the Ranch," said Six Zeta to anyone within earshot, "we slept four to a 2 m x 3 m stall, tethered and handcuffed. There was a drain where we tried to pee, but the fillies in positions one and four couldn't get there because the tethers weren't long enough. So appreciate the mattress. Appreciate the pillow and the sheets. And for God's sake, appreciate the air conditioning. When horses lived in the stable, they used it, but when it was converted to a slave prison, they turned it off. You have no idea how lucky we are."

"I called you in to talk about your headaches," Mr. Faisal told Seven Alpha.

"Yes sir. Every morning I wake up with a huge headache and nothing gets rid of it. The nurse has tried everything, sir. Sometimes everything gets blurry, so I think I probably just need eyeglasses, sir."

"They are no longer permitted. In any case, the x-rays show that you have a brain tumor pressing against your optic nerve. We will therefore be transferring you to the Zephyr facility."

Stunned silence. "The breeding farm? But sir, my performance has been in the top ten month after month."

"This is not a disciplinary transfer, it is simply a transfer. We're not punishing you for anything, just sending you to a more appropriate location."

"Do you mean to say, sir, that I'm going blind?"

"It's almost inevitable, yes."

"And that's why you're sending me to the Zephyr?"

A hard slap. "His Highness can do whatever he likes with you, whenever he likes, and you are not to question his decisions. The van is waiting. Good day."

"But sir–"

Another slap. *"Ikharhus!* Just shut the hell up! Trevino, escort her to the garage." He handed the eunuch her file.

When they were out of earshot, Trevino said to her, "Too bad. Half the girls there have been devocalized or blinded or maimed or have gone completely insane; all they care is that your reproductive system is in working order."

"But I've been a good slave," she said between sobs. "I've done everything they said. It's just not fair. And why don't they let the girls wear glasses?"

"A couple of years ago, a girl smashed hers and used the pieces to try to slash her wrists. That's how it works sometimes. *Hafiy zaka Allah min alaza.* May God preserve you from harm."

The van drove off, its passenger weeping bitterly.

Prince Ibrahim was not happy. A twenty-two million-dollar cobalt deal had just fallen through due to unrest – again, sigh – in the Congo. He checked the schedule to see which posterior would be entertaining him for the evening, and it was Eight Delta. He groaned. Tonight, he needed to forget the lost contract. Tonight, he needed consolation, comfort, solace, fun. He needed someone like Mukhmala who could make him forget everything except the pleasure of the moment.

Then he realized something that should have been so obvious, he couldn't imagine that he'd overlooked it for more than twenty years. Yes, he'd usually summon one girl at a time according to the tidy rotation, but he *owned* them, and *yarham 'abuuk,* good grief, he could do whatever he wanted.

"Abdul?" he said, "I'm feeling down. Tonight I want you to send me eight girls. Random selection, in addition to the one on rotation."

"Certainly, Your Highness. Any special way you want them?"

"The way nature made them."

"How do you wish for me to deal with the rotation in the database, Your Highness?"

"Oh. Good point. Well, Eight Delta is the principal here; just note the others as accessories."

"I knew it, I knew it, I knew it. You see? He *is* turning us into whores, just like at The Office," griped Eight Beta as she prepared to be escorted to His Highness. "I

59

told you. The second Mr. Abdulaziz came on the scene, this whole whore business started. I don't mind staying in a harem, but I resent the hell out of being turned into a whore."

"How else did you plan to spend the evening? Hey, at least it's something to do."

"And the man is cool in bed, not to mention, absolutely gorgeous. That streak of silver in his hair? Those beautiful shoulders? Oh! Could be a lot worse. A lot worse."

"I need cheering up today," he told them as they filed in. "And I could think of no better way than to enjoy the company of the most beautiful girls in the world." He gave them a big smile. "All right. Four Beta, come over here and give my sore feet a nice massage." He smiled. "Nice job, my dear. Now you will give me a nice long blow job, a really nice BJ. Let's see if the new training has been beneficial. Giuliano, bend the other girls over the barre, stuff them with wiggle worms, and have them entertain me."

Six Alpha prostrated. "Yes, my dear?"

"Master, please, may I request your urgent permission to go to the bathroom? I'm terribly sorry, master. I have diarrhea."

"Yes, of course, permission granted."

She jumped up, returning moments later panting with relief. Giuliano strapped her into position and she began to gyrate with the others.

The Prince started to moan, but was still coherent enough to tell Giuliano to get the shackles ready. Eight Delta's eyes bugged open – she knew better than to say anything – and soon she was spread-eagled, wrists and ankles firmly secured to the corners of the bed.

"You look so helpless, so beautiful," said the prince. "His Hardness loves seeing you like that." He looked between her legs, but even after ten minutes, nothing had happened at all. He sighed. Dutiful wasn't what he wanted. Submissive wasn't what he needed. "Giuliano, send her back. No bonus points, no demerits." He surveyed the beauty around him. "Undo them and have them all come over here and kneel. Who among you likes restraints, and I mean, really likes restraints? No, you don't. I remember you. You're just trying to manipulate me. Haven't you learned by now that I hate that?" He turned to Six Zeta, who had raised her hand. "Hmm. You really do, don't you? Okay, shackle her down and put the nipple-nibblers on her to speed things along. And the rest of you, resume the position of eager anticipation."

Six Zeta smiled. It only took a few minutes for her to be panting with desire.

More like it. His Hardness slid happily into the warm little part of her reserved exclusively for him, a part forbidden to all others, a part carefully guarded that he could enjoy whenever he felt like it. *Hareem* – forbidden places – were wonderful, wonderful inventions, where you could shelter parts like that from unwanted attentions and have them ready for your pleasure at the drop of a tunic.

She responded to him, not as a slave submitting to her master, but as a fully sensuous woman giving herself to her lover. He soon had her screaming with delight. He lay panting, spread out upon her, infused with ecstasy.

"Master, please?" said Six Alpha, kneeling beside the bed.

He groaned.

"Sorry, master, do I have your permission to go to the bathroom again? Sorry, master, sorry."

"Yes, Giuliano, let her go."

When she returned, he called her over. "Why do you have such bad diarrhea?"

"Thank you for asking, master. I have celiac disease, which means that I can't digest the gluten in bread, and I'm lactose-intolerant, which means that I can't digest milk products like yogurt."

"Has the infirmary been treating you?"

"Yes, master."

"Then why does it persist?"

"Because they are reluctant to exceed the recommended dosage of the medication, and it doesn't last all day."

"But why do you keep getting it?"

"I'm required to eat everything on my plate, master."

"Oh, we do give exceptions for medical reasons. We don't ever want to hear 'oh dear, I can't stand that,' but for medical reasons, certainly."

"I requested an exception, master, but Mr. Faisal said no."

"I will instruct him to give you an exception on medical grounds. What do you do during parties?"

"I'm never allowed to participate, master. Mr. Faisal said I'd ruin them. Thank you thank you thank you, master. I've been living like this for three years. You are a very nice master."

"You may kiss my feet. Giuliano, summon Firenze; she may return to the harem. And let the other girls come over here and kneel." When they'd gathered round, he startled them by asking, "What do you girls think about the tokens?"

Fidgeting. Playing with hair. Nervous coughs.

"Well?"

Finally Four Alpha had the nerve to ask, "Master, do you want us to tell you what you want to hear? Or what we really think?"

He smirked. "I see." He studied them for a moment and decided to take a chance. "Let me hear the truth. No demerits, no discipline, no corrections. The truth."

"They stink, master."

"They're horrible, master."

"They make us feel like slaves instead of like harem girls, master. We hate them. They're really annoying. And some of the girls find them sexually stimulating but then they can't do anything about it, so they get really frustrated."

"Let me ask you this: what's the difference between a slave girl and a harem girl?"

"Oh, lots, master. Slave girls are much lower rank. They do laundry and scrub floors and stuff. And they get beaten a lot."

"Harem girls only serve one master, sir. They're prized for their beauty and maintained in luxury."

"Semantics, if you ask me," said Two Kappa. "Either way, your life is basically over."

Ibrahim looked at her reproachfully, but kept his word.

"Very interesting. But you ladies keep forgetting about me. What would you suggest that I do to remind you that I exist?"

Shrugs. "Use the tokens for punishment. And give privileges for rewards. Like chocolate. Or tv."

"Toblerone, especially."

"Television, especially."

"No no, computer games."

"Ice cream, especially."

"Starbucks."

"Oh, master? We're sick of the training DVDs, too. Can we have some new ones, please? Please?"

He laughed. "This has been very interesting. Thank you for your candor. You may kiss my feet. Thank you."

"It was brave of you to ask, master."

"Giuliano, give each of them ten points and send them back. You gave me courageous and honest answers, and I wasn't expecting that. Good night."

"Ladies ladies ladies, I got the scoop," said Four Kappa. "Firenze told me the whole story."

"Firenze? He never knows *anything*." Two Alpha couldn't believe it.

"This time he did. He told me everything. Okay. There was this American girl named Mukhmala who belonged to Prince Ibrahim, and he leased her to The Office, and she was so amazing in bed that she made him pass out. One of the members there, an African ambassador, fell in love with her, but the Prince kept renewing her lease – she was making him tons of money – and he wouldn't sell her. Then she and another girl there murdered Dr. Hassan, and–"

There were high-fives all round. "You go, girl!"

"Yes, but she didn't commit suicide fast enough, and she was still alive when they sent security up, and they sentenced her to be tortured to death at the Rodeo, and the ambassador found out and rescued her, and actually married her and took her back to Africa with him, and now he's Minister of Foreign Affairs, and she's living *la dolce vita*. But Prince Ibrahim is depressed because she doesn't belong to him now. And that's why he's started, you know." She raised an imaginary glass to her mouth.

"I was on rotation just the other night," said Five Alpha. "He emptied one glass of prosecco after another, and oh boy. He had six of us there – what's this mass stampede about, all of a sudden? It used to be whoever was on rotation, and that's it. Anyway, he had a BJ contest. Winner got thirty points, second got fifteen, third got five. Fourth lost five points, fifth lost fifteen, and last lost thirty. One Xi placed last, and she started bawling because she's already had performance problems and this almost ensures that she'll have the lowest score this month. Then she got docked four more points because she was crying. And he also sentenced her to be strapped to that awful simulator every day until she can do the program in less than an hour."

"Good grief! I'm pretty good at blow jobs, but it usually takes me nearly an hour and a half. I've seen girls stuck there for more than three hours, tears streaming down their faces. If you stop to breathe, the damned timer goes backwards, and if you don't do it right, it gives you shocks. I hate, hate, hate that damned thing."

"At the Ranch," said Six Zeta, "one of the overseers quit. A mean one, too; he used his bullwhip a lot. When Nine Two died, he needed to make the notation in her file and noticed that she'd been abducted from a park in London when she was eleven. She died at twenty-two. He told Mr. Thibodeau right in front of us that it really rattled him because his own daughter had just turned eleven, and it suddenly hit him that we prisoners had once been actual human beings with mothers and fathers and hopes and dreams, not just nameless, faceless assemblages of body parts. The Archangel Jibril (Gabriel) appeared to him in a dream and told him to reevaluate his life. He decided to go back to Alexandria and rethink everything. I admired that."

Five Delta smiled indulgently, served herself another glass of tea from the samovar, and took a bite of an almond cookie. "While we were there, he spent a lot of time on the phone tracking down an eight he'd heard about. He finally located her owner, a physics professor. He refused to sell her. So his next call was to give orders to kidnap the professor, gouge his eyes out, devocalize him, have him hot-iron branded, and send him to work as a homosexual whore at the King's Club."

They stared at each other in horror.

Three Gamma rolled her eyes and sighed. "I wasn't on rotation, but a couple of weeks ago, Mr. Abdul sent me to him and he had what he called a blossom contest. There were eight of us, and he had us all in the position of eager anticipation, which in his twisted mind is supposed to turn us on." She glanced up. Without missing a beat, she said, "This guy was just balancing the final apple on a huge pyramid display, and a lady accidentally rammed me with her cart, and I went crashing into the apples, and they all tumbled down, and the produce guy couldn't help it and burst into tears." The others dutifully laughed. Trevino moved on. "Well, if your blossom had swollen the most after twenty minutes, you won. The prize was getting into bed with him. Six of us lost – no effect whatsoever. He was furious. Accused us of refusing to cooperate. Cost us each ten points."

"We've got to do something, ladies, this man is out of control."

"Like what?" Four Kappa said sarcastically, "mount a slave revolt?"

Three Gamma's glass slid out of her hand and landed on the carpet. Five Delta's mouth fell open. Something clicked. Something changed.

"There are more than a hundred of us. He wouldn't dare, um, lose his entire collection all at once…"

"Let's do it," said Three Gamma.

"Are you with us?" they asked Six Zeta.

"With you about what?"

The others giggled. Six Zeta lived in her own space, her own world. She'd only spent six weeks at the Ranch, but they had really affected her. She said it was so awful she didn't want to talk about it, but she rarely talked about anything else. They understood.

The housekeeper who rushed over to clean up the spilled tea saw only perfect pictures of innocence, and moments later Napoli walked by and smiled at them approvingly, seven well-behaved little harem girls, politely socializing in the elegant salon.

Next evening, Prince Ibrahim was even more depressed. A titanium deal was fast falling apart, Habib had screwed up and an uncooperative idiot had escaped with a six-two nine-point eight, and the never-ending staffing issues at The Office were causing more and more headaches. "Abdul? Who was the girl here last night?"

"Six Zeta, Your Highness."

"I like her. Send her back to me tonight. Fifteen minutes? All right."

He soon had her shackled in place like the night before. "You're hungry for your master again, aren't you?" She nodded. "All right, my dear, you and I are going to have a feast. His Hardness can't wait to nibble on you."

Five times he made love to her that night, and five times she shrieked with delight. Once, she actually wept. They had to take her back to the harem on a golf cart, and she spent a full day in the infirmary recovering. She'd earned herself thirty points, and a star by her name in Prince Ibrahim's database.

But she didn't make him pass out. Only one girl had ever done that. Oh, he missed Mukhmala so much. Why, why had he let her go? He crash-landed onto his easy chair, feeling very tired, and exceedingly, exceedingly Mukhmala-deprived.

Next thing he knew, a glass of steaming hot tea had been set next to him. "Oh, hello, Roberto, if you're on duty, it must be morning already. You know, today I want coffee. Strong. With a shot of grappa. And tell Luciano to make me a smoked salmon frittata with goat cheese and chives."

"Coming right up, Your Highness." He picked up the tea and looked at the Prince, who had That Look about him. Roberto smiled affectionately. "You really want that pretty American back, don't you, Your Highness?"

Ibrahim stared straight ahead. "That idiot ambassador had to go and marry her."

Knowing that she was making another man pass out in her arms was just too much to swallow. Roberto was right. He really did want her back. But she was no longer a slave to be bought and sold like a camel, she was a married woman. Why did life have to be so complicated? *Yaa salaam,* good heavens, he wanted her back. Somehow, some way, she must be returned to where she rightfully belonged.

CHAPTER THREE

As the household's newly appointed Minister of Education, Tammy loved her daily sessions with the children. She'd grown up wanting to be a diplomat, but she was drawn more and more toward teaching. She had a special place in her heart for sixteen-year-old Samira, a strikingly beautiful girl with Aïssatou's soft intelligent eyes and Yerima's smooth athletic grace. She was very shy, very insecure, and completely oblivious to how meltingly attractive she was. She made excellent grades, but had no idea what she wanted to do when she finished school. She'd shrug. "Get married, I guess."

"Sweetie, even if you're married, you need a way to make a living. What if your husband dies? Or takes another wife and neglects you? Or, you just never find quite the right man? You must never, never be completely dependent on a man. Never. If you have a skill, he'll respect you more. And he'll know you'll be just fine even without him. If you don't, he'll take advantage, knowing that you have no other option."

"But I'm not good at anything."

However, her eyes lit up whenever they mentioned food. One day, after they'd had a long conversation about the previous night's dinner, Tammy had an idea. "Let me check with your mother, but if she gives the green light, how'd you like to learn to cook? I mean, really cook? Chef Emmanuel is a terrific teacher, and I bet he'd be tickled to have another pair of hands in that crazy kitchen of his."

"Oh, Néné Sudari, that would make me so happy."

Permission was granted. Tammy still resented asking permission for everything – it reminded her how she used to have to request permission even to pee – but it was almost always forthcoming. And, as lowest-ranking wife, she had to go out of her way to keep everyone placated.

Within weeks, Samira was bragging about how she'd learned how to make *pommes duchesse*, an elegant spin on mashed potatoes where they were piped to look like carnations and lightly browned, and *poulet hollandais*, and *gigot farçi*, and *tarte Tatin*.

"Chef Emmanuel says you have a real flair, Mira. He loves how thorough you are, how much pride you take in peeling that carrot until it's absolutely perfect, how excited you get when you learn a new skill. Have you thought about going to culinary school?"

"Abi wants me to get my *bac*."

"He's right – you should – but one doesn't preclude the other. With your *bac* you can always go to university if that's eventually what you decide to do." They practiced writing nutritionally balanced menus, calculating food costs, and, with the chef's help, drawing up work plans so that dishes for sample menus would all be ready at about the same time. Chef Emmanuel was so impressed that he soon put Mira in charge of taking the daily inventory and making the shopping list for the following day.

"Saves me a good hour," he said, "and she does a great job."

Ismaëlou, fourteen, resented being lassoed into additional study time, which interfered with what he really loved – soccer. And his twelve-year-old brother

Kadry, nicknamed Ditto, followed his lead. Their grades were okay, but they needed motivation to improve, especially their writing skills. "Why don't you two write a book about soccer?" Tammy suggested. "We'll make it look really good, with graphics and everything, and show it to Abi. I bet he'll be stinking proud of you." There were lots of spelling errors, and quite a few grammatical problems, but they finally had a document they were pleased with. Ditto turned out to be a whiz with the graphics. "Now let's really open up the audience for this and translate it into English."

Yerima was blown away. "I'm impressed, but you left out one really important point. I wasn't too shabby a player in my day, you know. When the other team has the ball, close in on it, and when your team has the ball, spread out. Add that, and it'll be perfect. Great job, guys. I mean, great job."

"I wrote a book about soccer," Tammy overheard Ismaëlou bragging on the phone one day, "me and my brother Ditto. Sure, I can get you a copy, but it'll cost you a thousand francs. I'll even autograph it for you."

Thirty-six pages, but hey, it was a book. Christine at the bookstore agreed to carry it, which thrilled the boys no end.

Oumoul was eleven, and had inherited her father's gregarious gene. She was funny, thoughtful, and concerned about everybody, but was so busy taking care of her numerous friends that her schoolwork had taken a slide. She adopted a three-legged margouya lizard, fed every stray dog that ventured into the compound, saved stale bread to feed to the birds, and came over almost every day to play with Titi and Cleo, who positively adored her.

"What kind of work do you want to do when you grow up?" Tammy wanted to know.

"I don't know. Maybe play with a rock band, maybe be a movie star."

"You know what I think, Oumoul? I think you're Abi's girl. I bet you'd be a phenomenal veterinarian like him. Phenomenal."

A light bulb went off. "You mean, take care of sick animals?"

"You really love animals, and connect with them so well. Think about it. But you need to be good at science. Let's have a look at your homework, *ma petite biche*."

"He says that when I'm twelve, he'll teach me how to ride. I love horses. I *love* horses, Néné, well, the way you love cats."

"Only, I don't recommend letting a horse curl up on your lap."

"And I don't recommend riding a cat."

They laughed. "Let's make sure you stay on top of your homework every single day. And I'll tell you what. Let's surprise Abi. Look at this diagram. Did you imagine a horse had so many parts? Crest, withers, croup, stifle, fetlock. Don't tell anybody what you're doing, though, let's make it a surprise."

"I'm going to be a veterinarian like Abi," she told her six-year-old sister Aminatou.

"He's not a vegetenarian, silly, Abi's the Minister of Boring Affairs."

"Yes, but before, he was a veterinarian. Néné Sudari told me. So there!"

Ten-year-old Bintou was lost in Oumoul's shadow. They were less than a year apart, so they naturally hung out together, but it was Oumoul who decided on their games, Oumoul who cooked up the pranks they played, Oumoul who always evaporated when it was time to be scolded. It took Tammy weeks to figure out that Bintou had a gift for languages and a vivid, highly creative imagination. With Tammy's support, Bintou wrote a hilarious book about a mouse that sneaked onto a spaceship headed for the moon, and the ghost who lent him his bicycle, and the lollipop farm there that supplied most of the solar system. "Why do we always write books about boys?" Tammy asked. "Why can't it be a girl mouse?"

"Yes!" said Bintou. So the name was changed from Khalidou to Khalidatou. The book was nine pages long. They translated it into English, into Spanish, and into Arabic. Then Bintou drew illustrations, and Tammy ran them off and had a copy placed at each place at Sunday dinner.

"What have we here?" said Yerima.

"By Bintou Abdoulaye," said Amsaou, "you're amazing. Absolutely amazing. Your Arabic is suddenly far beyond what you've learned at Koranic school, and I didn't know you could speak Spanish at all."

"Estoy aprendiendo," said Bintou, with a fine accent. I'm learning.

Yerima gave Tammy an approving wink.

Aminatou was six, and looked so much like Amsaou that it staggered the mind. She was really into dolls, so she and Tammy gave them vocabulary lessons so they could throw around grown-up words like voluminous and gargantuan and unprecedented.

Amsaou almost fell over one morning when her six-year-old daughter told her at breakfast, "Néné, I'm rather averse to going to school today. Louise was positively odious yesterday and I'm henceforth not prepared to tolerate her incessant provocations."

Later Tammy admitted that she and Aminatou had practiced that sentence for days. "But she does really know what all those words mean!"

Aliatou was barely four, and could write her name, but within two months she could write the entire alphabet, upper and lower case, cursive and block letters. And count to ten in six languages.

Cathy was also four, very dainty, and unbelievably squeamish. She'd throw up when she'd see a squashed worm, say "ewww" three times every five minutes, and would only color with blue crayons because they were the only ones that were "clean." But she was also endearing. She could write her name with no trouble, but always made the Y upside-down. Finally Tammy realized that this was no accident, and asked her about it.

"The poor Y gets tired holding its arms up all day," Cathy explained earnestly.

"That is very, very thoughtful of you, Cathy, but that's how the Y is made. It doesn't get tired, honest." And henceforth, Cathy wrote Y's right-side up.

"My mommy says you used to be a, uh, I can't remember."

"I used to be a slave. It's a person who belongs to somebody else and who has to do whatever that person says, whether they want to or not. It's a really awful job, because even if people are mean to you, you can't do anything about it. And when you're a slave, they're mean to you a lot. But your daddy rescued me, and now I'm not a slave. That made me very happy."

"That's not the word."

"Did she say whore?"

"Yes, that's it. What's a whore?"

"It's a woman who gives personal services to men. Usually, a whore gets paid, but since I was a slave, only my master got the money. Sometimes they even forgot to give me food. It wasn't any fun at all, Cathy."

"You mean sex?"

Never underestimate a four-year-old! "Yes, sweetie, that's exactly what I mean. Sometimes sex can be beautiful. When a man and a woman love each other, it makes them love each other even more. But it can also be really ugly, and hurt something awful. And when you're a slave, men don't care one bit whether it hurts or not, and you're not allowed to complain. What's the job you hate the most, Cathy?"

"Changing Michael's stinky diaper."

"Okay, Just imagine for a moment that that's sex, and you're a slave. As soon as you change one stinky diaper, he poops again. You change that one. And then he poops again. All day long, every day. And if you say, Listen, I'm sick and tired of this, I don't want to do this any longer, they beat you up, or they don't let you have anything to eat. That's what it's like, being a slave."

"Yuck!"

"Yes, sweetie, you understand. Yuck!"

House phone, extension one. Tammy smiled. "Hello, darling."

"Babe, can you put on something nice and meet me in fifteen minutes? I want to take you somewhere. A fun surprise."

She appeared a few minutes later at the main house wearing a long dress in a red-and-yellow feather print that flared at the knees.

"Babe, wow! You look good enough to eat."

"On va où?" Where are we going? Oumarou inquired as he started the engine. Dieudonné, the gendarme/body-guard, slid into the front seat and saluted.

"We're going to take this beautiful lady to the house on the mountain."

Mount Fébé, wreathed in raphia palms and jacarandas, was about fifteen minutes' drive out of town. A winding road took them past the luxury hotel and golf course. They rounded a curve and the view of the city on the sparkling clear day took Tammy's breath away. Yaounde was much larger – more than two million inhabitants – and much nicer, than Tammy had imagined. Built on rolling hills, it enjoyed a pleasant climate even though it was less than four degrees north of the Equator. They arrived at a stone-fenced compound where a gendarme saluted smartly and pressed a button to open the gate. The car had barely pulled to a stop when two butlers rushed over to open the doors. Tammy looked at Yerima inquisitively but he just smiled, took her by the arm, and they mounted the stairs. Another butler bowed and ushered them inside. "He's in the upstairs parlor, Excellency."

"How's my man Theodore?" Yerima asked.

A big grin. "He turns four next month, Excellency. He's into everything. Drives us nuts."

"Means you should be grateful that he's a healthy, intelligent child. By the way, George, this is my new wife Sudari. And Sudari, this is George Foncha. Don't even think about basketball one-on-ones with him. He creams everybody in sight."

"Even you, Yerima?"

He made a face, and she laughed. "By the way, his grandfather was the single most important reason why the former British Cameroons and French Cameroun became a united country."

"I never quite understood what happened."

"The Germans lost Kamerun in World War I and it was split along occupational lines. The French got most of it and the British got a couple pieces that bordered Nigeria, which is why some people still say The Cameroons. They administered them as part of Nigeria, which made us mad, because Nigeria was a colony, and Cameroon was officially a mandated territory under the League of Nations, and later a trust territory under the

78

UN. In international circles, Cameroon is known for petition after petition to make France and Britain respect the special treatment we were supposed to get.

"Anyway, when independence was imminent, John Ngu Foncha went from village to village by bicycle and warned people that Nigeria was a tinderbox ready to explode and that it would be a mistake to remain part of it. And when the referendum took place, most people agreed with him. Besides, English-speaking Cameroonians, or Anglophones – we jokingly call them Anglo Saxophones – have far more ethnic affinity with the peoples of French-speaking Cameroun. It became independent in 1960, and in 1961, when Nigeria gained its independence, all but one of those pieces joined back with the French part.

"For a while we had a federation with two states, but it was like trying to have a federation composed of Texas and, like, West Virginia. Just too imbalanced. It served a purpose for a time, but now we have a unified country that still happens to be bilingual. And of course, he was right, only a few years later, Nigeria went through a horrible civil war."

"You must be very proud of your grandfather," said Tammy.

"Yes ma'am, yes indeed. He was Vice President until 1970. Welcome, Madame Abdoulaye. Welcome to Cameroon."

Yerima and Tammy climbed the graceful curved stairway.

"Grandpa grandpa grandpa, you're just not doing it right." A very exasperated girl of about eight was scolding a gray-haired man in a cotton coffee bean-print tunic and matching pants. They were sitting on leather poufs with a video game. She sighed. "You're hopeless, grandpa, hopeless."

"Rascal!" said Grandpa with a delighted smile.

"Scoundrel!" said Yerima.

Grandpa rose and clasped Yerima in a huge affectionate hug. When they released, he took a long look at Tammy, grinned, and held out his arms. "You must be Sudari. You rascal, she's even more beautiful than you let on. Welcome, welcome, welcome." And he gave her a crushing embrace.

"This is my hopeless cousin Antoine."

"Ohmygod," Tammy said, eyes opening wide. "Such an honor to meet you, Your Excellency, such an honor," she stammered. The President of the Republic himself had just given her a hug. "Now I know why you looked familiar. Your picture is on the wall in Yerima's office, but somehow Grandpa doesn't look quite the same as the President."

"Grandpa, are you going to finish this, or not?"

"Excuse me just a second." He sat back down. "Show me again, Marielle? Maybe this time I'll do it right." After a few moments the game chimed victory. "Aha! See? I'm not so hopeless after all."

The little girl had been completely focused on the game, but finally noticed Yerima. *"Tonton!"* Unc. He swept her into his arms and gave her a super-long, slobbery kiss.

"How's my favorite ballerina? Marielle, meet my wife Sudari."

She shook Tammy's hand very importantly. "*Tonton*, how many wives do you *have*?"

"I'm allowed to have four, so I have four."

"If they let him have a hundred, he'd have a hundred. Sudari, please make yourself at home, my dear. I'd love for you to meet Solange, but her sister has taken ill and she's gone to Mbálmayo to look after her. As you've no doubt guessed, this is my private home. If you want, Marielle, you can stay, but now I need to talk to *tonton* and *tata.*"

"You always have to talk to somebody," Marielle complained.

"That's my job."

"And you're always, always, always working."

"I have twenty million wonderful people I need to take care of, and that's a lot of work."

Yerima planted his stocking feet on the coffee table.

Antoine poured two snifters of Courvoisier. "Oh my, how rude of me. What would you like, Madame Sudari?"

"Courvoisier is fine. Thank you, Excellency."

And the President of the Republic served her himself.

"So, how is this rascal treating you?"

"So far so good, sir. I've managed to put up with him for two months now."

"You're really beautiful. If you ever get tired of him you can just move in with me, okay?"

"Okay, sir, you have a deal, but don't hold your breath. I have no plans to go anywhere." Yerima put his finger on her nose; she grabbed it and kissed it.

"I'm getting really good reports at how you're handling Foreign Affairs, Yerima." Antoine settled back in a recliner as Marielle climbed onto his lap and snuggled against him. "Your sense of humor goes over well, as does your heartfelt respect for other people, even on the other side of the table."

"I love the job, but it's exhausting. Receptions almost every night. I hated being ambassador, so far away, and without my family, but this is loads of fun. I love it."

"Sudari, Yerima told me about your background. I'm so sorry you had to live through all that."

She shrugged. "Thanks to Yerima, it's behind me, sir. It wasn't any fun, but at least in my case it had a happy ending. A very happy ending." She kissed her husband's finger again.

"I'm very interested in hearing more about this. I've heard stories of abductions and human trafficking right here under our noses, but I confess I know very little about it. I do hope that you're writing a book?"

"Yes sir, but it's still in the early stages. I can work on it for an hour or so, and then I start to shake, but I'll get it done eventually. It's hard, reliving everything."

"What's the most difficult thing you had to do?"

"Besides put up with Yerima?" They laughed. "Do you realize, sir, that seven of the eight first times we saw each other, I ended up in the infirmary?"

Yerima looked at her in astonishment. *"What?"*

"You didn't know that? I couldn't even walk. Nurse Musa laughed his brains out. Called it a case of severe over-enthusiasm."

Antoine went into gales of laughter.

Yerima was dumbstruck. "This is the first I'm hearing about it. Why on earth didn't you tell me, babe?"

Tammy thought it over. "You know, darling, you're right. I was forbidden to mention it."

"Because?"

"Because it might have been construed as criticism, and you know how protective of members' egos they are."

"Antoine, they even taught them to fake it. Fake it! I was appalled."

"Another way of protecting the members' egos," she said. "See, the rare man who knew what he was doing made all the others look bad." Yerima groaned. "I'd been at The Office for more than a year, and he was the only member who figured it out. I was so naïve I didn't even know what I was pretending to do; I was just following orders. He pushed me out of bed, slapped me up, and told me to get the hell out. I had no clue why he was so pissed. We finally got that sorted out, and he took me in his arms and, well, sir, well, he transformed my life."

Antoine threw his head back, eyes closed, laughing. "Yes," he sputtered, "Yerima has been known to transform the lives of hundreds and hundreds of young ladies. Fulfilling his destiny as rescuer of womankind."

83

"But Excellency, teasing aside, I still haven't answered your question. I had a master who was so domineering, so controlling, I mean, every single molecule was devoted to control. One time he kept me blindfolded and chained to the bed for eight days."

"I didn't know about that either, babe," said Yerima, sitting upright, knitting his brow in confusion. "How many more secrets have you been keeping from me?"

"No more than a couple million. That was after–"

"Okay, gotcha."

"He was also extremely vindictive. I overheard phone conversations where he'd order someone destroyed. A pilot refused to sell him a girl he wanted, so he had him fed to a crocodile. A contractor screwed up an installation, and he had the man turned into a female and set to work in a brothel. One man hung up on him, and he ordered him to be hamstrung and his eyes gouged out."

"And he got away with it?"

"Again and again."

"Yerima, I thought you said it was an extremely vengeful society, an eye for an eye, obsessed with family honor and all that."

"It is indeed."

"So how'd he get away with it?"

"Intimidation. Connections. But it won't work forever; one day he'll get what's coming to him."

"Maybe," said Tammy, not entirely convinced, "maybe not. This is how he's done things for more than twenty years. Anyway, sometimes he had slaves put to death just to underscore the extent of the power he had over them; other times, he had them executed because he was having a party and needed a few fresh corpses so he and his guests could have sex with them."

"A necrophiliac! You've got to be kidding! You mean, they actually exist?"

"Yes, Your Excellency, they really do. He's very low-ranking as princes go, but he's such an embarrassment to the royal family that they excluded him from the remotest possibility of succession. Anyway, he was tons worse when he'd had a few glasses of prosecco. The hardest thing I ever did in my life was tell him that his drinking was getting out of hand."

Antoine sat bolt upright, almost knocking Marielle off the chair. He looked at Tammy, at Yerima, back at Tammy.

Yerima said, "I've told you before, she has more balls than I do."

Antoine was still staring at her. "Either extremely gutsy or extremely foolhardy, I'm not sure which."

"Of course, he blew up, and I was in tons and tons of trouble, but then I gave him, I mean, in bed, um…"

"She made him pass out," supplied Yerima. "Using techniques I taught her, she went and made *him* faint. How do you like that? Hey, babe, that's still on your to-do list for me, you know."

Antoine was slapping the arm of the chair, howling with laughter. "So, I assume, he forgave you?"

"Give me time," she told Yerima, "just give me time, dear sir. Yes sir. He said he was going to build a beautiful harem just for me and cover me in diamonds and give me slaves of my own. Just what I always wanted, my own slaves, right?"

"A question here, please. I asked you what was the hardest thing you ever had to do, but I don't understand that you really had to tell him. Excuse me, Sudari, but it seems to me that you took a highly unnecessary risk."

"Good point, sir, but his drinking was getting worse and worse, and at least once before he'd killed a person he loved very much while he was drunk, and I knew that within a few weeks or months he'd kill me as well. My grandmother came to me in a dream and warned me that I was in grave danger, and I've learned to take her warnings seriously. So I could have kept quiet, and been killed, or speak up, and merely run the *risk* of being killed. Anyway, he traveled, and while he was away, my friend Zima and I finally got our revenge on a man who had constantly tormented us, and–"

"They murdered him," Yerima said. "They couldn't take it any longer, so when he got so drunk he passed out, they shackled him to the bed, sawed off a particularly annoying part of his anatomy, and slit his neck. He was Chairman of the Board of the men's club."

Antoine held his head. "Sorry," he said, "I'm having a hard time absorbing all this. First we're talking about necrophiliacs and psychopaths and now you're telling me that Yerima's sweet Sudari committed cold-blooded murder? With those soft ladylike hands?"

"No, Your Excellency, it wasn't cold-blooded at all. Actually, we had the time of our lives, the second-most fun I had in one thousand, nine hundred and four days. We'd set him up for months and months to make him think we wouldn't dare. Anyway, it's not highly recommended for a slave to assassinate an Arab, especially Chairman of the Board, and I was sentenced to be executed by torture. That's when Yerima rescued me. I owe my very life to this wonderful man, Your Excellency. Three months ago I was a slave on death row, and I still can't believe how lucky I am that he set me free, and here I am drinking cognac with the President himself." She wiped a tear from her eye.

"Yerima, my man," Antoine said with a wink, "I strongly recommend that you avoid getting this lady mad at you." He poured refills. "Wasn't that psycho owner of hers upset that you ended up with her? It sounds like he was downright obsessed. I mean, eight days?"

"He was very gracious. For our wedding, he gave Sudari a diamond necklace that appraised at $482,000, and he gave me a gorgeous stallion worth approximately the same. We were surprised, actually, at what a good sport he was."

"Let me clarify," Tammy said quickly, "that we sold both the necklace and the Arabian. We're not keeping a penny. We plan use the money to finance a foundation to combat human trafficking."

"You sold an Arabian, Yerima? Worth a half-million dollars? *You?*"

Yerima shrugged.

"His dream stallion," said Tammy, "I was extremely touched. And to put things in perspective, sir, three years earlier, Prince Ibrahim had paid one hundred and thirteen thousand dollars for me."

"So the horse…oh my." Antoine shook his head and groaned.

"But," Yerima added, "to put things in additional perspective, an architect who fell in love with her offered eight hundred thousand for her, and was turned down."

Antoine sat back and smiled approvingly. "I like what I see between you two. I like it a lot. How are you adjusting to being number four, Sudari?"

Tammy chuckled. "I adore Aïssatou, who's really taken me under her wing. She's strict, but she's also very loving and supportive. Amsi has become my best friend. Yerima told me that even the towels at the hotel are in love with her, and I think he's right. What a dynamite lady." She hesitated.

"And?"

"And then there's JoAnn. Beautiful weather we're having today, right, sir? I hope your sister-in-law will soon be better, sir. Um–"

Antoine roared, while Yerima made a face. "I naïvely thought that since they were both Americans…" He rolled his eyes.

"Sudari, please, I know it's not easy, but find a way to get along with her. Please. For my favorite rascal here, if not for yourself." Antoine grew pensive. "But back to your stallion guy. The more I think about him, the more nervous I get. I know a thing or two about human nature, and I just can't imagine that he's let go. My gut is rarely wrong. Be careful."

88

They sat in silence a few moments.

"I've said almost exactly the same thing to Amsi. I try not to think about it, sir."

"Sudari, you've just given me an idea. I'm going to set up a Presidential Task Force on Human Trafficking, and I'd like for you to serve on it. Would you be willing?"

"Willing, Your Excellency? I'd love to."

"Marielle, can you please go find Martine for me? Tell her to bring a notepad."

"*Tonton*, it's at least five," said Marielle, scowling. "There's Tata Amsi, there's Tata Alizée..."

Yerima laughed. "You're right. But Tata Alizée decided she didn't want to be married to me anymore. So it's still just four. He turned back to Antoine. "Commissaire Yayá would be perfect. And so would Jules N'nang, you know, who cracked the smuggling case."

"Great ideas, Yerima. And Alice Mpondo, the human rights advocate. And we need somebody from the military..."

"How about Annette Mveng, the major who promotes the opportunities that military service offers girls?"

They batted more names around as Tammy became more and more excited, watching a presidential task force materialize before her eyes.

"Martine, please, I'd like for you to meet Yerima's latest vict – I mean wife – Sudari. Martine Atángana is my last tenuous link to sanity. She's my *Directeur de*

Cabinet, or what in English you call Chief of Staff, my top, top aide. She's a constitutional lawyer, knows three-quarters of the population on a first-name basis, and somehow manages to keep thousands of documents and hundreds of projects on track. She also won't let me get away with *anything*."

He'd said it in jest, but there was a brief explosion of tension, and Tammy smelled a story.

"Martine, love, I want to create a Presidential Task Force on Human Trafficking, and I'd like for the decree to go out this coming week. Madame Abdoulaye has already agreed to serve on it, and here are a dozen or so other names of potential members. I'd like to extend a personal invitation to each one."

"So happy to meet you, madame. I love this job, and consider it a high honor, but here it is Saturday afternoon, and of course, I'm at work. Your Ex, I love this idea. You hear stories, you know, like that German tourist who vanished from the beach at Kribi, and that French model who disappeared from the resort at Limbe. And our own girls too, who somehow never get the same level of media coverage."

"It actually happened to Madame Abdoulaye."

"Mon dieu! Really, madame?"

"Yes, some day I'll show you the stainless steel collar that was soldered around my neck. This handsome gentleman here rescued me."

"Collar?" said Antoine, completely taken aback.

"Yes, Your Excellency. I wore a collar and cuffs; it made it easier to strap me down. I saved them to be able to show people."

"I hate to break this up, but we need to be going, babe. Embassy of Canada tonight."

"Always with Aïssatou, never with me. I try not to be jealous, but…" She sighed.

The President rose to see them off. "So, you made your owner pass out, did you? Yerima, my dear cousin, my very able Minister of Foreign Affairs, my lifelong friend, may I borrow her?"

"No way in hell," was the swift reply. The cousins laughed and hugged goodbye.

"I want to see that manuscript, Sudari. And thanks again for agreeing to serve on the task force."

"Thank you for everything, Excellency. I can't wait for it to be up and running."

In the car, Tammy leaned over and kissed Yerima's cheek. "Do you remember, the first day we met and you told me to give you a cat-bath, and I started licking you, and you asked me to tell you how you tasted? And I said, influential. I had no idea how right I was."

"You're going to make a huge difference, Sudari, I just know it. You've seen how these scumballs operate from the inside out. You know names, places. They count on the fact that once they have you, you never get out. I had no idea that Antoine was going to come up with that idea, but it's a great one."

Tammy snuggled against her husband and sighed contentedly. "But a certain hero rescued me and messed up their plans." A quick kiss. "Martine sure seems like a neat lady."

"You don't know the half of it. Just a couple of months ago, Antoine got sick of waiting for the National Assembly to act on a piece of labor legislation, so he decided he'd simply issue it by Presidential decree. She told him in no uncertain terms that he didn't have the constitutional authority. That made him furious, but she dug in her heels. They went several weeks barely speaking. It was Solange who got Martine to calm down and got Antoine to come to his senses. I mean, either the constitution means something, or it doesn't.

"That's another neat lady for you. Solange has a doctorate in microbiology from Stanford. I think I told you that Antoine spent twelve years in Washington with the International Monetary Fund? While they were there, she worked at the World Bank, managing environmental projects. Her father had an accident with a corn grinder when he was a child, and was missing all the fingers on his right hand, so she's also very active in organizations that help the handicapped. She and Aïssatou are very good friends. Don't worry, you'll meet her. I think you two will really hit it off."

"Did the Assembly ever pass the labor law?"

"Nope. The opposition is pretty fragmented, but on this particular issue, they got together and deep-sixed it. And Martine told Antoine it was exactly what he deserved."

Tammy laughed. "I like her more and more. Gutsy lady."

"The second-gutsiest lady I know," he told her, giving her a long and loving kiss. "I'm so proud of you, Sudari, so proud. You were completely at ease with the President of the Republic. You just can't be intimidated, can you?"

She laughed. "Maybe it has something to do with the fact that for three years I served generals and oil tycoons and princes and mega-zillionnaires – as well as the occasional stray ambassador – and you know what? They're all just guys." She thought for a second. "What made me shake in my boots was meeting your other wives. Now *that* was scary."

It was his turn to laugh.

It was still sinking in. He's the one who's proud of *me*? she marveled. Wow.

The President looked resplendent in an ivory damask gandoura and brimless maroon felt hat, quite a departure from his usual conservative suits and flashy Italian ties. He struck a gavel. "Ladies and gentlemen, I'm delighted to call to order the kick-off meeting of the Presidential Task Force on Human Trafficking. This is a topic that we're all vaguely aware of, but its significance really struck home when Yerima Abdoulaye, our Minister of Foreign Affairs, introduced me to his wife Sudari – here present – who had herself been a victim of this horrendous crime and spent five years in slavery. I'd like to start by going around the room. Everybody introduce yourself and give a brief indication of what you can contribute to this task force. And, Madame Abdoulaye, I think it most appropriate that we begin with you. Give us an idea of what you lived through."

"Thank you profoundly, Your Excellency, for creating this task force. It means a lot to me and I hope it will be able to make a difference. I for one pledge my fullest cooperation and dedication to further its goals.

"When I was eighteen I went to visit some friends who lived just outside Marseilles and was abducted. Next thing I knew, I was on the Persian Gulf.

"My first master was Sheikh Khalid. He was 81 years old and I was in his harem only briefly, because he blew up when he discovered that I wasn't the voluptuous Swede he'd ordered. My next master was Sheikh Ahmed, who assigned me to his son, Sheikh Saud. Saud is actually a very nice person and we eventually became friends. He is opposed to the institution of slavery and when I told him on my wedding day that I hoped to establish a foundation to combat human trafficking, he offered to endow it. Anyway, at his house things were very complicated. After about a year, against his loud pro-tests, I was sold to a family friend, Sheikh Fahd.

"Sheikh Fahd owned the most beautiful harem in the entire Middle East, the Rainbow Harem. There were six girls there and we wore fabulous gowns and jewelry. But we were also each dyed a different color. I was Miss Green, and although I left there more than three years ago, my system is still suffering the toxic effects. When Sheikh Fahd's little daughter finally lost her battle with leukemia, he went insane with grief, and became a very scary person. Thank God, Miss Purple managed to poison him.

"My new master was the Prince Macabre, so called because of his fondness for fresh corpses. The technical term, in case you're wondering, is necrophiliac. The prince leased me to a high-class men's club called The Office, where I was obliged to work for more than three years. Here are the collar and cuffs that I wore. These are all I wore, by the way. I was working sixteen or seven-teen hours a day, seven days a week, providing services that were not only disgusting, but often painful as well. If it were a pleasant job, they wouldn't need slaves to do it, right?

"Finally my friend Nenzima and I had had enough. One day a psychopath we really hated had so much to drink that he passed out, so we put him in the same shackles he had just used on us. We sawed off a certain very annoying body part, stuffed it down his throat, and slit his neck. It was very, very sweet revenge. Zima wisely committed suicide right away, but I thought things over too long and when security came up, I was still alive.

"Of course, they aren't exactly dainty with slaves who commit murder, so I was sentenced to be tortured to death at a scary snuff club called The Rodeo. I was put in a big glass pot and a lid was bolted down around my shoulders."

She'd managed to relate everything so far in a matter-of-fact tone, but now her voice broke and she struggled to maintain her composure. "I was supposed to be boiled in oil." She took a deep breath. "That is when my beloved Yerima stepped in and rescued me. Emancipated me. And by the grace of Almighty God, married me." She fought back tears.

"How did you meet him?" one person wanted to know.

"He was a member of the club. It wasn't just a brothel; it had a bowling alley, four restaurants, a cinema, enter-tainment like belly dancers, a gym, a pool, squash courts, all sorts of stuff. When I worked Reception I had to kneel and wash the members' feet, and sometimes we'd talk."

95

The truth and nothing but the truth.

"Can you pass those cuffs around?"

"Sure, here. A surgeon had to saw them off."

"How on earth did you stay sane?"

"I didn't. I got so depressed I wanted to commit suicide, but they monitor you so minutely I couldn't figure out how. Either I was on an assignment, getting ready for an assignment, or strapped to a display table to sleep."

There were more questions, but the President said, "We need to move on. Thank you, Madame Abdoulaye, for a riveting, moving, and disturbing presentation. Your courage impresses all of us." There was a warm round of applause. "We look forward to hearing more details as time progresses, and I encourage everyone to stay after the meeting if your schedule permits to chat. Commissaire Yayá, tell us what brings you here."

"Thank you so much, Excellency, for establishing this task force. I head up a police department specialized in crimes against girls and women – genital mutilation, forced child marriage, rape, domestic violence, and human trafficking. We know what's going on, but it's difficult to fight this crime, especially since, ahem, we are so, ahem, severely underfunded."

The President rolled his eyes as everyone chuckled.

"I was myself a victim of forced marriage when I was eleven years old and became a widow at sixteen. It's only semantics, the difference between a slave and an unwilling child bride. So, Excellency, if we have more resources at our disposal" – more chuckles – "we'll be able to do a much better job of running down leads and bringing these reprehensible criminals to justice."

"Anybody else here underfunded?" asked the President with a good-natured smile, and a half-dozen hands shot up.

"Excuse me, Excellency, I have an idea," Major Mveng said. "There's a small stipend that comes with serving on this task force. I for one would like to waive it and contribute it to the commissaire's department."

A chorus of "me toos" filled the room.

"Martine, love, find a way to transfer these funds from one line item to another without making Seydou have conniptions, will you? And that is a very generous gesture on your part, all of you. Are you happier now, Madame le Commissaire?"

"It's not very much, Excellency," she said pointedly, "but I really appreciate the members' generosity, and of course, every little bit helps."

It was an interesting group of eleven members, most of whom clustered around Tammy when the meeting concluded.

"Please," she begged, "this isn't about me. Do you think I like telling everybody hey, I used to be a slave in a brothel? But if anybody believes I volunteered for the job, they're out of their minds. Yerima keeps reminding me that I have nothing to be ashamed of, that I simply did what I needed to do to stay alive. I'm one of the rare girls who got out, thanks to my amazing husband, and I'm lucky to be able to speak for all the ones who spend years in this horrible underground, completely cut off from the world."

Maïmouna Yayá took both of her hands. "Sudari, you and I are going to be an awesome team, and the two of us are going to do some serious damage."

"Could I volunteer to work with you? I'm dying to go back to school, but it doesn't start until October, and meanwhile, I bet you could teach me a lot."

"Get Yerima's permission," advised the commissaire. "I know he'll say yes, but you'll get wife-points for asking, and it never hurts to have a few in your account."

"I'll ask him tonight," said Tammy. "I'm trying to write a book, but it's so hard, I can only write a few pages and then I have to stop. I've already checked out half the books from the Cultural Center library. And I spend two hours a day teaching the children, but that's really all I have on my schedule. It'll be good to have something meaty to do."

"What would you like to help with?"

"Well, to start off with, maybe help you organize paperwork. I'm good at that. But I'd like to sit in on strategy sessions and contribute what I know from the inside about how this whole underground operates."

"My filing box is an embarrassment. Sounds wonderful. And I'll get this cleared with my higher-ups. I doubt that it will be a problem, given the chair of this task force, but I need to take care of that formality." They exchanged phone numbers and promised to be back in touch the next day.

"Before we get going," Yerima said, "I have a disturbing and highly confidential announcement. There was an attempted *coup* Sunday night." Everyone gasped. "Four colonels and one general faced the firing squad yesterday, including, I'm very sorry to say, my good friend Pierre Nkom."

Amsaou's hand flew to her face. "Oh no! I have to go see Sandrine. That's just terrible!"

"No," said Yerima firmly. "Call her, or send her a note, but a visit would be out of line. Who was her husband trying to take down? And who is my boss?"

"Oh, oh, of course. But that's so *sad*."

"Military Security had been tipped off, so it was put down in less than fifteen minutes. Thirty-some other officers got prison terms. Just a little reminder that Antoine is not universally adored. Issa, we should organize occasional bunker drills." He sighed. "All right. Madame Prime Minister, what's the deal on the warehouse roof that the storm last week messed up?"

"It didn't make the news," Tammy observed. "It didn't make the news at all."

"It won't," Yerima said. "So don't talk about it, all right? Rumors will abound, but don't confirm them. You've heard something, don't know anything for sure."

Hmm, thought Tammy, this is most definitely not Washington.

"I got a contractor here," Aïssatou said routinely, "but he was a strange sort and I finally sent him away. He was asking all sorts of questions about you, Sudari. I have someone else coming on Wednesday."

Yerima and Tammy exchanged puzzled, nervous glances. "Thank you, Aïssatou. Your turn, Amsaou, for a report from Finance."

"Sorry to say that we've been having some pretty serious overruns in Education. Dari, darling, you're way over budget again – again! – and I'm missing a bunch, a bunch of receipts."

Tammy was hardly paying attention; she was still stuck on Aïssatou's comment. Her heart was in her toes.

"She's been buying books and supplies for the children. I authorized it."

"You're a naughty boy, Yerima, you didn't tell me that you authorized an overrun like this."

"That's because he just this second decided, as usual, to do anything to keep perfect little Miss Sudari out of trouble," spat JoAnn. "How much longer is she going to be a special case, Yerima? How much longer do you plan to give her special treatment? She's been here nearly six months and I'm sick and tired of the favoritism you keep showing her."

"All right, JoAnn, let's talk about this. Right after the meeting I will transfer you to the servants' quarters and we'll hang a sign on your door that says Open for Business, eighteen hours a day. You will not voice a single word of complaint, no matter how disgusting the man or how revolting the service. You will kneel or even prostrate to show him how much you respect him, even if you really hate his guts. In return he will slap you around, beat you up, kick you, or strap you down. Or in the case of Ibrahim, put you in shackles just because he likes the way it looks. You live like that for five years, JoAnn, and we'll see if you don't deserve special con-sideration when you finally resurface. Now apologize."

"I'm sorry, Yerima."

"No, to her."

JoAnn studied Yerima for a moment. He met her gaze. She sighed. "I'm sorry, Sudari."

"It's okay, JoAnn, I have a lot of things to work on. Readjusting to normal life is harder than I thought." She was close to tears. "I figured that I'd sort of, like, push a button, and be myself again, but it's a whole lot more complicated than that. I was confined to very small spaces for a long time, and the real world is over-whelming. It's big, it's confusing, and it's really scary. I'm trying, and God knows I want to do this right, but it's a lot, a lot tougher than I ever imagined."

"Another rude outburst like that, JoAnn, and I will deprive you of one of the principal benefits of marriage for a very long time. Do I make myself clear?"

"Yes sir."

"Amsi, I have a pile of receipts for you on my kitchen counter. I just keep forgetting to give them to you," Tammy said.

"Then you're a naughty girl too."

"Yes, I am, and I'm really sorry."

"What about Agriculture?" Yerima asked JoAnn.

"Wait a sec, please," said Amsaou. "We have two houses with issues. House Seventeen is now seven months behind on the rent. You were going to talk to them, Aïssatou?"

"Yes, I did. Special situation. It would be cruel to evict them, so I think we should just wait. They'll catch up."

"We'll trust your excellent judgment," said Yerima.

"Okay, and House Nine has needed eight plumbing repairs in eleven months. I strongly suspect that the kids are putting things down the toilet."

"Can you confirm that with the plumber? We should bill them for whatever repairs were due to negligence. Finished?"

"Yes sir."

"Agriculture?"

"The vegetables are sprouting; we can start harvesting in five or six weeks. What a great place to live, with three growing seasons a year! And I've started planting the hibiscus around the north fence."

"Fine job," said Yerima. "Education?"

"I meet with two or three children every day, and it's a lot of fun. What wonderful kids! Samira has gone from a 12 in history to a 16, and Ditto got a 19 on an English test the other day and couldn't believe it."

"They love you," said Yerima.

"Of course," sniped JoAnn. "Everybody loves perfect little Miss Sudari."

Tammy was still so focused on what Aïssatou had said that she let the snide remark pass. What in the dickens was Ibrahim cooking up? And why was that knot in her stomach growing bigger and bigger?

CHAPTER FOUR

The four conspirators were in their usual far corner of the salon, deep in thought. One would say something, and the others would think it over and start shaking their heads. Then a different one would say something, and they'd think about that, and shake their heads again.

Mr. Faisal, brow knitted, watched them from a distance. "Trevino," he said, "those four are up to something. I want you to tell me what it is."

"It's hard to listen without being really obvious about it, sir, the way they've positioned themselves."

"Hmm. They think they're clever, don't they? Well, try this. Work your way over to them very slowly, from the side. And pretend that you're interested in some other conversation."

Twenty minutes later, Trevino was back. "They're speaking very softly, sir, couldn't hear a thing. May I make a suggestion? Bug the flowers on the table next to them."

"His Highness isn't crazy about using such devices – a lot more trouble than they're worth. But I think in this case, we'll go ahead. Good idea."

No one thought anything about it when an hour later, a smiling housekeeper brought a fresh bouquet, set it on the table, and removed the old one.

Next day, Mr. Faisal had to strain to make out the fuzzy conversation, but one telling sentence was clear: "His dinner knife; it's the only way."

"Trevino, keep a close eye on them. I think those ladies are planning an assassination."

The three new girls were sitting in Mr. Sayeed's office, where they had been served tea and pistachio cookies. Two had puffy red eyes, but the third was smiling excitedly.

"Welcome to Il Giardino Posteriore. You are now the posessions of His Highness Prince Ibrahim. He is an extremely handsome and generous master and if you behave yourselves, you should be happy here. Many girls here are madly in love with him, by the way. This is a very prestigious harem and you should be honored that you have been selected for it. It is large, however, so we have a few rules to keep things pleasant. First, you will learn the affirmation of submission by heart. His Highness frequently visits the harem and he often requests that all the girls prostrate and recite it.

"It goes like this: 'You are my master, and I am your slave. You rule me completely and absolutely, and I must obey whatever you command me to do immediately, fully, and willingly.' You will memorize it today. You will also write it one hundred times in Arabic, and one hundred times in your own language. Please note that we already have it in forty-four languages, so there's no cheating."

"*Prostrate*, did you say?" asked the willowy platinum blonde. "Curtsey, yes. Stand at attention, yes. But *prostrate?* I've *never* had to prostrate before."

"You will address me as sir. Yes. Prostrate. With your arms fully extended and your forehead planted firmly on the floor. Yes. Prostrate. He requires it."

"I don't speak Arabic," said the petite brunette.

"You too will address me as sir. Then you will learn it. And you will learn it quickly. We offer classes, four different levels. And you will write the affirmation in Arabic as required, even if it takes you all day and all night.

"Second, you must always wear the tunic that corresponds to your rank. Any breach of this rule will get you forty strokes, since everything here is organized by rank. By the way, you will each receive temporary rankings that correspond to vacancies; your actual ranking will be assigned to you after the annual physical review. Also, you must eat everything on your plate whether you like the food or not; this violation will get you ten strokes. You must never touch your own body or the body of any of the other girls; you all are here solely for the pleasure of His Highness and we enforce this rule very strictly. Fifty strokes. No fighting with the other girls; you will always comport yourselves as dignified, refined ladies. You will also hold your arms still by your side as you walk, no arms swinging like chimpanzees.

"Each month, you will receive a performance evaluation based on several criteria: cooperation, submissiveness, refraining from complaining and crying, and most of all, how pleased His Highness is with you when he summons you to his bedchamber. You start the month with eighty points. You can earn bonus points for outstanding behavior, or you can get demerits if you break rules or behave in a manner unbecoming to a girl hand-picked to grace a royal harem.

"When His Highness summons you, you will be escorted to his bedchamber. When you are in his presence, you say nothing until he greets you. You will prostrate in recognition of his absolute authority over you as well as your willingness to do whatever he wishes. His sexual tastes are usually pretty standard, but he does like being in full control." He sat back in his chair. "Any ques-tions?"

"When do we get to meet His Highness, sir?" the statuesque honey blonde asked eagerly.

"Whenever His Highness pleases," was the curt reply. "All right, Mr. Firenze will take you on a tour of the facility and answer any more questions you might have. Again, welcome, and have a pleasant day."

Firenze was showing them the refectory when the brunette blurted, "Excuse me, is it true that Prince Ibrahim has sex with corpses?"

"None of your business. Now over here is the infirmary—"

"They call him the Prince Macabre, you know," said the platinum blonde.

The brunette covered her face with her hand. "So, the answer is yes. I don't believe that I belong to a sicko now. My last master was—"

Firenze said, "That's a good way to get into trouble here, both of you. Showing disrespect toward your master. First offense, a warning. Second offense, thirty strokes and five days in detention. Third, fifty strokes and ten days. First we paint your rear with nettle extract, then we strap you to this thing over here; let me show you. Usually, after two or three days you can turn over again. And after five or six, walk."

A girl was already strapped in place.

"What is that sign around her neck?"

"It says, 'I displeased my master and will therefore be executed in three days.' She had the lowest performance evaluation of the month. She's kept like that for four hours a day and you can earn two points by paddling her five strokes strong enough to register on the sensor. The rest of the time, she's tied to that pillar over there. They put that canopy to keep it in the shade; before, several girls died from the heat before they could be properly executed."

The platinum blonde was aghast. "You mean, he executes a girl every month?"

"Yes, of course. Just a little motivation for you to behave yourselves and to be especially accommodating when he wishes to exercise his proprietary rights. Sometimes, even more. Occasionally he points to you at random and says that today you're going to die. And, well, you die. And if you commit a capital crime, of course. A couple of years ago, two idiots attempted to assassinate him and were dispatched to the Rodeo. Now, like I was saying, this is the infirmary."

"What's the Rodeo, Mr. Firenze?"

"A snuff club where disobedient slaves or other criminals are executed in, shall we say, entertaining and imaginative ways." The girls exchanged horrified glances. "Each girl gets a complete check-up once a year as well as a visit from a dentist. Nurses are on duty sixteen hours a day and you are free to consult them anytime you wish."

"How is this poor girl going to be executed?"

"By drowning in the fountain. Over here is the salon, and off the far end is the interfaith prayer room, back there is the garden, and of course, this is the courtyard. By the way, when outside men need to come into the harem, the gong will sound three times. This means that you must immediately drop whatever you are doing and go into the salon. We close the curtains and lock the doors until they leave. A few weeks back, for example, a repair crew had to come and fix the walk-in freezer. The gardeners and other male staff come at night, by the way, when all the girls are in the dormitory."

"Mr. Firenze, I was surprised that the harem has male managers," said the blonde. "Isn't that, I mean…?"

"There are six eunuchs, and the managers are required to wear special sheaths so that they can't mess around with royal property."

"And you're one of the eunuchs?"

"Yes."

"How long?"

"None of your business."

They crossed to the other side of the courtyard. "Behind this wall is the detention area."

The inductees saw two high-ranking discplinarians barking orders to seven detainees. "Kowtow. Prostrate. Okay, now, forty knee-bends. Kneel up. Kneel down."

110

"They spend ten hours a day like that when they're on detention. And they get half rations. The rest of the time, they're locked in the detention room. See? Just benches and a toilet. And no, it isn't air-conditioned, and the windows up there by the ceiling don't open."

"Where do they sleep, Mr. Firenze?" the honey blonde asked.

Firenze shrugged. "On a bench, on the floor, wherever. It's a jail. It's not meant to be luxury accommodations."

"Dark gray," said the brunette. "How depressing."

Then he showed them a row of six cells, two of which contained girls who were forlornly staring into space. "This is the Arrividerci Ragazza unit. Goodbye girl. In other words, Death Row. The one on the left has been here for two months, and the other for five."

"When and how will they be executed?"

"When he throws a party, obviously," said the brunette.

"You've been here less than an hour, and you're already asking for trouble. Be careful, or you're going to be the next one with the sign around her neck. No date has been set."

"What did they do?"

"One screamed insults at His Highness, and the other categorically refused to say the affirmation of submission. When he decided to send her to the Ranch, she made matters worse by cursing him."

"What's the Ranch, Mr. Firenze?"

"A prison where cowboys can play with the inmates. And they play rough. Ask Six Zeta about it; she was there for a few weeks. His Highness noticed her at a branding party and brought her here."

"What did she do?"

"Runs in my mind that she bit a customer."

They walked over to the dormitory, and Firenze unlocked a door.

The girls gasped.

"They call *that* a dormitory?" the brunette said. "Six girls to a room the size of a closet? Not even a window? My last master owned more than 200 women, but we all had private suites, a bedroom and a bathroom. With a tv. We only got two channels, but at least it was something."

This time, she got a slap. "You have one week to settle in and get used to the rules. And His Highness takes his rules seriously, believe me. The bunks are narrow and closely stacked because he disapproves of lesbianism. You remember what Mr. Sayeed said about not touching another girl? He means it."

"Prince Mohammed did, too; we just weren't allowed in another girl's room."

"How long were you there?" asked the honey blonde.

"Six years. And I never once laid eyes on him. Where were you before?"

"I was given as a birthday present to a fifteen-year-old sheikh, but he threw a tantrum because he had clearly specified that he wanted girls who were one meter eighty or taller, and I'm only one-seventy-seven. Before that, I belonged to an eighty-two-year-old prince, who died. I was in his harem for four years and I saw him exactly once. What about you?" she asked the platinum blonde.

"I belonged to Sheikh Abdullah. I was there for three years and he slept with me twice. The rest of the time we had to sit quietly with our hands folded and just wait. I thought I was going to go nuts. A girl who had the nerve to say 'Wow, am I ever bored' got forty lashes."

"Here," said Firenze, "girls serve His Highness on a rotation according to the date of acquisition, so you'll be in his bedchamber at least two or three times a year. Now. Back to the morning routine.

"A buzzer sounds, which unlocks the door for three minutes. You get up, fold your nightgown neatly and place it on the pillow, put your tunic from yesterday in the laundry basket, and stand at attention outside the door. If you aren't outside by the time it locks again, you have to stay in the dormitory all day, so be sure you get out on time. Then you shower and brush your teeth, after which, attendants will apply make-up and do your hair.

"After that, everyone goes to the refectory for breakfast, then to the Training Room where you watch instructional videos for one hour. Then you may take Arabic or another elective. One hour of aerobics, then another hour of practical instruction – staggered, to allow for individual attention – and another hour of electives. Then you may sit in the garden, socialize in the salon, relax in the courtyard, whatever you wish."

"Except, have a life," the brunette said blackly. This time, Firenze slapped her twice.

Dr. Lolowah finished her induction examination of the platinum blonde. "Padlock?" she asked as mildly as she could. Not the first time she'd seen it, and probably not the last, but it was disturbing nevertheless.

"Yes ma'am. Sheikh Abdullah died, and his son Sheikh Habib inherited us. Then he went absolutely wild buying more girls. Before, we each had our own room, but soon there were three, and even four to a room, and there was only one small bed, and stuff started happening that he didn't approve of, so he had us all padlocked shut.

"But the matron got overwhelmed trying to keep track of everything. Half the time the kitchen ran out of food, we could only shower once a week because there was no hot water, on and on. A total disaster. Then the matron got sick and died, and nobody knew where she'd put the keys. Probably a hundred and fifty girls, and they could only find five or six keys. So yes, doctor, here I am, padlocked."

Dr. Lolowah shook her head. "I'll have to saw it off you, and it isn't going to be easy."

The pay was good, but being a harem doctor was often so depressing, she didn't know how much longer she could do it. The things men did to women just because they could! She sighed, and took out her surgical saw.

"At the Ranch," said Six Zeta, "if you had big frontal projections you were a heifer instead of a filly, and wore a cow's head mask and a cow's tail. But they were kept in the barn where I never went and I have no idea how they were handled in the rooms. Nobody ever told you anything, of course. In fact, they never even spoke to you. They'd just say, 'take four-three to room 414,' or 'bring sixteen-one to the corral for her weekly paddling'; you never went anywhere or did anything on your own. You got taken places and you endured what they did to you and that was the end of it. Even so, a few inmates managed to misbehave – don't ask me how – and got themselves flogged. I heard one of the floggings when I was in the corral on display. It was a gelding. No screams, because of the pacifier, just the sound of a whip tearing into flesh. They took out the pacifiers for the branding parties, though, because screams were an essential part of the entertainment."

"*Ta'aal huna,* come over here," Prince Ibrahim said to the frightened girl who'd just been delivered to him. She prostrated awkwardly. "Smile at your master. You may kneel."

One Rho closed her eyes – never a good sign – and fell to her knees. Her lips quivered, but never actually formed a smile.

"How old are you, my dear?"

"Eighteen, master." Her voice trembled.

"And how long have you been in this harem?"

"Not quite three years, master."

"Where are you from?"

"Hamburg, master."

"*Zehr gut,* very well," he said, trying to help her relax a little. "You will start by massaging my feet. Then you will feed me dinner."

It was one of the worst massages he'd ever endured.

"Forget it," he said at length. "You're not going to catch the plague if you actually touch me, you know. Abdul? One Rho is totally incompetent. Remove her entirely from the rotation and dock her twenty points. I don't want to see her here ever again. And you, my hopeless little *jaria*, are dismissed."

"You've banned me from your bed, master?"

"Yes."

"*Jawohl!*" she said under her breath, but not softly enough.

"*Komm zurück! Schnell!* Come back here at once! "On your knees!" His slap knocked her several feet. "Abdul, forty strokes and ten days for gross insubordination. Get the hell out of here before I do serious damage."

He sank back down into his chair. You give them instructional DVDs. You even hire a trainer. And they still act like they've never seen a male before. "Abdul, send me the next one. She'd better not be such a total disaster."

Fifteen minutes later, Giuliano ushered in Zero Alpha. Ah. She walked with dignity and prostrated with real respect.

"It's so good to see you, my dear. How have you been?"

"Quite well, thank you, master. How may I give you pleasure tonight, master?"

"I want you to feed me my dinner, give me a bath, and then a nice massage. Would you do that for me?"

"With pleasure, master."

"You may sit on my lap while you feed me." He grabbed a breast and licked her nipple. "You look much nicer than the last time you were here."

She gave him a wry smile. "I'm delighted that you find me pleasing, master."

"Do you like your new shape?"

She gulped. Cast her eyes downward. "Here, master, some nice risotto."

A small slap. "You're not answering me."

She began to tremble.

"I asked you a simple question and I'm expecting an answer."

"I'm glad you find me pleasing, master." She closed her eyes. "Some asparagus, master?"

Another small slap. "Now you're stalling."

She shrugged. "Please, master, some fresh mozzarella."

"You're not going to say anything else, are you?"

"I owe you respect and obedience, master." In other words, don't ask any more questions, because I'm scared to death I'll give you the wrong answer.

He sighed in exasperation. "One of the girls told me that the device is uncomfortable. Is that true?"

"It is an honor to be selected for this harem, master." She stiffened and her breathing was labored.

Nobody had the nerve to tell him the truth. Either they told him what he wanted to hear, or avoided the issue altogether. He sighed, and chuckled when he remembered how shocked he'd been when Mukhmala had looked him squarely in the eye and given it to him straight. Who has a bigger dominator, me, or the professor? *The professor*, she'd told him without hesitation. Who's better in bed, me, or the professor? *The professor.* But how can that be? I make you scream. *Yes, master,* she'd said, *but the professor makes me faint.* He laughed again when he remembered how deflated he'd felt – sometimes the truth isn't fun to hear at all. But she'd explained that she was refusing to flatter him out of respect, that he'd immediately figure out that her answers were empty flattery, so she preferred to tell him the unvarnished truth. The only girl who'd ever, ever had the guts to do that.

There was nobody like Mukhmala, nobody. How could he, a royal prince, let that damned slave occupy such a big place in his thoughts? But they'd passed out together in each other's arms. And he'd finally made *her* faint, so he no longer had to swallow being second-best. But she'd also had the nerve to criticize him for drinking. Stepped way, way over the line, that time. Damn, damn the insolent *imara moshaakis!* Bitch!

Giuliano ducked as the bottle of prosecco came flying across the room. "Your Highness?"

"Send this girl back. No bonus points, no demerits. A total waste of my time." He sighed.

118

"May I feed you the rest of your dinner, Your Highness?"

"No thanks, Giuliano, I've just about lost my appetite. I'm so sick of spineless *mutamalikin,* yes-men, and fawning *jariaat*, slave girls, and answers that aren't really answers, and calculated flattery. Obey orders, yes. Show due respect, yes. Give diplomatic answers, of course. But this is ridiculous." A half-smile. "The girls talk to you sometimes. What's going on?"

Giuliano hesitated ever so slightly and closed his eyes. Then he plunged. "They hate the bras, Your Highness. In fact, I've heard that they're planning a revolt."

"You're kidding."

"They hate them, Your Highness."

"But I thought they'd love having beautiful bosoms."

"That's not the issue, Your Highness. Apparently they hurt. A lot."

The Prince absorbed this information. "I love my girls. I'm not trying to hurt them. They told me there was mild discomfort, but not pain." He picked up his phone. "Abdul? Ditch the stupid rotation for tonight. Two duds in a row. Send me a girl who'd like to have some fun, not a dutiful automaton. Ten minutes? All right. Oh, by the way, have you heard rumors of an impending revolt?"

"Every few months we hear such rumors and they never amount to anything, Your Highness."

"Have any of the girls complained that the devices are painful?"

"We implemented the program exactly as directed, Your Highness."

Prince Ibrahim groaned and hung up the phone in disgust. Yet another spineless baboon.

A few minutes later, Three Zeta appeared. "I'm so happy you let me come serve you tonight, master." She broke the rule – he was supposed to address her before she spoke unless she simply acknowledged him by saying Master – but he liked what he heard and let the violation pass. She gripped his ankles and fervently kissed his feet.

This was more like it. "Would you care to give this tired master of yours a nice massage?"

A big smile, a tremor of anticipation. She hummed happily as she worked the lotion into his taut skin, coaxed the tension from his muscles. It felt good. Really good.

"Thank you, my dear. Giuliano, shackle her to the A-frame. Just a little slack. Do you enjoy being restrained, my dear?"

Giuliano snapped the last leg iron in place.

"With you, master, it's okay. You just do it for fun. I had one master – well, he didn't do it for fun. But master, please, one problem: my nose is suddenly itching something awful, and I can't rub it."

He laughed. "I think I can take care of that for you. There, is that better?" She nodded.

He liked the way she said master, as naturally as if it were simply his name, not like the girls who gagged on the word. She'd fully accepted the fact that she was his possession. A promising start.

"Now I plan to rub somewhere else." His practiced fingers soon had her writhing with desire, but the chains kept her in control. Beautiful. Eager. Completely helpless. An intoxicating combination. She was almost at her destination when he mounted her. He sensed she was coming, and pulled back. Again, more intensely, and he pulled back yet again. He kept building, and drawing back, and building, and drawing back. When she was almost in tears, he allowed her to explode. Wild with pleasure, she strained futilely against her bonds. So defenseless, so powerless. So responsive. Completely under his control. He let himself go and fell onto her, staying fully engaged until the throbbing had subsided and her shrieks had turned to happy whimpers.

Not bad. Not bad at all. This was what owning girls was all about. But *laa samaha allaa*, heaven help her, she was still no Mukhmala.

CHAPTER FIVE

Sheikha al-Jauhara's black eyes were flashing thunder-bolts. "You have the nerve to call yourselves men," she demanded, "when your father has been branded, blinded, devocalized, and forced to work in a brothel? And you just sit there? I'm ashamed of every last one of you. Every day when he wakes up, he's no doubt thinking, at least I have three fine sons who will avenge me and redeem the family honor. But you're nothing but spineless *jabaan.* Cowards. You're an embarrassment, all three of you."

"But Mother..." began Talal.

"Don't you dare 'but mother' me! So? His cousin Prince Daood is a big-wig at the Police. Make it look like an accident."

"Mother, do you really want us to end up like the others? Nawwaf was sent to the Rodeo. They brushed his skin with acid so it burned off. Gouged out his eyeballs and fed them to him. They tortured him for three weeks! Then there was Mustafa. They put him in a cage, pumped him full of female hormones so he'd grow boobs, hamstrung him, put a little pink ribbon around his dick, and–"

"In other words, Ibrahim has succeeded in intimidating you. Since he's such a big *futuwah,* bully, everybody just stands back and lets him get away with outrage after outrage."

"Mother, everywhere he goes, he has four bodyguards. Four! He knows that half the kingdom hates his guts."

"You boys are sitting there like Wednesday in the middle of the week, like bumps on a log. Two slave girls were finally able to take out Dr. Hassan, and the only resource they had was courage. We have plenty of resources, but you're missing the key element: guts. Now go out there and pretend – at least pretend – that you're worthy to be called men. Are you going to let two slave girls show more courage than you? *Slave girls?*"

Salman, the youngest, finally spoke up. "The others were idiots. They tried to kill him here. He travels a lot. His defenses are probably down when he's overseas."

The sheikha set her cup of *gawaha* down with a clatter. "First sensible thing anybody's said all day. Find out everything you can about these trips – where he stays, what the set-up is. Everything."

Fahim sat up sharply. "Why not join forces? I think I know someone who knows the son of the pool contractor."

"And I know one of the sons of the pilot who was fed to the crocodile," said Salman.

"The hand of God is with the group. Are you going to do this?"

"Yes, Mother, you can count on us."

Sheikha al-Jauhara took a decisive swig of *gawaha* and smiled with satisfaction. Maybe they'd turn out to be actual men after all.

"At the Ranch, the cowboys could choose from several dozen DVDs that all, of course, had Western themes. The rocking horse where the filly was attached was programmed to match the DVD, so it would walk, or canter, or gallop, or even buck, depending on the DVD. There were built-in spurs – I still have marks on my sides – and sometimes the cowboys would wear extras on their elbows. I hated them. I also hated the riding crops, which most of the cowboys used.

"In the corral, we were displayed over a raised log. When a cowboy whacked you on the rear, that meant he wanted you harnessed up and taken to his room. The handcuffs they used on us were adjustable, so they could pull our elbows back, then they'd slide a command bar through your elbows behind your back. Then one eunuch would grab one end and another would grab the other, and they'd propel you along. There was nothing you could do except go where they took you. They'd put you on a cart and insert the bar into special grooves so that you were completely immobilized. Riding backwards, they took you to the room, where two more eunuchs would lock you into whichever position the cowboy wanted. What an awful, awful place."

"Hi, Charles," Tammy said into the phone. "Would it be possible, please, for you to pick me up here at the Cultural Center now instead of an hour from now?"

"I'll pass you to Madame JoAnn," he said.

"Hi, JoAnn. Listen, the person I was supposed to meet fell and broke her arm, so she's headed to the hospital instead of here, and I've already checked out all the books they'll let me check out, and I don't really want to sit here for another hour. Is there any way Charles could pick me up now, please?"

"You're always messing with the schedule and there's no way we can keep up with all your outrageous demands."

"I'm not always messing with the schedule, JoAnn, I'm just trying to live a life that occasionally needs adjustments. Where are you now?"

"I'm on my way home to pick something up, and then I'm heading right back out again."

"Can you swing by and pick me up, by any chance?"

"Sorry."

"JoAnn, I'm not asking for the moon, here. I hardly ever have the car, and every now and then I need it for something besides school and church and work. You keep it, like, eighty percent of the time."

"I outrank you, so, too bad."

"I acknowledge that. And I try to be reasonable. But you're not being one bit nice, or one bit fair."

"Tough shit, Sudari, tough shit."

Tammy hung up the phone, eyes blazing, and turned to the Cultural Affairs Officer. "Angela, isn't it ironic? I get along great with my two Fulani co-wives, but it's the American who's driving me nuts."

"I'd ask Hans to drop you off, but he's picking someone up at the airport."

"No big deal, I'll just take a taxi. Aïssatou will throw a hissy-fit, but so be it. Won't be the first time, and it certainly won't be the last."

"May I see you for a second?" Aïssatou asked Tammy several days later as they left the women's dining room after breakfast.

"What can I do for you, ma'am?" Oh brother, another scolding. Three, four times a week. Couldn't Aïssatou see how hard she was trying? And how difficult it was?

"I've had several people tell me recently that they've seen you getting into taxis. You're a wife of the Minister of Foreign Affairs, Sudari. What possesses you, my dear, to take taxis when you have a car and driver at your disposal?"

"Ma'am, I'm the *fourth* wife of the Minister of Foreign Affairs, and that's the problem. Have you ever tried to share a car with JoAnn? It's only occasionally that she condescends to do me a huge favor and let me use it. If I can get something onto the schedule a week or two in advance, ma'am, I can get the car. But if I just need to go somewhere, she always has it, and gee, sorry, there's no way she can rearrange things. She usually keeps the car from nine to four, and Charles has to stay with her the whole time, even if I just need it for forty-five minutes somewhere in the middle. I can get to school, I can get to the commissariat, I can get to task force meetings and church, but that's it. If I want to get a haircut and haven't scheduled it way in advance, I take a taxi. Anything else, I take a taxi.

"Yes ma'am, I agree, it's ridiculous, but instead of making scenes eight or ten times a week, I just get into a cab. If you calculate how often she has it, I bet she has it eighty percent and me twenty percent, or even eighty-five and fifteen. I'm not really used to riding around in a chauffeured Mercedes and I'm not too snobbish to take taxis, so that's what I've been doing. Tell me, ma'am, what should I do? I'd appreciate your advice."

"I'll talk to her. I didn't realize it'd gotten this far out of hand."

"You told me to defer to her, ma'am, and that's exactly what I've been doing, but it's getting harder and harder. She's being absolutely contemptible and frankly, I'm running out of patience. Three or four times a day she finds ways to put me down, flaunt her superior position, or remind me that I used to be a whore. I'm polite to her, I'm deferential to her, I adore Cathy and Michael even though they're hers, but it's not going to take very many more taxi rides, or very many more deliberate insults, for me to get fed up. I don't think I've ever done anything mean to her, ma'am, but I married Yerima, and that's all it took. I can't remember one single time that she's been civil to me, not one."

"I understand. The three of us will sit down tomorrow and work out a schedule for the car. You should absolutely, positively, not be riding around in taxis. Yerima would die of embarrassment, and besides, it's simply not safe. Next time you have a problem, call me, and I'll mediate."

"Even when you're presiding over hearings? I don't mind bothering you occasionally, ma'am, but I hate being a tattle-tale. If I told you every time I had an issue with the car, I'd be an absolute pest."

"Text me, and I'll find a way to deal with it. I'm sorry, Sudari. She's exceedingly jealous of you, feels like there's no way she can compete with your, um, background. Neither one of you grew up in a household like this, but I'm sure we'll be able to work out something."

At her wedding Tammy had promised to respect Yerima's other wives. But she never imagined that it would be this hard. She thought she was so inured to putting up with crap that everything would just roll off her back. Most of the men at The Office treated her like she hardly existed, looking through her rather than at her, and she finally got used to being invisible, merely an object. But these were deliberate, calculated, premed-itated put-downs. Grinding her under her foot. Rubbing her nose in her low rank. Going out of her way to be nasty.

A package deal, though. You marry Yerima, you get his other wives. She sighed. She went back to her apartment and clutched Titi so hard she squealed. "Titi, I can't just continue to hate my co-wife." Titi tilted her head in a way that somehow reminded Tammy of her mother and her favorite dictum, When everything else fails, try love.

Of course.

Love JoAnn? Tammy rolled her eyes and sadly shook her head. Nice theory, but in this case, no way.

A few days after returning from a conference in Tokyo, Yerima took a stair wrong, wrenched his knee, and wound up having surgery to repair the damage. Tammy was almost glad, because it meant that he'd have to cut back on his grueling schedule, which was spinning farther and farther out of control.

"He's such a big baby when he's sick," Amsi said. He's whining, he's helpless…"

"Yerima? Helpless? I can't even picture it."

"Allah!" She rolled her eyes and laughed. "Dari, darling, you have no idea. Oh, sweetheart, can you do this. Oh, sweetheart, can you help me with that. It's like he can't even feed himself any more. He really milks it. His mother said that when he was five, he hurt his finger, and when he didn't get sufficient amounts of sympathy, he held his finger and *limped*. He hasn't changed one bit!"

But he asked JoAnn to stay with him in the hospital, and JoAnn to stay with him as he recovered at home.

"He's trying to salvage a strained relationship," Aïssatou explained.

"But, ma'am, he's straining his relationship with me because I'm excluded from all this. He's my husband, too, and I'd like to be able to take care of him, at least some of the time."

"Il faut supporter, ma chérie," she said. Just put up with it, my dear. "JoAnn thinks he favors you far too much. He's trying to reestablish a balance. It's not always easy, sharing a husband, but he's a good man, and he tries very hard to be fair. Trust him. It all works out in the long run."

"It hurts, ma'am," Tammy said. "I'm surprised at how much it hurts. I'm not proud of it, but I can't help but notice that it hurts."

She could picture her mother staring at her expectantly, reproachfully. Try love? *Love?* "Mother," she said out loud when she got back to her apartment, "Nice idea, but believe me, you obviously don't know JoAnn."

"The hibiscus along the fence look absolutely fabulous, JoAnn, you've done an incredible job with them. Huge improvement."

"Thank you, Mr. President. But may I please point out that half my plans are on hold because Education got such a huge chunk of my budget." She threw Tammy a scathing look.

"Are you still sore about that? Zheesh! It's all right. We understand. Unusual circumstances, and we had to take unusual steps. Besides, her entire budget is only one-quarter what yours is, so don't overstate your case."

"Ever since she's been here, it's been Sudari this and Sudari that. You're supposed to treat us all equally, and you used to do a pretty good job of it, but I've had it. I thought I could live in a polygamous household because I trusted you to be fair, Yerima, but this has gone too far."

"That's strange. Alizée used to complain that I was always favoring you."

"Just because I don't know how to make you faint doesn't mean you have to treat me like I'm second-class."

"Oh, *that's* what this is all about. I don't expect you to make me faint. And you're most assuredly not second-class. Listen, this is our weekly household meeting. Let's talk about personal matters afterwards."

"I'm unfortunately not a professional whore like perfect little Miss Sudari."

Tammy rose and hung her handbag on her shoulder.

"Sudari! Where the hell do you think you're going?"

"That was her five millionth intentional provocation, Yerima, and I'm sorry, but that's my absolute limit. I've been as patient can be, and as deferential as I know how, but I'm not going to sit there politely and take it anymore. Good day." She threw back her shoulders and stalked out.

"I strongly recommend that you retract that last statement, JoAnn."

"See, Yerima? There you go again. She *was* a professsional whore, dammit."

"JoAnn, not now. Let's get back to the order of business. Amsaou, how's the budget faring?"

"We're–"

"I'm not finished, Yerima. I'm sick and tired of this. You can go to hell with your Ministry of Agriculture. You can go to hell with your Ministry of Education. And you sure as hell can go to hell with your darling little professional whore."

"Think it over, JoAnn, don't be rash."

"I've thought it over, Yerima, and I'm out of here. I'll love you with my whole heart until the day I die, but this just isn't the kind of marriage I had in mind."

"I'm sorry. I'm very sorry. Shall I ask Maître Anagho to draw up the papers?"

"Might as well."

"Do you plan to go back to New York?"

"Why should I? I love it here. Cathy and Michael are here. I love my job. I feel needed, like I'm actually making a contribution. If a certain cabinet minister could arrange for me to get a permanent resident visa, I'll stay here."

Yerima rested his forehead in his hand and sighed. "Meeting is adjourned," he said sadly.

"The stable at the Ranch where they kept you was air-conditioned when horses lived there, but these days, since it's just slaves – prisoners – they shut it off. It was so hot it was almost suffocating, but they didn't care. One day a filly actually passed out, but they dragged her off to work anyway.

"They called me Four-Three, fourth stall, third position. There was a beautiful sign over the stall that said Baab al-Samaa', Door of Heaven. I think that was the name of the horse that used to live there. Much nicer name than Four-Three, that's for sure.

"I overheard the overseers one day talking about Sheikh Mohammed, who used to own the whole complex. He decided to sell just at the time the Circuit wanted to add a snuff club and a prison, so the Rodeo is just on the other side of the parking lot. In the complex is also a greenhouse commercial vegetable production center, a Halaal slaughterhouse, and a bone meal plant. When I figured out where some of the bones came from, I threw up.

"I'm so lucky that Prince Ibrahim rescued me. I still have screaming nightmares about that place."

Tammy was in Aïssatou's apartment, helping her organ-ize her case files. The senior wife moved a stack onto the dining table. "They're piling up and piling up and it's not fair to the litigants. I wish you could help me write the judgments, but I'm afraid that's something I need to do myself."

"Is it?" asked Tammy. "Why don't you just tell me what to write, and I'll draft something, and you can edit it, and we'll get this backlog all caught up. Show me a few samples, and I'll take a whack at it. If we can do two or three a day, in a month we'll have waded through this whole stack." She sat down, notepad in hand.

"Would you do that for me, my dear? Honest?"

"Of course. And it's not just for you, it's for all these people who are trying to paste their lives back together. We need to get caught up."

"Tell you what. I'll go through each one and stick a note to it, and we'll give it a try." She smiled at her young co-wife. "For that, you deserve a nice cup of citronelle. Fatimatou? Can you brew us a pot, please?"

They sipped quietly, reflectively. Finally Aïssatou said, "Yerima's giving JoAnn three months. House Four should be vacant by then, so he's turning it over to her. He's asked me to see if you'd be willing to raise Cathy and Michael. JoAnn wants them raised as Christians, and Amsaou and I aren't able to do that. I know you adore them."

"I don't mind, Aïssatou, but I'm the last person on earth she'd want to take her children. She'd positively break out in big red splotches. Plus, I'm not Catholic, I'm Protestant." She thought a second. "Has the court already decided on custody?"

"The father almost always gets custody unless the children are very small, and then, the mother only has them until about the age of five. Now, before you decide how unfair that is, remember that it's a rare woman here who can afford to support a family herself. Furthermore, from a cultural standpoint, the children are part of the father's family. And JoAnn even signed a pre-nup to that effect.

"All right. When she leaves, the children will move in with you. I'm glad that's settled." She set down her cup. "It's too bad. They really love each other and for nine years got along reasonably well. It's just since... since..."

"Since I came on the scene. I know. She's casually men-tioned that fact to me at least twenty thousand times. I don't know what to do, Aïssatou. I've tried my best to be nice to her, but she's so jealous that I've just about given up."

"We've all had a problem, actually, since you arrived. Yerima just isn't himself anymore. He's so wound up in that job, and so focused on helping you settle in, that he just doesn't concentrate on his marital responsibilities the way he used to."

"You too? All those blankety-blank phone calls at all hours drive me nuts, and Yerima's so obsessed with that job he always takes them, no matter what we're doing."

"You mean you have the same issue?" Aïssatou threw back her head and laughed. "All this time we thought it was because he was spoiling his new bride, and you do have, um, your background, so we thought you two were having a great time." She laughed again. "I've tried to bring it up a few times, but he always blows me off."

"I'm going to talk to him. And good grief, am I ever going to live my 'background' down? Actually, I've tried talking to him too. But now, I'm going to pull out all the stops. This just can't continue."

"Look out, my dear, he's not going to want to hear it."

"Hey, this isn't nearly as hard as telling Prince Ibrahim he had a drinking problem."

"Maybe not, but I'll be on alert for the mushroom cloud. Maybe he'll pay attention to you; he most decidedly doesn't want to listen to Amsaou or me. And he's so protective of you he won't listen to a thing JoAnn says."

Her heart grew sweet. Dear, dear, protective Yerima. "But this just has to stop. You're so gentle, and so respectful, and so deferential, that he doesn't realize how serious you are. But I'll tell him. No bones about it."

"I've noticed something, Sudari. Do you realize you haven't called me ma'am in more than two weeks?"

Tammy sat bolt upright and her hand flew to her mouth. "You're right. I didn't think of that. I'm sorry, ma'am. I'm very sorry."

"Don't apologize, my dear, it's a good thing. I think it means that you've become a normal person again." Tammy tried to absorb this information. "I'm very, very happy for you, but I must point out that this means your grace period is over. You will henceforth be subject to disciplinary measures whenever you break the rules. Remember how I've cautioned you a number of times about your rebelliousness? Take heed, my dear, there will be no further warnings."

When the alarm went off at four-forty-five, Tammy just couldn't drag herself out of bed. First she thought it was simply the early hour – even the parrots weren't yet squawking – but then she realized she was just plain feeling rotten. Well, maybe today she'd skip the pre-dawn Ramadan breakfast. After all, she wasn't fasting, and she'd made appearances at several others to show her respect for the household religion, but today, they'd have to get along without her.

She'd laid in supplies of yogurt and *pains au chocolat* – her own! – and she still had leftovers from last night, so she wouldn't starve even though the kitchen wouldn't serve again until thirty minutes after sunset. It was Wednesday, and Fatimatou would come at two to clean the apartment and do her laundry. She shook her head in amazement. Here she was, planning her own day, organizing her own meals, making her own decisions. Even after ten months, she was still marveling. Freedom was good. Freedom was very good.

Fatimatou was a wonderful housekeeper and delightful young woman, but had never been to school a day in her life, and her French tickled Tammy no end. The French word for vacuum cleaner is *aspirateur*, or "aspirator," but she always called it a "respirator." And Tammy was still trying to figure out how to translate her way of saying "this is no joking matter" that would convey not only the meaning but also the hilarious grammatical construction. *S'amuser* is literally, to amuse oneself. But Fatimatou, unaware of things called reflexive verbs and how it was spelled, made a reflexive *noun – Ce n'est pas de s'amusement.* It is not amusement oneself. Another favorite expression of Fatimatou was *jusqu'à...fatigué.* Until...tired. As in, I have scrubbed this pot and scrubbed this pot until I'm sick of it.

Tammy staggered out of bed about nine, quickly emptied a mug of coffee, and poured herself another, hoping it would perk her up. She sat down at her computer and held her head. She was exhausted. Maybe it was because she was reliving ugly events, experiencing for a second time what no one should have lived through even once. As usual, Cleopatra was curled up on her knees and Nefertiti was draped around her shoulders, purring softly.

"Cleo, I just can't get this stupid paragraph to strike the right balance. I don't want to sensationalize what happened, but I also don't want to gloss over things. Like my nice Taymoor used to say, I'm either completely in the dark or with two lanterns."

Tammy suddenly felt a presence behind her. Aïssatou was standing in the middle of the living room.

"Oh! Sorry, Issa, you startled me."

"I've been here for several minutes, my dear. We missed you at the *suhuur* this morning."

"I'm sorry. When my alarm went off I just couldn't drag myself out of bed."

"Why was your door locked, by the way?"

Tammy shrugged. "I don't know. Why not? It's my apartment; I can lock the door if I feel like it."

"It gives us the impression that you're doing something you shouldn't. By the way, I have a key, and so does Yerima. I'll leave the door unlocked and strongly suggest that you keep it that way."

"Okay, sure, if you say so."

"I think you like the sense of power it gives you."

"Power? Me?" She laughed.

"Symbolic power. You used to be locked up, and now you can lock other people out."

Tammy thought for a moment. "I never thought about it that way, but you're probably right. You're dead-right about an awful lot of stuff. You're amazing."

"I'm a judge, and I've learned a lot about human nature. Sudari, my dear, no married woman is completely free. When you agreed to marry Yerima, you gave up much of your freedom in exchange for financial security, prestige, and regular access to the bed of an extremely virile man. Fulani wives are less free than many, partly due to Islam, and partly due to centuries of our own tradition. I know that *obey* is a word you associate with your years in slavery, but a Fulani wife obeys her husband without question and graciously accepts being under his control.

"If you have a problem with that, my dear, you aren't going to stay married to Yerima for very long. He's quite liberal as Fulani men go, but he does expect his wives to accept his authority. Even to the extent of not locking the door."

Tammy deflated. "Every now and then it really gets to me. It's not easy."

"I know you're trying. What is it that Ibrahim used to make you say? Some sort of affirmation?"

"The affirmation of submission. I had to say that I would obey him immediately, fully, and willingly. He loved hearing that."

"Don't you think your husband, whom you love, deserves better than your master, whom you feared?"

"That's a good way of putting it. But like you say, the word obedience reminds me of painful times. I'd never dream of rebelling against Yerima, Aïssatou, I'm just rebelling against my memories of enslavement."

"I understand, but it's still rebelling. You're doing a fine job on the big things. You're great with the children. Your comportment in public is exemplary. You're good with the staff. But you're having trouble with little things, like locking your door, or always making Yerima wait fifteen or twenty minutes when he summons you, or your nonstop bickering with JoAnn that's driving all of us nuts, or going over budget again and again. I'm sure that you're still just trying to prove to yourself that you're no longer in slavery; nevertheless, rebellion of any sort will not last long in this household. Are we clear?"

"Yes ma'am. I'll try harder. Really, I'll try harder."

"Are you all right? You look pale to me. Extremely pale."

"Good question. I started bleeding this morning. I sort of had a period a few weeks ago, but this doesn't feel like a period at all, and I feel awfully weak."

"Do you think you can walk over to the infirmary? It's Wednesday morning, so Dr. Ayissi should be there. Have you met her?"

"Yes ma'am, when I cut my foot. She's very good."

A few minutes later the doctor grimaced. "I'm sorry to say, madame, that you've just had a miscarriage."

"Miscarriage, doctor? I had no idea I was even pregnant."

"It looks like you conceived only a few days ago and the pregnancy never really established itself. I'm very sorry. I know how much you want children."

Tammy broke down in tears. "Those damned chemicals, and those damned shots. I've been away from all that for months now, and they're still screwing me up."

"Don't worry, madame. They'll work themselves out of your system eventually. The human body is amazing. Sometimes the best medicine of all is to stand back and let Mother Nature work her magic. Tell you what. I'll monitor you, and we'll see how things go. Don't give up. You're young, you're healthy, and we'll soon have your tummy out to here. All right?"

Tammy gripped her hand. "I gave my life to Yerima, and giving him children is just one way – an important way – that I can show my complete commitment to him. It's not an option for me, it's an obligation."

"It's okay, madame, we'll do this. Don't worry."

"Tonight, babe, you're going to do the Ibrahim thing for me. I've waited for months, and I'm not going to wait any longer. Period." He propped himself up on his elbow and played with her hair as heavy rain beat down.

"You're sort of, kind of, involved in that yourself, you know, my beloved *jaumu*."

"I recall that you two were playing one of our games – my games – but I can't remember which one."

"Contrition, *jaumu*. The problem is, ahem, I've been such an exemplary wife, that you haven't had any reason to punish me."

"Well, you did walk out of our meeting the other day. I wasn't happy about that at all. Yes, JoAnn was rude to you, but walking out in a huff was rude to all of us, and you deserve to be disciplined. You're right. We haven't played that game in a long time, and it's a really good one. Now listen, you naughty girl, on the floor, in the position of contrition. And make it snappy."

"Na'am, jaumu." She lay prostrate on the rug, arms extended. She didn't even know if the game would work anymore, it'd been so long. Had her body forgotten all the games they used to play? The way they'd drive each other crazy with desire with cat baths, massages, playing dozens of games he'd devised to ensure hours of delicious, glorious passion? At The Office, they could enjoy each other without urgent phone calls, pressing engagements, or trying to squeeze in a few hours of love-making after a late reception. But now, there was call after call from Antoine or other officials. And there was always that infuriating stack of files that covered his desk, overflowed onto chairs and onto the floor.

Within a few minutes she realized that while she might have largely forgotten how to play the game, her body had not. It fondly remembered the delight in store, and as she lay there for the twenty-eight minutes of her sentence, her need for the gorgeous man she'd married – the gorgeous man who was back to signing those damned papers – grew and grew. Finally the buzzer on his cell phone went off. She stood, awaiting orders.

"Already? Wow. Well, has the naughty girl–"

The phone rang. "Hey, cuz. What? A shrimp boat? An invasion? What the hell? They're out of their stinking minds! Unbelievable. Okay, thanks for letting me know; I'll get on it first thing in the morning." He hung up. "Would you believe that? A shrimp boat hits a reef just off the coast of Málabo, sinks, and the crew members swim to shore. And the government arrests the crew and accuses them of mounting an invasion." She stared at him. "Cameroon means shrimp, by the way. From the Portuguese. So, back to my naughty girl. I hope you've had–"

The phone rang. "Yes? Oh, the second time? Same stunt? All right, good to know."

Tammy took Yerima's bathrobe, put it on, and sat on the bed. "Yerima. Darling." She made the time-out sign. "They aren't going to stop, are they?"

"What, the phone calls? No, they're not. They come with the territory."

"Immediately, fully, and willingly. Ibrahim would approve."

"That was uncalled-for," he scolded.

"It also happens to be entirely accurate. If you don't have the guts to tell Antoine to cut them out, I will. Darling, they've already destroyed your marriage to JoAnn, and we other three are on the verge of mutiny. I'm here trying to make love to my husband, but the man who's here is a stranger who happens to be the damned Minister of Foreign Affairs. This guy sitting on the bed surrounded by mountains of files isn't the man I married at all. I was used to magnificent feasts, and now I'm barely getting sandwiches. Nice sandwiches, but I was used to seven-course banquets.

"Look at these, darling. Change of category? Authorizing maternity leave? Your Secretary General should be signing these, not you. Delegate, for heaven's sake. You should be worrying about why the Chinese

144

bring in their own workers whenever they build something, and so-called shrimp boat invasions, not administrivia. This isn't an embassy with a few dozen people, darling, this is an entire ministry. You can't do everything by yourself anymore."

He stared at her in stunned silence.

"Would you like to salvage your marriage to JoAnn? I've figured out her problem."

"Yes, of course. As I've told you many times, for me, marriage is for life. I'm still totally committed to her. And she's pregnant, you know."

"I didn't know, and I don't really care. Plus, I don't know why I'm telling you this, because she's not exactly my favorite person, but I think if we can get JoAnn back on track, maybe it'll improve things with the rest of us. I'm going to do the Ibrahim thing on you, but not the one you think, and you're not going to like it one bit."

She stood up, swallowed, and cemented her resolve. "Yerima, my love, you know how much I adore you, and how eternally grateful I am that you saved my life. Remember, I even offered myself to you as a servant, just to be near you. This is absolutely, positively, the last thing I expected as a problem. I thought I'd have trouble adjusting to polygamy, but except for JoAnn, that's actually not going too badly. I thought I'd have trouble adjusting to life in Africa, but I positively love it. Working with Mouna has shown me such need to help women, and I find it very gratifying. I was nervous about taking on your children, but I adore them. What has totally taken me by surprise, though, is my disappoint-ment here, right here in this bedroom. When we got married, I thought, wow, we've got this sex

145

thing nailed. But it's been months, and if anything, things are getting worse. You're as addicted to that damn job as Ibrahim was to his prosecco.

"Do you remember Toril and Monika the day we escaped from The Office? I told them, on a scale of one to ten, you were a twenty-five. They didn't believe me, but it was true. Oh God, was it ever true. The most incredible lover on Planet Earth. Do you remember, darling, how we'd spend hours and hours making love? And we'd both come five, six times? Now, I come maybe twice, and you only occasionally make me faint, and I'd come to expect that almost every time." Tears welled in her eyes. "Now, I'm sorry to say, you're about an eleven. Comparatively speaking, a pale shadow of what I'd come to expect. I grieve that you're not living up to your own standards."

"An *eleven?*" he squeaked.

"You were appointed Minister the very day we were married, so JoAnn thinks that you're expending all your energy on me. She doesn't realize that it's the job, not me. I have exactly the same problem she does, and Aïssatou and Amsaou have it too, but are too respectful, too Fulani, to make a big deal of it – to you, at least. At The Office, remember, you wouldn't even turn on the television because you wanted us to focus totally on each other. You keep bringing up the fact that I haven't ever made you faint, but it's because we have to start all over again fifteen times every night. Even when the damned phone isn't ringing, I hear you thinking, oh rats, I need to do this, and I forgot to do that.

"You require total surrender from me, and you showed me how wonderful the rewards for that can be. But I'm only getting fifty percent from you. Yerima, I'm not getting what I need, and far, far less what I grew to expect. I'm sure Antoine doesn't realize how disruptive his calls are, but we have a meeting of the task force next week, and I'll be glad to pull him aside and give him your wives' perspective. Or would you rather talk to him yourself?"

He stared at her for the longest time. "An eleven?" he squeezed out again. He gulped. "No wonder JoAnn's so pissed."

"She, uh, somehow, uh, got the impression that I make you faint every time I see you, and I confess that I, uh, I, uh, haven't exactly disabused her of this idea, and that, uh, probably hasn't helped."

He covered his face with his hands and groaned. "You little vixen, you. I have more trouble managing you two than I do the whole damned Ministry. You're fighting all the time. All the time. And it's got to stop. I'm giving you a stern warning here: if there's not significant improvement immediately, I'm going to take you both off the schedule until it does."

"Hey, she outranks me, but that doesn't mean I can't out-psych her. And besides, she's checking out." She suffered a quick pang of guilt. She hadn't made the slightest effort to love JoAnn. Not the slightest.

"I mean it, Sudari, I'm sick and tired of the bickering." He shook his head. "Holy shit." A pause. "Holy shit. I'm rewinding a few conversations, and now I see what you all were trying to tell me. I'm furious, I'm insulted, but I'm also feeling overwhelmingly guilty. I hate like the devil to admit it, but I think you're right."

"I was scared to death that you were going to explode."

"I came very close. Aïssatou keeps telling me to get my temper under control, and I'm trying hard. Now that I'm MFA, I can't just keep flying off the handle."

"I told her I was going to talk to you, and she said she'd watch for the eruption." Tammy moved the files off the bed and stacked them in the corner. "Get a special emergency number. Tell Antoine that after nine o'clock, you're off duty. He can send you emails. He can text you. But these phone calls have got to be history, or you're going to wind up a bachelor again." She shut the phone off and lay it on top of the files. "Tell you what. Why don't I just go back to my apartment? At least there, I can get some sleep without being interrupted twenty thou-sand times." She reached for her panties.

"You'll do nothing of the sort. Come right back over here. I'm going to show you that I'm not an eleven. I can't believe you. Do you remember when you faked it and I was so outraged that I hit you? Well, you just succeeded in infuriating me more than that by a huge margin. I repeat. Come back over here. Now."

"No, Yerima. Sorry. I'm really, really mad at you. And you still haven't told me that you'll talk to Antoine."

"I ordered you to come back here. Are you defying me?"

He wasn't joking in the least, but she detected a promising glint in his eye. Put her hand on her hip. "Just maybe I am."

"All right, woman, you're asking for it." He leapt out of bed and grabbed her, but just got an armful of robe. He threw it on the floor and chased her into a corner. She almost managed to pull away from him, but he held her

148

firmly and marched her smartly to the bed. "Now maybe you'll do what your husband tells you."

"What? Submit to an eleven? When I married a twenty-five?"

"Insult your master, will you? Now you're really going to get it." She fought. She struggled. Bit by bit, he was overcoming her. "Surrender."

"Not on your life."

The hurricane bore down upon the lone palm. It resolutely stood its ground as the wind hurled itself against it, remained steadfast as the rain tore at its roots. But the howling gale was relentless, and the powerful downpour continued unabated. The tree bowed at length. The only way to survive the onslaught was to become one with the whirlwind and to give itself over completely to the rain. The moment came that the tree absorbed the mighty wind and hungered for more, soaked up all the glorious rain and thirsted for more. A flash of lightning, and the sky grew black.

When he came to she had already recovered and was waiting, smiling, to plant kisses all over his forehead.

"Welcome back, Yerima, my love, my hero, my darling. Welcome back."

Several days later, after some serious and overdue praying, Tammy knocked on JoAnn's door.

"What the hell do you want?"

"JoAnn, we got off on the wrong foot. I'd like to invite you over for dinner tomorrow in my apartment. Seven o'clock?"

"What's your angle, Sudari?"

"I just want to clear up some misunderstandings. I'm trying to help your marriage."

"You? Help me?"

"Yes, me. You love Yerima, I love Yerima, and we've caused him a lot of grief. I'm really doing this for him. Plus, I'm not the horrible person you think I am. Seven?"

JoAnn laughed incredulously. "Okay, this I gotta see."

Chef Emmanuel made JoAnn's favorite, Hawaiian huli-huli chicken, baked in barbecue sauce, fresh ginger, pineapple juice, sherry, and soy sauce. Tammy had never heard of it, but it was wonderful, and provided a welcome topic that she and JoAnn could agree on, at least for a few minutes.

"I still don't understand why I'm here tonight," JoAnn said at length, an edge to her voice.

"I can see why you're suspicious. My mother's favorite mantra is, When everything else fails, try love. So I figure it's time to try. I tried this with Sheikh Saud, and it completely turned things around. I tried it with Prince Ibrahim, and in a way, it turned things around. And I'm hoping it will help with us."

"Hmpf. I think that things are way too far gone, but I'll listen."

"That's all I can ask. Yes, JoAnn, I was a whore. I was a trained, professional whore for three years. I positively hate the word, because it implies that it was a voluntary career choice. More exactly, I was a slave in a brothel, but most people think of girls in brothels as whores. Period. As you know, I didn't exactly volunteer for the job, but it was part of my life and I'll never be able to escape that fact. I'm not ashamed of it – I did what I had to do to survive – and praise God, I survived.

"But I think you'll be surprised to learn that it was Yerima who taught me almost everything I know. In fact, until I met him, even though I'd been in the brothel for months, I hadn't ever had an orgasm. I was so naïve that the first time we were together, I faked it, just the way I'd been trained, and he blew up. I panicked, because he was going to give me a terrible evaluation, and I was already in loads of trouble – I was always in loads of trouble – so I groveled. Begged him to tell me what I had done to offend him.

"He looked at me only the way Yerima does – you know what I mean – as if he's x-raying every last cell in your entire body to see if you're telling the truth, and he saw that I was completely clueless. He apologized, took me into his arms, and that's when I became a woman."

"You too?" They laughed. "Do you know Dalida's old song, *Ti Amo*, where she says 'I was born in your bed?' I know exactly what she means."

"I don't know the song, but I sure do understand the sentiment. So, he started me on his course of instruction. I couldn't get over it. Months later, I was still only partway through the introductory curriculum."

151

JoAnn was smiling. "He's really something, isn't he?"

"That's for sure. A few months later, my master, Prince Ibrahim, whom I'd never met, summoned me for the first time, and immediately realized that I knew stuff that the Training Department never heard of. He's a member of the Board at The Office, so he went into my file and in a flash figured out who'd been teaching me. He called him the professor. So yes, I was a professional whore, but Yerima taught me what I know, not The Office. What I'm saying is, you've had exactly the same professor as me, but you've known him for ten years, and I've known him for three, so you probably know lots and lots more than I do. May I ask you an intensely personal question?" Without waiting for an answer, she plunged on. "Have you ever had anal sex?"

JoAnn flinched. "Yes, exactly once. I wanted to kill my boyfriend, it hurt so bad. Plus, I got an infection when he switched back. Not my idea of fun."

"Well, that was my assigned specialty – emphasis on *assigned*. I hated it too, JoAnn, really hated it. But that's how I spent eight or ten hours a day for three years. Members were encouraged to use lubricant, but a lot of them didn't want to. I was in the infirmary due to bleeding at least once or twice a month. Most of the rest of the time I spent giving BJ's, which I also hated."

"What's a BJ?"

"Blow job. Yerima has tried to describe what a horrible life I led, but understandably you latched onto the idea that because I used to work in a brothel, I could give Yerima better sex than you. If you want any tips about giving BJ's or being sodomized or groveling, or how to deal with being paddled or harnessed or shackled, I might be able to help. But except for that, I could no doubt learn a lot from you."

"Sodomized? Eight or ten hours a day? Shackled? Oh God." She held her head in her hands.

"I'm not asking you to feel sorry for me. Like I say, I did what I had to do to survive, and thanks to Almighty God and to Yerima, all that's behind me. Uh, no pun intended."

"Oh God."

"Something most men are reluctant to ask their wives. But slave girls, that's altogether different. One of the other girls said that we were just like toilet paper: no matter how disgusting the job, they simply used us and didn't think twice. Slavery isn't fun, JoAnn."

JoAnn sighed, and the way she looked at Tammy showed a degree of more respect. "Tell me something. How do you make him faint?"

"I don't make him faint every time, by the way. Resist him. It turns him on big-time."

"Resist Yerima? And *survive*?" She laughed incredulously.

"One of his games. Especially the game of contrition."

"He's tried that with me, but I was scared he'd kill me."

"It's delicious. All right, next issue, JoAnn, and this is the biggie. I'm having exactly the same problem as you other three. You all thought he was spending his energy on me, but he's so wrapped up in that damned job that he's neglecting me too. He was appointed MFA the very day we were married, so it was only natural for you all to think that I was the problem. It's the job, JoAnn, it's not me. I'm mad at him too, especially about all those blankety-blank calls at all hours from Antoine."

JoAnn dropped her fork. "You mean…"

Tammy nodded.

"Oh God. All this time, I was sure, I was convinced. I mean, oh God."

"I understand, believe me. I'm sure I would've come to the same conclusion."

JoAnn started to cry. "I love him so much, but it's been so difficult. So difficult."

"I know. And I'm sorry I've been so snotty to you."

"Same here. Oh God, Sudari. I had no idea. Oh God."

Wife number three and wife number four hugged for everything they were worth.

"Thanks."

"I should've done this a long time ago. A long time ago."

Several days later, Yerima announced that the paperwork for the separation had been suspended and that they had decided to give their marriage another chance.

Aïssatou, Amsaou, and Tammy applauded. Yerima gave Tammy a knowing – and very grateful – wink. JoAnn looked at Tammy and actually smiled.

154

Prince Ibrahim had high hopes for Office whore 518, with her nine-six ass and sweet but somehow gloomy Finnish smile, and she was okay, sort of. She'd given him a nice bath and a decent BJ, but otherwise, she'd been a disappointment. Just like everybody else.

He sighed. "Fernando, give her a Satisfactory and send her back to Central."

Nobody'd been able to please him like Mukhmala. Sweet, steamy, smoldering Mukhmala. So innocent, so wholesome, so unlike a whore, with those big soulful eyes and little-girl smile, but no little girl at all in bed. A woman who knew, like none other, how to drive a man wild with desire and turn that desire into pure ecstasy.

He wanted to kick himself. Why, why, hadn't he found some loophole in the idiotic lease? Why hadn't he simply pardoned her and taken her into his harem right then? Now it was so complicated. Whoever imagined that the idiot ambassador would have the nerve to buy her – royal property, no less – and marry her? But he'd bought her under false pretenses. The Rodeo sold her to execute, not to emancipate, and the sentence had never been carried out. So technically, she was still rightfully his own.

He'd briefly considered marriage, but most assuredly, it wasn't the solution. Princes do not marry slaves. It diminishes the quality of the royal bloodline. It compromises the prestige of the prince himself. It insults the family. It offends all aristocratic families whose daughters deserve a princely husband. Plus, it puts stupid ideas into the heads of other slaves.

Furthermore, her family wasn't the least bit aristocratic – butchers and farmers, flower brokers and tradesmen – and he'd checked her Dutch ancestors all the way back to the 1700s. There was nothing but one lowly baron, and the footnote said, "title fraudulently obtained and subse-quently rescinded." Maybe in Africa, the son of a minor sultan like Abdoulaye didn't have to maintain such high standards. Obviously, if the idiot had actually married her.

She'd never really belong to Abdoulaye, so-called married or not. He and Mukhmala had passed out together in each other's arms. She was far too special to waste on anyone else. She belonged to him, and she was going to make him faint again and again, and that was all there was to it. Take her back into his legitimate possession. And return her to his bed, the place she should rightfully be.

Yes. Mukhmala definitely belonged to him, and him alone.

CHAPTER SIX

Zero Eta was delivered to Prince Ibrahim as scheduled, but as usual, he was on the phone. He told her to lie down and that he'd be with her in a few minutes. The tungsten deal was complicated, however, and the conversation dragged on and on. She didn't intend to, but after waiting for nearly an hour, she fell asleep.

Next thing she knew, she was being flung from the bed onto the rug.

"Is this the insolent way you act in the presence of your master?" he bellowed. "Not only were you snoring, but your back was toward me and your knees were together. If you are in this room it is for one reason, and one reason only, and you should always be cognizant of – and eagerly positioned for – that reason."

"I'm so sorry, master, no one ever–"

"Giuliano, time to teach this idiot a lesson. Get the spreader bar and put it on max." Master and slave both gasped, but for quite different reasons, as her knees were locked into position very, very far apart. "Now tie her wrists to the bed. Stretched. Good. Oh, I know what, get that new pacifier. I love that thing. Have to suck it for at least one minute out of every five or it deflates and buzzes. Keeps the girls quiet. Keeps them busy. Gives them practice on a desirable skill. And makes them very, very obedient – fifty strokes for every buzz after the first one. Every hour, let her have five minutes' rest and some water, but we're going to keep her like that for 48 hours. I strongly recommend, my dear little idiot, that you not fall asleep."

Zero Eta managed to get through her sentence with only one buzz, and was returned to the harem. But the following morning she fell asleep during Training, which got her twenty strokes, and fell asleep again at lunch, which got her ten more. It took two days in the infirmary to more or less recover from both the paddlings and the "lesson."

She was limping along beside her friend Two Alpha toward their usual bench. "Before," she said, "I actually liked Prince Ibrahim. But now, I positively loathe the man. Two days sucking the goddam pacifier. Two days with my knees stretched so far apart I think that a year from now, my thighs will still be aching. And my arms still hurt like crazy from the way I was tied down. I don't know how, but I swear, I'm going to kill the man."

Trevino, who'd been only a few feet behind, said simply, "I rather doubt that." He grabbed her and hauled her before Mr. Faisal.

"Hmm. That wasn't very smart of you." He placed a quick phone call to his boss. "He has sentenced you to ten years at the Ranch." She began to sob. "Don't worry. You probably won't live that long. I saw the figures just last week. Actually, life expectancy there is up three days from what it was last quarter – it's now four years, seven months, and four days. You know, not quite enough food, not quite enough sleep, minimal medical attention, a few too many ice-water enemas, a few too many branding parties, cowboys who play a little too rough. Put her in the holding cell until the van gets back." He handed Trevino her file and, as she was handcuffed and taken away, muttered to himself, "Females are such complete idiots."

"You eat three decent meals a day here," commented Six Zeta. "At the Ranch, they stuffed a feeding tube down your throat twice a day and the glop gave me such bad diarrhea I was in the infirmary for days and days until my system adjusted. Okay, we're not exactly getting five-star cuisine, but the food isn't bad. I really like the spiced spinach with chick peas. It could be a lot worse, believe me."

Prince Ibrahim was in a smiling good mood, joking with Mr. Faisal, winking at his girls, relishing the remarkable beauty surrounding him. For a while he let them go about their activities, but finally he had Mr. Faisal sound the gong. This time, he had them line up in order of height, the tallest to the right and the shortest to the left.

"Good afternoon, my beauties," he began.

"Good afternoon, master," they chorused.

"If you have been in this harem for ten years or more, kindly step forward."

Nine girls looked nervously at each other and obeyed.

"Remove your tunics and let me see how beautiful you are. Walk single file in front of me."

They complied, not sure where he was going.

As each one passed he said "Nice, very nice, good, excellent. You are taking very good care of yourselves, and I congratulate you. You may all return to the assembly. Now. All the fours will kindly step forward." Eleven girls did so. "Who would like to volunteer to die today for her master?"

Four Lamda raised her hand.

"Why are you volunteering?"

"To show my master how much I respect him."

"Good girl. What is your choice? Hanging, or drowning?"

She gulped. "But master, last time–"

"That was last time. This is this time. How?" She began to tremble and did not respond.

"All right, it will be by hanging. Torino and Trevino, please proceed."

Before the shocked assembly her tunic was removed, she was handcuffed, a silken noose placed around her neck, and within minutes, her lifeless body was hanging from a fig tree in the garden.

The prince continued routinely. "Do not – do not – try to manipulate me; there's nothing that infuriates me more. Now I want each of you to curtsey to me and I recommend that you do so with a full measure of devotion."

As each girl curtsied, he signaled that she should return to the assembly. He wasn't happy, however, with how three girls had performed the obeisance and told them to stand to one side. "These girls were insolent, Faisal. Detention for two weeks and Level One probation for six months. Good day."

"When I was at the Ranch," said Six Zeta, "to make sure we were totally anonymous, nameless bodies, they put horse head masks on us. In the seven weeks I was there, only one cowboy ever removed it. I was amazed. No pacifier, no bit? Well, guess where he ejaculated.

"They also used wood stain to stencil designs on us to make us look like pinto ponies, and of course, one spot covered three-quarters of your face.

"Everything there was meant to be demeaning. When they'd take us to a room in the Redwood Lodge, we'd ride on our knees, facing backwards, locked into place. I'm so lucky that Prince Ibrahim rescued me. I still have screaming nightmares about that place."

It had been months since instituting the bosom-enhancing devices, and the time had come to inspect the results. Many girls had already graduated, but several dozen remained in the program. Prince Ibrahim had all of his girls line up, this time in order of height, and had the devices removed so he could see the progress.

"Faisal," he said, "We're going to need another hierarchy, tits. On some of them it's worked really well; on some I can barely see any results at all. Get the photographers to take interim shots."

The girls passed slowly before him. He beckoned a few of them over so he could cup their breasts in his hands, groaning with pleasure, but most walked by unnoticed.

"All right," he said, when the last one had filed by, "time to put them back on."

The eunuchs prepared to padlock them back in place.

"No sir," said Six Alpha.

"No sir," said Three Eta.

"What?" said Prince Ibrahim.

"No sir," said Eight Alpha and Three Mu and One Phi.

"No sir," said Ten Beta and Three Iota and and Zero Tau.

"You dare say no to your master?" snapped Mr. Sayeed.

"We've had it," said Eight Delta.

"He's finally gone too far," said Two Lambda.

"What?" said Prince Ibrahim, looking accusingly at Mr. Faisal, whose mouth had dropped open. "Everything is screwed up, like a coil of rope and the end is lost. What the hell is going on?"

Mr. Faisal couldn't say a word.

"On your knees," said Prince Ibrahim.

Fewer than two dozen obediently knelt. The rest stayed defiantly on their feet.

He was shell-shocked, but regained his senses quickly. "Document this," he told the photographers. "You will all return to your dormitories immediately and be on full lockdown until further orders. You are dismissed."

Many of the girls refused to move, and the eunuchs had to drag them away.

"We won't be treated like this anymore."

"You've way overstepped the line."

"*'Aani 'aadmi, muu shalib*. I'm a human, not a dog."

The photographers continued to snap pictures.

"I asked Abdul about this, and he assured me that nothing was going on. Faisal, prepare a letter of dismissal for gross negligence. And have it on my desk no later than noon tomorrow."

Two days later, the prince assembled his girls to announce how they would be disciplined.

"On your knees," he commanded. "All of you. Now!" All but six obeyed. The eunuchs grabbed them and held them down.

"The three ringleaders, Four Kappa, Three Gamma, and Two Alpha, will be devocalized and hot-iron branded on the soles of both feet. They will each also be paddled fifty strokes a week for the next six months. And I'm putting them on Level Three probation for two years.

"The three deputies, Eight Epsilon, Five Alpha, and Five Delta, will also be devocalized and hot-iron branded on one foot, and paddled fifty strokes a week for the next four months. They will be on Level Three probation for one year. The six leaders will draw a token. One, chosen by lot, will be executed at the Rodeo, and another, also chosen by lot, will receive a life sentence at the Ranch. In addition, to emphasize my displeasure, they will all suffer the humiliation of shaved heads for the duration of their probation.

"They will also eat two meals a day: one, bread soaked in lukewarm water, and the other, a puree of scorched turnips and Brussels sprouts and chick peas, which they will lick like dogs from a bowl placed on the floor. They will not be allowed to participate in any of the recreational activities and instead will spend two hours a day on the BJ simulator. Every day they will also write one hundred affirmations of submission in Arabic and one hundred in their own language. They will write firmly, neatly, and correctly, and if upon review Mr. Faisal or Mr. Sayeed does not consider what they write satisfactory, for each violation, the probation will be extended by seven days.

"The girls who participated will be paddled fifty strokes a week for four weeks and will be on Level One probation for one year. They will each draw lots and three of them will be hot-iron branded on one foot.

"Now. For the nineteen of you who remained loyal and obedient, I will give you each a special bracelet. Every week before her correction, each rebel will be obliged to kiss each of your asses. You will henceforth be allowed to choose your meals from a special menu. And finally, I'm creating a special lounge where you'll be able to watch authorized television broadcasts for up to three hours a day."

The six ringleaders drew tokens from a jar. Three Gamma drew the Ranch token and slumped in despair. The Ranch. For life! One of the deputies, Eight Epsilon, drew the black ball. She gasped and crumpled into a heap in the courtyard, while the others hugged and wept in relief.

"Any more idiots planning a rebellion? You are dismissed."

165

Attendance at the brandings was obligatory, two or three a day, once a week, over several weeks. Right after breakfast, the expert borrowed from the Ranch immobilized the girls in branding cradles with one leg raised and the toes pulled back to ensure taut skin on the sole of the foot. The actual brandings, however, didn't take place until after lunch.

"Those poor things must be absolutely terrified," said Seven Delta.

"That's the whole idea," said Eight Beta.

When the moment came, each rebel was required to say loudly and clearly – under threat of permanent transfer to the Ranch – "I defied my master and richly deserve the punishment I am about to receive."

Screams. The sickening smell of burning flesh.

Each time, spectators passed out. Vomited. Many were overcome and had to sit down.

"The devocalizations will be carried out after the brandings are complete," announced Mr. Faisal.

"Of course," said Six Zeta. "They want us to hear the screams, just like at the Ranch."

The rebels were allowed to recover in detention until they could once again climb the ladder to bed. And the paddlings were carried out right on schedule.

"I've never seen anything so cruel in my life," said Seven Zeta. "Never."

"If you're obedient," said Mr. Sayeed, who had overheard, "you have absolutely nothing to fear."

She waited until he was out of earshot. "I have reason to be very afraid," she said, mostly to herself. "He hasn't seen anything yet."

The gong sounded, and the harem girls assembled in the courtyard. Mr. Faisal said he had just one brief announcement.

"His Highness has decided to completely revise the system of rotation. He is sick and tired of being poorly served in this area and has concluded that after he has exercised his proprietary rights at least four times, he will honor with his attentions exclusively those of you who sincerely want them. You have twenty-four hours to think this over."

This announcement was met with total disbelief. "Condi-tions apply. First, your decision will be irreversible. Once you have opted out, or opted in, it's final. Second, if you opt in, you will automatically get fifteen bonus points every month; if you opt out, you will get fifteen demerits. You are dismissed."

The women couldn't get over it.

Next day, each girl was interviewed. If she opted in, a gold bracelet was attached to her left hand; if she opted out, it was made of silver. Thirty-one girls opted out. Some were extremely disturbed when they learned that opting out also meant that they would undergo a clitoridectomy.

"If you're not giving it to His Highness, you no longer need it," Mr. Faisal explained. "Besides, you'll feel less stressed. Many masters do this routinely to the women

167

they own. A skilled midwife is coming day after tomorrow to carry out the procedure."

The four conspirators all agreed to opt in. Changes or no changes, they decided to move forward with their plans. Now they just had to find a way for all four of them to be on duty at the same time.

Prince Ibrahim was a dead man. He just didn't know it yet.

CHAPTER SEVEN

Amberine, the former *jaria* from Georgia who'd married Sheikh Saud's brother Farook, sent Tammy pictures of her new baby Saud and his proud big brother Ahmed, almost three. Her emails sounded so happy, co-publishing articles on monetary policy with her husband. "Now that I have my doctorate," she said, "I can actually do stuff in my own name, although I have to publish overseas because nobody here will take me seriously. They pretend they do, but there's always some reason why they can't publish this particular article at this particular time. Then we submit the same article under Farook's name, not even changing a comma, and bingo, they snap it right up. In other words, they had instantly dismissed it because it had a female author."

She and Farook had attended a conference in Brussels, where they met two sister Ph.D.'s who, of course, needed a male relative to escort them whenever they traveled. They decided to play a joke on the authorities by asking their mentally retarded brother to go with them. To their consternation, since he was male, he was a perfectly acceptable chaperone. "They thought it was hilarious," said Amberine, "but I told them it was absolutely outrageous. Now that I'm in the real world I see what women here have to put up with day in and day out, and it's unbelievable. Would you believe that a thirteen-year-old girl got 80 lashes because she took a cell phone to school? Eighty lashes! They finally granted women the right to vote – we're in the year 2011, right? – but it won't go into effect for a few more years.

"And did you hear about the girl who was gang-raped and then her brothers killed her to save the 'family honor'? You need four witnesses, so it's virtually impossible to get a conviction for rape, but if a girl says she was raped, she's automatically guilty of illicit sex. If her family doesn't kill her for 'shaming' them, she's likely to go to prison. Unbelievable."

By the miracle of Facebook, she'd managed to re-establish contact with her brother Steven, whom she hadn't seen in eighteen years. She wasn't the least bit surprised that he'd become chef at a barbecue restaurant in their home town of Savannah, but he was aghast at what had happened to her. They were planning for him to visit, and she was very excited.

But all was not well. She'd discovered a lump in her left breast, and it turned out to be Stage III cancer, and the chemo and radiation treatments were not having the desired effect. "I'm going to beat this," she said, "I have two little boys and one big one who depend on me, and I'm not about ready to let them down."

"Can you come over here, babe? Right now? And I mean, right now?"

"You don't sound like a very happy chappy, Yerima."

"I'm not. The story hit, and Antoine is pissed as hell."

"No problem, darling. We knew it would happen sooner or later, and I'm ready."

"You don't know our journalists. Vultures."

"They can't possibly be any scarier than the ones in Washington. I'll be right over."

A glum Philippe Essomba from *la Présidence* – the Office of the President – was sprawled dejectedly on an easy chair in the main parlor. "This is a major embarrassment," he scolded. "It's giving the President a black eye."

"It doesn't need to, sir," said Tammy. "You're letting the journalists manage the story, and naturally they're putting things in the worst possible light. There's a very good story here that's going to make the President look wonderful. One of my father's best friends back in Washington is a spin doctor – someone who takes a mess and turns it into a public relations *coup* – and while I was home last year I talked to him about how we should handle this. On my wedding day, I asked Yerima whether or not we should try to hide my background, and we decided that we'd be open about it. We knew it would come out sooner or later. Not fun, but we can deal with it.

"I'd like to call a press conference tomorrow morning, say, ten o'clock – with your kind permission, Yerima – and stop this dead in its tracks. I'd like to make three points: Yes, I was sold into slavery and forced to work in a brothel. Two, the Minister of Foreign Affairs rescued a real-live damsel in distress from a horrible life and an even more horrible execution. And three, the President was so moved that he established a special task force to combat human trafficking. What's so bad about that?"

Philippe was completely taken aback.

"Babe, a press conference? Are you kidding? They're going to eat you alive."

"No, they won't. Because I'm going to follow Fareez' advice and treat them like allies, not adversaries. I'm going to joke with them, smile at them, and tell them the God's truth. They're expecting us to waffle, to go into hiding, to start feeding them lies, to think of them as the enemy. That's what most people would do. But I'm not most people, and neither are you. This is my story, Yerima, and I can take care of it. But it would help a lot if you were there, not just to lend moral support, but to give me legitimacy. You're one of the most respected and beloved people in this entire country and just your presence there would speak volumes. And if you could say a few lines and introduce me, it would be even better."

"Give me a moment." He made a call. "Marie-Claire, sweetheart, can you move tomorrow's prep meeting about the offshore drilling thing to the afternoon? There's been an ugly news story about Sudari and we need to call a press conference as soon as possible to clear things up. You think you can? All right, thanks, doll." He turned back to Philippe and Tammy. "Where should we hold it?"

"Ideally, the steps of the Presidential Palace," Tammy said, "where the first meeting of the task force was held just the other day. If that would be all right with His Excellency, we can give it some great publicity."

"I'm pretty sure he'll agree. I want to see a written opening statement no later than eight tomorrow morning so I can clear it with the boss."

"I can give you one right now," said Tammy. "It meets with Fareez' approval, but if there's anything His Excellency would like to change, I'll be delighted to fix it."

"Can I see that?" asked Yerima.

"Oh, I suppose so," she teased.

"I like it," Yerima said, "but how in hell are you going to explain how I knew you? That I fell in love with you because you were my favorite whore at the brothel? Some ten-watt bastard's sure to ask."

"It was a real club, remember, not just a brothel. When I worked Reception I'd wash your feet like I did for all the other members. We talked. And if someone asks did you ever avail yourself of other services, I'll say yes, occasionally. And immediately change the subject – slightly, so it doesn't seem like I'm actually changing the subject – to focus on something positive and keep them from dwelling on that point."

He scratched his eyebrow. "There goes another headline, MFA frequents brothel."

"But you did, darling, and if you deny it, it'll make things even worse. You had very good reasons for it. Your wives didn't accompany you, you were in an extremely closed society where casual relationships were impos-sible, and you're a healthy member of the masculine race. It's not something you'd like trumpeted on the front page, but people will understand. What makes people mad is when you lie, and try to cover up. If you say Yes, I did, because of this and that, they almost always understand.

"One of my favorite stories is about Ronald Reagan when he was Governor of California. He announced his position on something and said that his feet were planted in concrete. Well, things evolved, and if he didn't change his position, he'd be really stupid, so he called a press conference and announced a 180-degree turn. And before a single solitary journalist could raise his hand and say 'uh…' he said, 'Oh, by the way, if you hear a funny noise, it's the sound of concrete breaking up around my feet.' Everybody laughed, and that was the end of it."

Philippe chuckled. "Pre-emptive strike. Brilliant. Maybe you're right. I'll stick this under His Excellency's nose and confirm the location. *Mes sieur et dame*, see you tomorrow."

About four dozen overtly suspicious members of the press, some with tv cameras, were waiting next morning when Yerima and Tammy strode confidently to the podium. They gave each other big smiles and Yerima took the microphone.

"Good morning, everybody, and thanks so much for coming on such short notice." A smile that would melt an iceberg. "My name is Abdoulaye, honored to serve this wonderful country as Minister of Foreign Affairs. Or, as my six-year-old says, Boring Affairs." He waited until the laughter subsided. "Anyway, I'm just here to introduce my wife. This is her story, and she wants to tell it herself. I respect that. And let me tell you, I have enormous respect for her. She was kidnapped, sold into slavery, and forced to work at a men's club.

"At the time, I was serving as Ambassador, and I was a member of the club, and when she was on Reception duty she had to kneel and massage all the members' feet when they came in. She would smile at me, joke with me, even tease me. And I thought holy shit, here's this slave, with one of the most horrible jobs anywhere on earth, and she still finds ways to make me laugh. That's an incredible testimonial to the resilience of the human spirit, and an incredible testimonial to one of the most beautiful and most courageous women I know. Ladies and gentlemen, I'm very proud to present to you my wife, Sudari Abdoulaye."

Dead silence. Shock. Confusion. Coughs. A few rustled papers.

Tammy gave her husband a dazzling smile, said, "Thank you, darling," then, still smiling, turned to the assembly. She looked stunning in a brown-and-gold two-piece traditional dress. "Good morning, ladies and gentlemen. I'd like to read a brief statement, and then I'll be glad to take your questions. I can't imagine that you'll possibly have any, but just in case, I'll take them." She added, "This is a really cool story, and I'm so glad you're here." Smiles all round. A few chuckles. So far so good.

> News has broken that I was once a whore. This is entirely true, but there's a lot more to the story than that.
>
> When I was eighteen years old I was abducted while visiting friends in Marseilles, and sold into slavery on the Persian Gulf. For two years I belonged to mega-wealthy sheikhs and kept in private harems, but then I was sold to a prince who leased me to an exclusive men's club called The Office. Yes, I was a whore, or more precisely, a slave forced to work in the sex industry; the word *whore* implies unfortunately

and inac-curately that it was a voluntary as well as lucrative career choice. During the three years I worked at the club, I generated in excess of eight million dollars in revenue for my master, but of course, I never saw any of it. In fact, sometimes I'd even go two or three days without food. I despised the disgusting work, but to survive I was obliged to swallow my pride and obey orders. I was slapped, kicked, put in shackles, and in general treated, as one of the other girls put it, with all the respect given toilet paper.

The Chairman of the club loved to humiliate me and my best friend, Nenzima, and we positively hated him. One day we reached the super-saturation point. When he fell into a drunken stupor we shackled him to the bed, sawed off an especially vexatious body part, and slit his goddam diabolical double-talking throat.

Nenzima and I called it our long-overdue sweet revenge, but The Office considered it murder. She wisely committed suicide immediately, but I waited too long and was still alive when they found us, and was sentenced to be executed by being boiled alive at a horrible snuff club. His Excellency, who was serving as Ambassador at the time, heard of my plight, mounted a success-ful rescue operation, and emancipated me. Several weeks thereafter I became his extremely grateful and happy bride.

Her voice broke and her eyes filled with tears. She pressed a hand to her face. Yerima gave her a discreet thumbs-up, and she continued.

The President of the Republic was so moved by this true-life saga of suffering and rescue that he established the Presidential Task Force on Human Trafficking and honored me greatly by asking me to serve on it. The kick-off meeting was held several days ago inside the Palace, and he graciously accepted for us to hold this press conference here on the steps to emphasize his commitment to fighting this horrendous crime. This is an all-star task force that has the purpose of preventing traffickers from condemning other women and girls – and occasionally men – to lives of unrelenting misery and despair.

I will be happy to entertain your questions.

A dozen hands immediately went up. "Oh dear," she said, "how can I possibly be fair? Well, the pretty lady in the beige dress. Yes ma'am, what would you like to know?"

"Did the Ambassador ever use your, um, personal services at the club?"

Yerima held his breath, doing his best to look dignified, detached.

Tammy shot her a conspiratorial smile. "Occasionally, yes ma'am, of course. His wives had responsible positions here and did not accompany him, and there, it's such a closed society that you can't even think of having casual relationships. Plus, he's a healthy male, full of vitality. And listen, just speaking as one woman to another, I made damned sure that I married the man before he could escape. He's amazing in many respects. I'll leave it at that."

Knowing laughter. Nudges.

Yerima exhaled. She'd deftly diverted the focus from an ambassador paying visits to a brothel to a woman appreciating his prowess. Subtle. And *inshallah*, God willing, effective.

"Did they keep you in chains?"

"Occasionally, ma'am, but not all the time. One of my owners loved putting me in shackles; they gave him a power rush." She smiled. "First question everybody asks, but the overwhelming majority of the time, no. And I was never flogged – although the threat was always there and I do know many people who were. I spent most of my life on my back, on my knees, or bent over. I will leave the rest to your imagination."

"Did you fall in love with any of your masters?"

"No sir. One was eighty-one years old, one was impotent, one dyed me green for his Rainbow Harem, and one was a necrophiliac. In case that word doesn't appear very often in your conversations, it means someone who makes love to cadavers. Sorry, but I didn't feel like falling in love with any of them. They were my masters. Period. Uh, correction. I became friends with one of them, who is a very nice person, and we're still friends."

"Which one was that?"

"The one who was impotent, sir. I helped him with his problem even though he tried to conceal it from me, and he was so surprised, and so touched, that it changed our entire relationship. My mother is profoundly religious, and she used to tell us, When everything else fails, try love. So as one human being to another, I extended a hand of friendship to a man grieving

179

profoundly over the death of his young wife. He recently remarried, which made me very happy. And not incidentally, he later financed the rescue operation that His Excellency organized – snuff parties are incredibly expensive – so, in a very real way, he was an important part of saving my life."

"Madame Abdoulaye, can you please tell us more about this club where you were supposed to be boiled to death?"

"It's what they call a snuff club, a place where they torture people to death as entertainment. They hold this nightmarish club over your head from day one, threatening you that if you don't do everything they say, that's where you'll end up. And it's the obvious choice for executing a slave who murders the Chairman of the Board."

"Did you ever try to escape?"

"Yes ma'am. It didn't work, and they beat the soles of my feet until they were so swollen I couldn't walk for weeks. Had to crawl everywhere. Not fun."

"When you were a whore, did you have a specialty?" The journalist who asked this question had a smirk on his face.

"Yes sir, an *assigned* specialty, being sodomized. I absolutely, absolutely, hated it, but when you're a slave, you're not allowed to express any opinions, so that's how I spent maybe eight, ten hours a day. Can you imagine spending ten hours a day doing something that is not only physically painful but positively revolting? Welcome to the world of slavery. The services I provided weren't ones that men could readily expect from their wives; they were over the edge, disgusting.

180

That's why slavery persists, because slaves can be forced to provide such services. No matter how repulsive, you say Yes sir, Gladly sir, Of course sir. Or you're in big trouble. And I did what I had to do to survive."

She shrugged. "May I quickly point out, many girls *don't* survive. Some slave owners are sadistic monsters who torture the unfortunate people in their grasp, and there are brothels that cater to every taste, many of them extremely brutal. In some of the worst, life expectancy is counted in weeks or even days. I'm extremely lucky to be able to stand before you today, one of the rare girls who not only survived but who was rescued and can tell people here in the real world what goes on."

Audible moans.

"Yes? The gentleman over here with the nice tie."

"How do you like Cameroon, madame?"

A soft question, to be sure. "Well, I haven't been here very long, and haven't had a chance to see much of it yet. But what I've seen makes my mouth drop, it's so beautiful. The people are very warm and welcoming, and I love it. Back in Washington I'd wake up to the blaring of truck horns and sirens, and here it's wild parrots. Goodness, they're noisy! But they remind me every morning that I'm in Africa, and I'm in Africa because I'm married to the extremely attractive and kind-hearted man who saved my life." She blew Yerima an enthusiastic kiss.

"Oh oh! I almost forgot. I wanted to show you the collar and cuffs I wore at the club. And they're all I wore, by the way. They made it easy for the members to strap me down. Yes, please, get a good shot of them. Anybody else? Listen, while I'm here, let me remind you what the fundamental story is. It's His Excellency the Minister of Foreign Affairs, who saved a real-life damsel in distress from a horrible life and an even more horrible death. And it's His Excellency the President, who has taken decisive action to combat the horrendous crime of human trafficking. Please. It's not about me, or what I lived through. It's a beautiful fairy tale, only it really happened. I'm sorry that this didn't turn out to be a scandal, because I'm originally from Washington, and I know how journalists love to get their hands on nice juicy scandals."

Chuckles.

"Slavery is horrible. But thanks to my wonderful husband, it's no longer part of my life. And thanks to strong leadership by His Excellency the President, this country is now firmly dedicated to combatting this dreadful crime." She smiled. "If there are no more questions, I'll just thank you once again for coming and wish all of you a very pleasant day."

A few journalists came forward to shake her hand. "So nice of you, ma'am. Thank you so much, ma'am. So nice to meet you, sir. My pleasure, ma'am."

The man with the nice tie waited until everyone had gone and introduced himself. "My baby sister disappeared three years ago walking home from school," he said. "Now I'm wondering…"

"Oh my God," Tammy said. "How old was she?"

"Sixteen. Beautiful."

"Listen, there's a lady on the task force who specializes in crimes against girls and women. Her name is Commissaire Maïmouna Yayá and here's her phone number. If anyone can help you, she can. Pretty cold trail by now, but you never know. You're in a good position to help raise awareness, Gérard. Collect similar stories. Publish them. Publish her phone number, or mine. Talk about the new task force. Get people interested and let them know what they can do."

"I'd very much like to write an article about you, madame."

"I don't want this to be about me. I was a victim, not a hero. That man over there is a hero."

"I understand, madame, but people need to know how you lived. Who your masters were, how you got along with them. What you had to do every day. People don't know. They really don't know. And if they knew, they'd be eager to do something."

"I'm trying to write a book, but it's taking forever. It's hard."

"Chapeau, madame," said Yerima, giving her a big kiss. Hats off to you, ma'am.

"Yerima, darling, this is Gérard Eyebe, and he'd like to write a feature article about me. What do you think?"

"It's up to you, babe. One way to get the word out."

"Do I have your permission to invite him to the house, dear sir?" He nodded. They set up an appointment and Gérard withdrew.

"'They're going to eat you alive,'" she quoted with a wicked smile.

"Okay okay, you had them eating out of your hands. If it weren't blatant nepotism, I'd hire you as my press secretary on the spot. You were amazing."

"So were you, dear sir. You set the stage just right, and pre-empted most of the nasty questions by coming right out and saying what they thought we were going to hide. What a team!" They gave each other high fives.

Philippe shook her hand, nodding. "You certainly turned that around, madame. I was really nervous about this whole thing, but I think it went just fine. And the President will appreciate your plugs about his task force."

"He's trying to do something, sir, and I want to support that any way I can."

The press conference had gone well, but the original story persisted. And a handful of journalists hadn't been thrown off track by the deft change of subject. One newspaper ran another story, "Wife of MFA confirms whore allegations," and two others, "Foreign Minister met wife in brothel."

"People are going to believe what they choose to believe," she told Yerima. "We kept it from getting out of hand, but some people are determined to be hateful and there's not really much we can do."

One day she was in the bookstore getting stuff for the kids and a customer recognized her from the telecast.

"Espèce de putain," he spat. Filthy whore.

Tammy remembered Aïssatou's directive to be polite to everybody, and just smiled. But it certainly didn't feel very good.

And there was a tailor who'd set up shop with his treadle machine on the sidewalk outside the commissariat who called her *putain* every time she'd come or go. She'd always smile and tell him good morning, and he'd always glare at her with utter contempt.

For the most part, though, the public was supportive, especially after Gérard's article came out. He'd done an excellent job, in three columns, of capturing the gist of what she'd lived through. Maïmouna went into the archives and saw that she'd received a missing person report about his sister, and had even questioned a suspect or two, but had not been able to pursue the matter further.

Within a few days Tammy had waded through all of the piled-up filing at Maïmouna's office, and started catching up entering cases into the database. She adored the commissaire, whose gentle nature, generous heart, and determined cheerfulness lay comfortably around a core of tough professionalism. The extent of the problems she dealt with was mind-blowing, especially case after case of domestic violence, considered a crime only if it involved bed rest of ten days or more. Tammy noticed that numerous cases couldn't be pursued because doctors had issued medical certificates for eight or nine days, even those involving broken ribs and jaws.

"The low-down bastards," she commented.

"Of course, men know the rules, and they protect each other. That's why we need more female doctors and more female police officers."

The cases that were the hardest to enter were the ones of child molestation and genital mutilation. One man had molested six little girls, the youngest only five, before someone spoke up and he was finally arrested. And there were dozens of cases of clitoridectomies.

"It's the women themselves who perpetuate this brutality," explained Maïmouna. "Somebody did it to them, so they're going to do it to their daughters. They call it beautification. Some traditionalist men refuse to marry a girl with her clitoris intact, because she's considered high risk for infidelity. We're making progress – good progress, in fact – but in some parts of the country, this barbaric practice still persists."

And the occasional manslaughter. One man suspected his wife of being unfaithful, so he tied her down and stuffed her with chopped habanero peppers. He was amazed when she died. "She wanted it hot there, so I made it hot there. All I wanted to do was teach her a lesson." He got four years.

Or criminal neglect. A wife hemorrhaged to death with her husband present, and he did nothing to summon medical attention. "She wasn't a very good wife," he explained, "and I decided I needed a better one. This way I didn't need to go hire a divorce attorney." But he could have used a better criminal lawyer: he got seven years.

Or forced marriage. A fourteen-year-old girl came to the commissariat bawling her brains out. Her father needed a big favor from the traditional ruler in his area, so he decided he'd give her to the chief. She got wind of his intentions and ran away, but none of her male relatives would take her in because she was disobeying her father. Mouna found her a place to stay.

"We have several girls like that in our compound," said Tammy. "Thank God for Aïssatou, who makes sure they have somewhere safe to live."

"Does Yerima know?"

"Sure. He's not what you'd call a flaming liberal when it comes to women, but Amsaou tells me he's light years ahead of his own father."

"That's for sure. Tidjani owned dozens of slaves and kept virgin girls in huge clay jars. When he decided he'd like one, they'd put a ladder down and let her climb out. Yerima's mother was a big influence on him. Cathérine was educated, you know, a high-school French teacher. She was Tidjani's third wife, and married him against strong protests from her own family, because he wasn't Catholic. She died a week before Cathy was born, so Yerima named her for his mother. She raised him to respect women, but the rest of society didn't really support what she taught him. I mean, how can you tell people that child marriage is wrong, when the Prophet himself married his last wife Khadija when she was only nine years old? It's a very, very complicated issue, especially for Muslims."

Maïmouna's pregnant cousin Hapsatou appeared at the commissariat one day, two small children in tow. "I gave her money for food," Mouna said. "Her idiot husband just took a third wife and all his money is going to her. Hapsi and the kids hadn't eaten in three days. I told her things were liable to get worse, and she'd better roll up her sleeves and find a way to make a little money herself, selling beans and rice or *ndole* or something, but she said her husband wouldn't let her. He's a shift supervisor at a bread bakery. What on earth is he thinking, marrying a third wife when he can't – or won't – even support the two he has?" She shook her head.

"Women aren't second-class citizens here, it's more like third- or fourth-class. In most cases, married women are considered legal minors their entire lives, and if they aren't married, people think they must be prostitutes. We're making steady progress from a legal standpoint – only a few generations ago females were actually considered saleable property of their fathers or husbands – but the laws are having to drag society along behind them. Things are getting tons better, which is the only thing that keeps me going. Of course, we police see the worst of the worst. And a big point is, finally, women finally have the possibility to come forward, whereas before, they had no options at all."

As requested by the Task Force, they began cataloguing all the reported cases of missing women and girls that could possibly fall under the rubric of human trafficking. They started to notice certain geographic clusters as well as striking similarities in the reports. Tammy admired the way Mouna systematically and painstakingly sorted through everything, identifying commonalities, trying to make sense of an overwhelming mass of information. She had a white board with red circles, blue checks, green x's, and a map with colored pins. And they were starting to see real patterns.

Tammy welcomed a frightened lady into her living room and invited her to sit down. "Tea, ma'am?"

"Yes ma'am, thank you."

They chatted a few minutes about the cloudy weather and rumors that the government was going to raise fuel prices again. In early 2008, it had set off widespread cost-of-living riots that had paralyzed much of the country for nearly a week.

"It's our own oil, our own refinery," Madame Kaptchouang grumbled. "The stupid government just wants more revenue."

"Well," Tammy said mildly, "costs go up for the govern-ment too."

Tammy refilled her cup and finally said, "So, how can I help you, ma'am?"

"My husband sells girls to rich men in northern Nigeria," she blurted out. "But if he finds out I told anyone, he'll kill me. I mean for sure, he'll kill me."

She spent nearly forty-five minutes providing details: names, addresses, methods.

"I won't tell anybody where I got the information, ma'am, but I'm very worried about you. I can help you find somewhere safe to stay if you don't feel comfortable going home."

"He doesn't know that I know. I'm good at playing the dumb little wife who serves beer and sugared peanuts and disappears. But I sit in the kitchen and listen."

"How long has this been going on?"

"Eight, ten months."

"Any idea how many girls?"

"Six or seven, it's about one a month, but he plans to expand, because it's good, easy money. Georges has a wholesale coffee business and makes a shipment every few weeks to Kano. There's usually a girl on the truck. A few francs to the border guards on this side, a few naira on the other, and nobody says a word."

"How did you know to come to me?"

"I read about you in the paper. How you suffered. And I thought *zut alors*, heavens, that's what's happening to these poor girls."

"Madame Kuissu, you're very brave to come tell me all this, and I certainly understand why you couldn't file a report at the station. But what are you going to tell your husband if he asks why you came here?"

"Good question. He was really *gratiné* when the President set up that task force, and I'm sure he knows you serve on it. We need a good reason."

"Do you work?"

"Not really, I make a few francs here and there braiding hair."

"That gives me an idea. Amsi? Are you busy right now? There's a lady here who does braids and I thought you might like to meet her." She hung up. "She'll be right over."

Tammy briefly outlined the situation.

"Can you come Thursday evening and do my hair?" Amsi said. "And bring extensions? Let me give you a pass so the gendarmes will let you in."

"Thank you, thank you," she said.

"Be sure to let me know if you need somewhere safe to stay," Tammy told her.

"I'll be all right. I'm so glad to be able to tell someone."

"Madame Kuissu, you've saved a lot of girls from horrible lives. Thank you so much for coming."

Tammy turned her notes over to Mouna, who was able to confirm after a quiet investigation that the information was entirely correct. Four of the five men involved were swiftly arrested and papers drawn up for prosecution. The fifth managed to elude police for several days before he too was apprehended, but it was too late for Madame Kuissu. Her bruised and broken body was discovered in a ditch with a note pinned to her that said, "Thank you, Whore Sudari."

"I feel terrible," she told Mouna, "terrible. I tried, but…"

Mouna hugged her close. "You did your best. You can't let it get to you. You never know. Maybe the gendarme at the gate was her husband's cousin. Maybe it was the taxi driver. You never know. In my job, this sort of thing happens all the time. I go home thinking, if I'd just done this sooner, or if I'd only followed up on that angle, or if I'd only figured it out on Tuesday instead of Wednesday. And it drives me nuts. If I can satisfy my conscience – which is tough – then I just let the rest roll off my back. Meanwhile, though, I'm adding murder to the list of charges. We have a rock-solid case, thanks to Madame Kuissu, and these guys are going to be locked up for a long, long time."

It was always fun getting emails from Heineken, the lovable Dutch eunuch from Sheikh Saud's estate. He'd finally been able to buy his dream cabin in Colorado and shared it with Angie, a devocalized girl whom Abubakr had rescued from the Candlelight Lounge. "Yesterday Angie tried to brush Tripod. Loved it, but he couldn't figure out what she was doing. Hilarious. Finally gave him the brush and he rolled over on his back and spent a good fifteen minutes examining it with all three legs. One well-educated raccoon, that's for sure. The shep-herds gave him a hard time at first, but now they're friends. Love playing ball together. The bobcat Robert won't have anything to do with them. He adores Angie, though, who knows just the right place to scratch behind his ears.

"Angie's planted flowers everywhere and the place looks great. You and Yerima should visit. Got a fancy loft in the cabin where you can sleep and we can feed you veggies we grow ourselves and incredible lamb from the farm right down the road. Fine life here in Colorado and I sure do miss you, dearie."

"Fine life here in Yaounde too," she replied. "And speaking of visits, my family was just here. I was so excited, because my mom and Wellie had never even met Yerima. He treated them like royalty. They didn't exactly mind riding around in a chauffeured Mercedes, and of course everybody knows him, and people would rush over and shake their hands just because they were with him, and they couldn't get over the fact that this beloved celebrity was actually my husband. My *husband*, Heineken. I still can't get over how lucky I am. I'm the wife of the Minister of Foreign Affairs, not a slave in The Office. The *wife* of a beautiful man, can you believe?

"They stayed at the guest house here in the compound where even the walls are made of marble. They were blown away. Y couldn't go with us because he had to

192

go to a conference in Addis Ababa, but he arranged for us to take a week-long waterfall tour. Heineken, this country has got to be among the most beautiful anywhere on earth. Every time we rounded a curve, we gasped. Then we rounded another curve, and gasped again. Absolutely stunning. Picture medium-sized mountains all covered with green, and rivers everywhere, and gorgeous, gorgeous falls. There's even a smallish one near Pygmy country that goes straight into the Atlantic. They loved it.

"And they couldn't get over the great climate. Here in Yaounde it ranges between about sixty and eighty degrees year-round. I've seen exactly one mosquito, whose GPS was obviously malfunctioning. It rains a lot – there's a big rainy season and a small rainy season – but you just go about your business and get on with life. Sometimes it looks real hazy and it's sand from the Sahara that's blown this far south by winds they call the harmattan. This country is bigger than California, so it's like winds from Oregon that carry sand all the way to San Diego.

"We spent two days in Douala, a port city and industrial center of three million. We positively cracked up when we learned that one part of town is called Denver. Mansion after mansion, named after the *Dynasty* tv show. Of course, I had to visit the big chocolate factory. Lots of great restaurants and really nice shops. But it's hot and muggy, because it's right on the coast. When it's not too cloudy you can see Mount Cameroon from there, an active 14,000-foot volcano.

"They met my three co-wives and were surprised that we get along pretty well. I told them it sure didn't start out that way! Although I must confess, a few cracks are showing up between JoAnn and me again. Caldwell –

no more Wellie – wants to work for the FBI in their human trafficking section, so he spent a couple of days with Mouna at the commissariat seeing how she does things. Mom still isn't working but she's doing a lot better and I think it did her heart good to see how happy I am. It was hard hugging them goodbye.

"I'm still working on my book, making decent progress. As months go by, it gets a little easier to write, but I don't want to wait so long that I forget how horrible it all was. Amsi has been a doll saying, I don't understand this, or tell me more about this, or you've said this twice. She's my best friend here, even more than Mouna. Cleo parks on my lap and Titi winds herself around my neck, and they purr at me. They're so much fun, Heineken, and I think of you every day. The best wedding presents of all. Books and cats and chocolate, what I missed the most. Bit by bit, I'm catching up on all of them.

"School starts soon. Yes!

Love to all of you,
Tammy

P.S. Tripod sounds like a hoot. I can't wait to see all of you."

At the second meeting of the Task Force, they were talking about how traffickers operated. Most of the members thought that in Cameroon, at least, human trafficking was largely a crime of opportunity: someone sees a vulnerable girl and grabs her.

"That may have once been the case, but these days I'm seeing otherwise," Maïmouna said. "I'm seeing targeted kidnappings and organized rings. It's becoming a well organized criminal industry, and I find that highly disturbing. We are seeing clusters of activity in certain areas, and the reports are strikingly similar: girls abducted as they walk home from school. It only takes a few seconds to grab an unsuspecting victim and force her into a car."

Tammy listened for a while, lost in thought, remembering her friends at The House, the Rainbow, and The Office. Most of them had been systematically targeted, lured, and trapped. "I think it's getting more high-tech, too," she said. "More and more young people are using the Internet, and traffickers are going to start doing exactly what they do in the States and Europe. They place ads on websites that teen-age girls frequent, offering glamorous jobs in movies or modeling or rock bands, and when girls respond, they grab them. My Norwegian friend Toril, for example – at The Office they called her Jiggle-Tits – answered an online ad for a bit part in a movie. She knew her parents wouldn't approve, so she didn't tell anybody what she was doing. When she got there, the office looked really convincing, with movie posters everywhere, and the guy was on the phone with an agent who was trying to cast the remake of some big film. She was thirteen, and of course, she was dazzled.

"He asked her if she had time to sit down and chat or if someone was waiting for her. She realized afterwards that what he was really asking was if she had come alone and unprotected, but she was so excited that he wanted to interview her that she didn't focus on that part of the question at all. He put her at ease and they chatted for a few minutes. Then he said he wanted to show her the studio. Well, it was a closet, and he shoved her in and locked it, and next day she was in a crate on a cargo jet headed for the Gulf."

"And we have a growing cinema industry," commented Jules N'nang, the Gendarme detective.

"If it isn't movies, it's modeling, and look at the burgeoning fashion industry around here now. Or trying out for a hot new band. They know what teen-age girls dream about. They don't care that they're destroying lives; they just want to make money. Most of the girls I knew on the Gulf were lured in and trapped that way. A few had responded to online propositions, and that's going to be more and more of a problem around here too. Look at all the kids these days who are on the Net for hours a day; it's really changed teen-agers' lives."

"I'm interested in knowing more about what happens to the girls once they get to the Gulf," said Alice Mpondo, the civil rights attorney. "That is the modern-day slave trade, and there's no other way to describe it. Girls stolen from Norway and Germany and then shipped as slaves to stock harems and brothels."

"And Maryland," Tammy added wrily. "Some harems are so big that the girls never even meet the man who owns them. I remember a friend of mine from Switzerland who spent more than eight years in a harem with several hundred other girls and never once laid eyes on her owner. He had eight or ten favorites and everybody else was just stockpiled there. She said she thought that harem girls were sex objects, but that in that case, they were just plain objects.

"A lot of girls are forced into brothels, and some of them are extremely brutal. When you combine unlimited amounts of money and people who are completely under your control, it seems to encourage indulging in every perversion and every excess. I was lucky. The Office had strict rules against brutality, but I was still slapped and kicked dozens of times a day. In a lot of the clubs they burn the girls with cigarettes, strap them down and whip them, spray them with attractants and let dogs loose on them …
Unspeakable."

Major Mveng inquired, "How at risk are our girls for this?"

"Not very high," Tammy said. "There's a huge bias there toward tall blondes; there aren't very many Africans except as domestics. Tall blondes are considered premium livestock and Arabs are prepared to pay a fortune for them."

"I've heard about something recently," said Antoine, "and it concerns teen-age boys. Predators look for kids who have ambitions to play professional soccer in Europe. Families scrape together the money to send them to France, and a small proportion actually get recruited by teams, and the rest are abandoned with no money, no resources, and extremely vulnerable. From what I under-stand, the 'pretty' ones end up in homosexual brothels, and others are turned into eunuchs and shipped to the Gulf to guard the girls in the harems."

"I've heard about that too," said Alice. "Thank God, a Cameroonian in France has created a foundation to help these kids, but he's always short on money and a lot of them don't know about him."

The President said, "I think we should focus on three things: preventing this crime, pursuing the perpetrators, and finally on helping people like Madame Abdoulaye who were rescued but then face huge challenges readjusting to normal life. Most of the problem here, as I see it, is domestic or regional, girls kidnapped and sold to rich men here or in neighboring countries."

"We've just put one ring out of business that was selling girls into Northern Nigeria," said Maïmouna, "and I'm glad to say that the trial got a good bit of press. I think that as part of this effort we should also continue to educate the public."

"There's a journalist who's doing an article on the topic every month now," said Tammy. "Instant results: that's how we found out about that ring."

Antoine grinned. "And you did a masterful job of following through, Madame le Commissaire. The Procureur (D.A.) was impressed by how thorough your investigation was and how carefully you had documented everything."

"We're making progress," Maïmouna said proudly. "We are actually making progress."

Tammy's heart swelled with pride. She felt important. Needed. Like she was making a serious contribution. It was heady stuff, and she took great pleasure in it.

October finally arrived, and with it, classes! Tammy enrolled in the Faculty of Law and Economics, and poured herself with gusto into her long-delayed academic education. Aïssatou advised her to be the best-prepared student in her class, but also the most self-deprecating. "Don't tell them who your husband is, or they'll immediately decide that you're getting favorable treatment. They'll eventually find out, but by then they'll know that you deserve the high grades you get."

Her criminal law professor, however, recognized her from the news coverage, and asked if she'd be willing to give a presentation on modern-day slavery. "I'm very sorry, Dr. Dipanda, but I'd really rather not, sir, especially early in the semester," she told him, "because Yerima's extremely sensitive about my earning my degree on my own merits, and I don't want to give anyone the wrong impression. In any case, Commissaire Maïmouna would be a lot more credible than me. She's an amazing lady – as sweet as can be, but tough! I can ask her, if you like, sir."

"I know her, but only in passing. Would you?"

Tammy called her on the spot.

Maïmouna dazzled them, starting with a global perspective, followed by general ways that the criminals operated, the applicable laws in Cameroon, and finally, the President's new initiatives. Then she drove her points home. "Does anyone know of someone who just disap-peared? Most particularly, a beautiful young woman?" A few hands went up. "Were you aware that one of your own classmates was sold into slavery and managed to survive more than five years of hell before her future husband rescued her?" Consternation. "Sudari, dear, please come up."

"Mouna, I hadn't planned–"

"Just don't say who he is," she said quietly. To the class, she said, "I'm sure you'd like to ask her a few questions. Ten minutes, professor?" He nodded.

"What was it like, being a slave?"

"It was scary, because I belonged to some real weirdos. One of them was a tyrant on his good days and when he was drunk, a monster. I was afraid every single day for my life."

"Would you explain weirdo?"

"Two of them in particular. One dyed me green – the chemicals are still screwing up my system – and the other liked dead girls. Weird enough for you?"

Incredulous laughter.

"How were you rescued?"

"My future husband bought me and emancipated me."

"Where were you?"

"I was kidnapped in Marseilles and shipped to the Persian Gulf."

"Do you speak Arabic?"

"Yes, I do. One of my masters had a doctorate from a university in Texas, so we spoke English, but I had to speak Arabic with everyone else. You learn a language real fast when your survival depends on it, believe me."

"What was the worst moment in those five years?"

"When I was sentenced to be boiled in oil and bolted into a big glass pot." Gasps of horror. "There was one psychopath I really hated, I mean, from his hair to his toenails, and I finally had the chance and murdered him. They decided to make an example of me by torturing me to death so that other girls wouldn't get the same idea."

"What was the best moment?"

"When I was pulled out of that pot and realized I wasn't dead after all. The second-best moment was slitting that low-down double-talking sadistic miscreant's neck."

Laughter. One student said, "Aw, Dari, don't be so shy, tell us what you really thought of him." More laughter.

"Did they ever put chains on you?"

She closed her eyes and took a deep breath. "At the gentlemen's club, yes. Chains, straps, leashes, tethers, harnesses, shackles, handcuffs, you name it. Not all the time, but frequently. I think that every single restraint ever invented was used on me at some point."

"Were your masters cruel?"

"One was extremely cruel to people who got in his way, but he wasn't cruel to me. He was extremely controlling, but not actually cruel. One of my masters was a very nice man, and we became friends. We're still friends. Most of them considered me simply an object for a particular purpose, used me for that purpose, and went on with their lives without thinking about me at all."

"What's it like, living in a harem?"

"Boring, boring as hell. The Rainbow Harem, where I was dyed green, had a great library – in the year I was there I went nuts and devoured more than five hundred books – but in most of them you're basically locked up all day with nothing to do and nowhere to go. A lot of girls go insane. Then the men say, you can't trust women with any responsibility, because they're mentally so fragile. It never occurs to them that if they were forced to lead totally empty lives, basically just sitting around waiting and waiting, they'd go insane at alarming rates too."

"What's been the hardest part of readjusting to freedom?"

"Handling money. Try going five years without a franc to your name, surrounded by people who own yachts, Boeings, Rolls Royces, huge estates... You lose perspec-tive, and what's worse, you have no idea that you've lost perspective. It's not until your husband says for the fifteenth time, babe, you know, they've invented some-thing called a budget, and you realize that you've screwed up again. I thought my overruns were such trivial amounts that I couldn't imagine it would be a problem. And another thing has been finding out about huge news stories that I knew absolutely nothing about because I was so completely cut off from the world."

"What kept you going?"

"My faith in God, the fact that I knew that my father was doing his best to get me out and hadn't abandoned me, and the love I shared with the wonderful gentleman who rescued me."

"So...if you're a whore and a murderer, and this dude married you anyway, may we assume that you must be phenomenal in bed?"

202

It was a physical effort for Tammy to resist the temptation to march across the room and smack him. She recoiled, but recovered and brought herself to her full five-eight height. She looked him square in the eye. "So…if you're focused on things that are none of your business, and if your mind is so resolutely in the gutter, may we assume that it takes a hand pump and Viagra to get you going?"

"Touché," someone said.

"Oooooooh, that hurts."

"So she's a whore, a murderer, *and* a bitch."

"Who's your husband?"

"He's a horse veterinarian by training, an extremely handsome and kind-hearted Fulani from Maroua."

"Thank you, Sudari. Very, very interesting. And many thanks to you, Commissaire Maïmouna." The class, with one exception, gave them a standing ovation.

Tammy grabbed her books and got into the waiting car as quickly as she could. "Late for work, very very sorry," she said over her shoulder to the cluster of students who wanted to continue the conversation.

"Must be one heck of a successful veterinarian," commented one student as the sleek Mercedes pulled away. "Wabenzi."

"Veterinarian, my eye, see the sticker? That's the car of Minister Abdoulaye. Wabenzi? What's that?"

"In Kenya we have an honorary ethnic group. If you ride around in a Mercedes Benz, we call you Wabenzi. Who's Abdoulaye?"

He laughed appreciatively. "He's the one who married the whore. Foreign Affairs."

"And she's the whore. Damn."

"Nice lady, though. And you know what? I never noticed before; she really has a great-looking ass."

When they were halfway to the commissariat, Charles made an abrupt and unexpected turn.

"Why are you going this way?" Tammy wanted to know.

"Don't turn around to look, madame, but there's a beige Fiat that's been following us. It tries to keep three or four cars back. Ah, sure enough, there it is, turned right after us."

"Wow," she said. "You're amazing. How did you ever notice?"

"I saw it when I was waiting for you at school. Two guys leaning on it, trying a little too hard to look nonchalant, and I began to wonder."

Tammy sighed. The knot in the pit of her stomach was growing to alarming proportions.

CHAPTER EIGHT

Mr. Faisal put in a call to his boss. "Your Highness, I just wanted to give you a quiet alert. Four girls came to me this afternoon and requested that they be sent to you together. The way they put it was this: one would give you a BJ, one would give you a massage, and the other two would be sucking your toes."

"Doesn't sound too bad to me." He laughed. "How soon can they get here?"

"Your Highness, I have a strange feeling. First of all, all four of these girls have had a long series of disciplinary issues. You're extremely perceptive, Your Highness: three of the four were the ones you had disciplined after the recent obeisances. Second, they've been spending a lot of time together, and several times Trevino and Firenze have overheard something about a knife. In fact, precisely what they said was, 'His dinner knife; it's the only way.' Then this morning, Napoli saw them whis-pering to each other. They did high fives and giggled."

"Hmm. Stupid, stupid, stupid, little girls. Schedule them for Thursday night. I'll be ready. But I missed one. Who was that?"

"Six Beta. The auburn-haired Irish girl with long legs."

"Oh, I know which one you mean. I've wondered why she's suddenly been sucking up to me. She's a real beauty. Too bad."

"By the way, Your Highness, inventory is down to 103."

"And we're on the verge of losing four more. All right, thanks, I'll talk to Nigel about restocking."

"May I respectfully ask, Your Highness, just out of curiosity, why you chose the number 111?"

"Two reasons: I just like the number, and also, my beloved nanny Lucia died on the eleventh of Muharram, the eleventh day of the first month, so it is in memory of her."

"I understand that in numerology, it stands for the Trinity."

"Indeed," replied Ibrahim, "prosecco, chianti, and asti spumante. Or tomatoes, garlic, and basil. Or the mouth, the pussy, and the asshole."

At the appointed hour, the four girls trooped excitedly into their master's bedchamber, big smiles brightening their faces. They prostrated with such devotion that Ibrahim had a hard time keeping a straight face. Four or five other times, girls had decided they could outsmart him. Each time, the Rodeo got more meat. They'd been warned. They knew perfectly well what risks they were running. But it'd be fun to mess with them a little, play along with their stupid, stupid little game. He discreetly drew his finger across his neck and winked to alert Giuliano of their intentions.

"It's so nice of you to offer me your collective services," Ibrahim began. "It sounds absolutely delightful. We'll get to that soon enough. Who would like to sit on my lap and feed me my dinner? All right. And who will be my beautiful footrest? Come. You other two, stay like you are. Cut me a nice piece of braciola. Careful, my dear, that's a very sharp knife. I wouldn't want you to injure those beautiful fingers." He pointed with his chin to the zucchini alla gorgonzola, then the mushroom risotto, then the panzanella. When Five Gamma'd fed him the last bite he set the empty plate on the table, the knife within easy reach. Giuliano started over to take the plate away, but Ibrahim almost imperceptibly shook his head.

"More prosecco, Your Highness?" asked the valet.

"Yes please." He took a swig and smiled. "So, just what do you beautiful girls have in mind?"

They exchanged excited glances. "We want to give our master an evening he'll never forget," said Eight Gamma. "If you would be so good, master, as to lie down, I will give you the best BJ you have ever had. Five Beta will massage your chest with her magic fingers. And Five Gamma and Six Beta will each take one foot and suck your toes."

"It sounds like you've given this some real thought. What's prompted this sudden devotion? You three failed to show me proper respect during the obeisances the other day, and you, my dear, have a list of disciplinary issues as long as my arm."

They all started to speak at once. "Wait. You first. You may kneel."

"I came to grips with the error of my ways, master. I wish to apologize, and this is a tangible way that I can do so."

"I see. And you?"

"Pretty much the same, master. I was very rebellious, but I'm finally reconciled to being here."

"And what about you?"

"I'm very remorseful, master. I owe you my very existence, master, and it has only recently hit home. I desperately want to make it up to you."

"And you."

"I've been so stupid, defying a master as handsome and as kind as you. I commit myself to being the most devoted slave you ever owned, master."

"We want very much to please you, master."

"I see," he said agreeably, lying down as they had requested. "Miraculous reform, and all four of you at the same time. How very interesting."

They exchanged nervous glances, but the moment passed.

"May we give our master even more stimulation, even more pleasure, by using these?" Eight Gamma pointed to the shackles that were permanent accessories to the bed.

"More pleasure, you say? Nobody's ever had the nerve to suggest that."

"Oh yes, master, it's very nice for a woman, but even more pleasurable for a man."

"Okay, why not? It's not as if you were planning to slit my throat."

Giuliano stifled a guffaw in the nick of time and a *frisson* of panic curled around the room, replaced by sighs of relief when the last iron was snapped in place.

Such pathetic, pathetic amateurs. Time to get rid of the valet. "Giuliano, please go to my study and bring me my tungsten file. I'm not sure exactly where it is; it's probably in the stack to the left on my desk. If not, look on the credenza."

Excited glances. What unbelievable luck!

Eight Gamma casually picked up the knife and, concealing it next to her leg, made her way over to him. Five Beta started the massage, Five Gamma and Six Beta began sucking his toes.

"We have something else planned for you tonight, master." The activities were suspended. "We would like to wish you a very pleasant journey to the life beyond." She touched the knife to his neck.

"Guards!"

Four bodyguards, concealed behind a screen, leapt into action. Screams of shock. Within seconds, all four girls were handcuffed and on their knees. One of the guards released Ibrahim, who put on his robe, sat down, and stared for a long time at the sobbing foursome.

"We saw you coming from miles away, you stupid, stupid, stupid idiots," he told them. "Do you think you're the first girls who ever had this insane idea?" He folded his hands. "The dog barks, but the caravan moves on. You were warned. You knew perfectly well what you were risking. Attempted assassination? I don't need to tell you what the penalty is. I've reserved places at the Rodeo for all four of you. Guards, the van is waiting."

Screams of dismay. The Rodeo? The *Rodeo?* They always knew in the back of their heads that it might be a possibility if they failed. It just never occurred to them that their plans wouldn't work. But now, it was going to happen. To them.

"When I was at the Ranch," Six Zeta said, "they posted the schedule for paddlings. The cowboys could watch, and they'd fight over who could take the filly up to their room. Cowboy Clint would come every Tuesday afternoon to watch me be paddled, then have me taken right up. It got him so excited. Here, after 40 strokes you're in the infirmary for three days and can't sit down for two or three more, but there, you're immediately hauled off to work. And once a day they use the Rocket. When they paddle you, it shoots you around a track like a roller coaster and puts you back in position just in time for the next stroke. Sometimes a cowboy would pick you out of the display and ask that you be rosied up for him, so you'd get twenty strokes for absolutely nothing. I can't believe how lucky I am that Prince Ibrahim saw me and bought me out of that place just in time. I still have screaming nightmares about it."

When they arrived at the snuff club, the girls were fitted with shoulder harnesses and leather hoods, and suspended by meat hooks on the edge of the arena. They could hear screams every night as other executions took place. They could hear the announcer whip the spectators into a frenzy as the unfortunates were ripped apart by hyenas, gradually lowered into a cobra pit, or sawed slowly into pieces. "A week or so of hearing this will put you in the proper mood for your own execution," the manager said as he had their wrists bound tightly with barbed wire and spiked collars fastened snugly around their necks. "The meat tonight is suspended by its arms over a bonfire. Leather baskets are attached to its ankles and knees, and the spectators throw weights into the baskets. Its arms will eventually be ripped off, and sizzle sizzle sizzle."

The executions took place over four evenings. For each, the five-hour preliminaries were the same: two hundred lashes over their entire bodies with a whip embedded with glass shards, then completely immersed in a hot pepper sauce, then rubbed with coarse salt. A twelve-inch pointed dildo was pounded into their rears. Then a barbed-wire girdle was hammered in until it almost entirely disappeared into their flesh.

Finally, it came time for the real show. None of the girls had been devocalized, so, as the club announcer put it, their screams would be "robust and gratifying."

The first evening featured Five Beta. She was spared the pepper sauce, only because the crocodile didn't care for it. She was placed head first on a five-meter-long greased incline that led to the crocodile pit. Two teams played tug-of-war; amid loud laughter, Team Up would pull a rope that wound onto a wheel, pulling her back an inch or two, then Team Down would make her descend a little. When the star member of Team Up tripped and fell, Team Down made rapid progress. "She'll soon take a dive," one member said excitedly. The crocodile spoiled their plans, however; as soon as he saw her, he heaved himself up onto the ramp and pulled her down. Total time, including preliminaries: six hours and fifty-eight minutes.

"Next time," the manager told the announcer, "we need a lot more of a drop into the pit. That was a real let-down."

The following evening, Five Gamma was suspended head down by eight sturdy ropes tied to her ankles over a tank of raw and extremely odiferous sewage. Spectators threw small curved knives at the ropes, fraying that one there, weakening this one over here. Of course, many of them missed. One became embedded in her thigh. Another sliced off a nipple, causing an explosion of delight. Another wedged in the back of her head. One by one, the ropes were severed. She was fairly lucky; the show only lasted six hours and seventeen minutes.

More spectator participation was involved in Six Beta's execution. She was attached spread-eagle to a metal frame on wheels. One team was equipped with branding irons, and the other tried to keep the meat away. Points were scored for branding particularly juicy targets: breasts, forehead, cheeks, inner thighs. When there was hardly any more unbranded skin, she was turned over, exposing her beautiful rear, which generated consid-erable excitement. But it also meant that she was lying on freshly-branded skin, and she kept passing out from the pain. Spectators complained bitterly. She had fainted repeatedly during the preliminaries, and as the program progressed, it became more and more difficult to wake her up and make her scream. Long before all the scheduled activities had taken place, she expired, which caused loud booing. Five hours and thirty-two minutes.

Eight Gamma was the ringleader, so a special treat lay in store for the spectators. They started by running her arms and legs through rollers that completely crushed the bones, then attached her to another A-frame on wheels. On another set of wheels was a rotating brass screw, nearly eighteen inches long and three inches in diameter. The spectators were again split into two teams, one controlling the meat, the other controlling the screw. Every minute that elapsed without a touch gave the meat team points; every time the screw came in contact, the screw team got points.

Soon there were long gashes all over, where the screw had sideswiped her. Finally, after more than two hours, while the meat team had unexpected trouble changing operators, the screw found its mark between her legs. It continued to rotate until the screaming stopped. Total elapsed time: seven hours and forty-four minutes.

As a side show, they brought out what was left of an oil executive who refused to sell Ibrahim three girls. He no longer had eyes, a nose, ears, lips, or his male parts – they'd all been ground up and fed to him. After the obligatory preliminaries, every bone in his body was broken with sledgehammers, and he was put in a glass box that contained hundreds of mosquitoes and botflies. A botfly would capture a mosquito, lay its eggs on her, and as she bit, the eggs would be deposited beneath the skin. The eggs hatched and became larvae, still burrowed under the skin, causing excruciating pain. He'd been bitten dozens of times, and bulbous lumps were all over his body.

This particular execution didn't provide the same drama as most at the Rodeo, so it couldn't be featured at a party, but the managers had assured Ibrahim that the level of agony over such an extended period would far exceed what most victims would endure. And he was brought out every now and then so that spectators could enjoy the look of intense anguish on his disfigured face. Now, when they placed hot coals where his eyes used to be, there was barely a flicker.

An adulterous couple shared a cell, each suspended in a glass cylinder. Facing each other, they were each tube-fed a diet of rats, cockroaches, pig entrails, meat crawling with maggots, and other treats. His urine and feces were piped into her cylinder, and vice-versa. They were already chest-deep and in another few days would finally drown in each other's shit. It was the woman's husband who created this ingenious technique – far more meaningful, he said, than merely stoning them to death.

When the required highlights video was shown at Il Giardino Posteriore, so many girls threw up, passed out, or became hysterical, that Mr. Faisal decided to show it in ten-minute clips rather than all at once.

"They went about it all wrong," Seven Zeta told One Pi. "What if the guards had just stood there and laughed?"

"But how could you ever engineer that? We're not allowed – uh, what nincompoops would ever try to assassinate such a good master? They got what was coming to them, that's for sure." Torino moved on. "We're not allowed to talk to them and they aren't allowed to talk to us."

"Mere details. They were stupid. I know what to do, and it's going to work," Seven Zeta repeated.

Pandemonium – literally "all the demons" – in the harem. The physical review had just taken place, and seventeen girls changed category. Two lost their nine-status altogether and were demoted to Il Giardino dei Fiori. Both of them were sobbing as they were issued pastel tunics, named Delphinium and Digitale (Foxglove), and loaded onto the golf cart for transfer.

The most stupefying demotion of all was that of Ten Alpha to Nine Beta. She was so shocked, she sat all day long in a corner of the salon, unseeing eyes cast straight ahead. She would not speak, would scarcely allow herself to be guided to the refectory to eat. Sometimes, unbelieving, she'd look at the silver border on her tunic, and go back to staring into space. She was no longer the most beautiful girl in the most exclusive harem in the world, and she was shattered.

Zero Iota, who had bitterly complained that she'd been misclassified, rejoiced when she learned she'd been promoted to Four Delta. But most of the reclassifications were downward, and a lot of girls were unhappy.

Mr. Faisal and Mr. Sayeed were doing their best to calm them down, but girls had to get used to tunics with different borders, dormitory assignments had to be rejiggered, and girls who'd been used to a particular cognomen – sometimes for years – suddenly had to remember to answer to a different one.

So it was a relief for everyone when Mr. Faisal announced that a party celebrating the grand opening of Il Giardino del Arcobaleno, or the Rainbow Garden, had been scheduled, and the girls from Il Giardino Posteriore would be featured entertainment. Finally, they could devote attention to a fun project instead of dealing exclusively with all the turmoil after the physical review.

The chaos resumed, however, when the review committee returned several days later, this time, to evaluate bosoms – not only size, but shape and overall appeal.

215

The graduates were each awarded ten bonus points and were told that they would be featured twice during the party, once for their rears and once for their breasts.

"What an honor," wrily commented Five Zeta. "Before, we existed only between our waists and our knees. Now it's between our *necks* and our knees. This is positively thrilling."

It took two days to get ready for the party. The bath attendants used special cream to make the girls' bodies glisten, and special conditioner to make their hair look like it was lit from within. Early on the morning of the party, the bath attendants gave each *derrière* a massage with pearlized gel, after which, no one was allowed to sit down. Then, each rear was dusted with ultra-sparkly disco dust, carefully blended so that colors moved gradually from violet to red and back to violet, echoing the rainbow theme. The same was done to the fifty-nine Fs, also arranged in order of height.

Two hours ahead, the girls were moved into place, lining both sides of the hallway that led to the Grande Sala de Balo, or Grand Ballroom. They were bent over a barre, their wrists attached to their ankles with velvet color-coordinated ropes. Then there was the time-consuming job of stuffing each rear with an electric wiggle worm programmed to selected music – carefully, so as not to mess up the beautiful make-up – and running the cord as invisibly as possible down the front of the leg.

Mr. Faisal was shaking his head, it was so stunningly beautiful. "Time for the test run," he said. The hallway was filled with the magnificent sounds of *Cielito Lindo*, and instantly, more than a hundred asses swayed in rhythm. "Your Highness," he said, "this is beyond magical. This is sheer genius. Your guests are going to be impressed beyond belief." He shook his head again, overwhelmed. "All right, everything works. Now we're just waiting for the guests."

The girls were allowed to stand up for a while; they were reattached just before the forty invitees were due to arrive. At least a dozen guests stopped in the hallway and just gaped. One was so overcome that he needed to be assisted into the ballroom.

Inside, garlands of flowers in rainbow colors were festooned between the pillars. Music was provided by an all-female mariachi band wearing sombreros, sequined high heels, and big smiles. A huge fountain with rainbow lights danced in synchrony to the music. Usherettes – wearing starched white collars and cuffs, colorful satin bowties, and gold high heels – showed each guest to his place at the banquet table. Rainbow-hued serapes, strewn with hibiscus and alamanda blossoms, supported arrangements of fresh fruit, accented by *cabochons* of amethysts, sapphires, emeralds, citrines, orange padpar-adshahs, and rubies.

At each place were four girls: one, defanged, under the table, to provide a long and luxurious BJ as the guest enjoyed the sumptuous feast. One on the right, one on the left, and one behind, to ensure that he never lacked for anything. A curtained booth behind the table pro-vided privacy if he chose to avail himself of the services of any or all of the attendants, but as more and more champagne was consumed, fewer and fewer guests took advantage of the booths and openly enjoyed the company of their companions.

Platters of chicken mole, beef enchiladas, cheese empanadas, and grilled veggie quesadillas with *queso*

217

fresco were quickly emptied. The tuxedoed butlers had to answer lots of questions, since Mexican cuisine was very little known, but oohs and aahs accompanied almost every bite.

Prince Ibrahim hadn't refused when his own attendants offered frequent refills of Perrier-Jouet – about $4,000 a bottle – so he was a little wobbly when he rose. "Gentlemen," he began, and the band went *pianissimo*. "We have some wonderful entertainment for you this evening. First, I hope you are enjoying the band. I learned an interesting story about how mariachi music got its name. When Prince Maximilian ruled Mexico, he wanted special music for his wedding. In French, the word is *mariage,* mah-ree-AH-zheh. By the time the word was pronounced in Spanish, it became mariachi."

Delighted nods.

"We have recently upgraded the allure of the girls in Il Giardino Posteriore, and would like to present to you, fifty-nine magnificent pairs of Fs as they perform to *Un Rinconcito en el Cielo*."

A curtain was raised, and fifty-nine pairs of breasts came into view. Each woman to whom they were attached was tied to a column by her elbows, to raise her bosom as far as possible. The rest of her body was veiled in pastel rainbow-hued tulle, so only her beautiful breasts were visible. The guests gasped. Each woman was standing on a special metal disc, and when Mr. Faisal pressed a button, the boobs began to bounce in time to the music.

One guest needed to be revived, and another had to be diplomatically restrained.

"And now, for our special treat, please meet the residents of my newest and most forward-thinking harem, Il Giardino del Arcobaleno, the Rainbow Garden. This harem was two years in preparation, and as far as we know, the only one in the world that includes six authentic albinos." He gestured, and another curtain opened.

Miss Purple stood at the top of a curved staircase, gowned in royal purple satin and weighed down with amethysts and diamonds. She smiled, nodded, and descended the staircase. She was soon followed by Miss Blue, Miss Green, Miss Yellow, Miss Orange, and Miss Red, until all six stood together at the base of the stairs.

At a signal, their gowns were gone, and six ladies, each dyed a different color, were standing naked.

The guests went berserk.

"Please continue to enjoy yourselves. You will each take home, as a souvenir of this evening, whichever of your four attendants you select. And, as a grand prize, we will also draw a name to receive one of the Fs, who is also, by the way, a nine-point ass."

The party started to wind down and guests thanked Ibrahim profusely and left, each with a new *jaria* in tow. *"Shukran,"* they said, thank you, and their host responded *"Afwan,"* you're welcome. They exited down the hallway, past more than a hundred asses simul-taneously gyrating to *Amor Eterno*. Prince Abdullah won the grand prize, a very somber Three Zeta, who dutifully bowed her head and, four respectful paces back, followed her new master out the door.

Mr. Faisal sounded the gong, and the harem girls assembled in the courtyard. It was a pleasant day – only in the mid-80s.

"Come on, come on, ladies, *yalla bil-'ajal!* Make it snappy! This should be brief."

"What the hell does he want this time?" growled One Omicron.

When they quieted, he began. "His Highness is instituting some new policies. Now, before you start moaning and groaning, hear me out. First, he strongly objected to your method, revolt, which he found insulting, because he is an extremely benevolent master who is always willing to consider petitions that are well reasoned and respectfully submitted. Nevertheless, he has heard you, and with immediate effect, the physical enhancement program will become entirely voluntary." He paused to let the cheering subside. "You will be awarded ten bonus points each month if you choose to continue, and if you choose to discontinue, ten points will be deducted. But it is no longer mandatory.

"Second, also with immediate effect, surrendering a privilege each day will be required only for the bottom twenty performers." More cheers. "In addition, the top twenty will draw tokens each day that will reward them with their choice a chocolate bar, an hour of approved television, a dish of ice cream, a tall of Starbucks coffee, or an hour of approved computer games." Deafening cheers.

"Third, he has provided Training with a completely new set of videos." The women were ecstatic. What had happened to Prince Ibrahim? Why was he suddenly in such a buoyant mood?

"Who cares? For once, the changes are really terrific," said Six Theta.

"I've heard that the harem for that girl is under construction," said Two Nu. "She'd better watch out."

CHAPTER NINE

"What exactly did you say about Viagra at school the other day?" Aïssatou demanded of Tammy one morning after breakfast.

Tammy couldn't believe her ears. "You heard about that? Good grief, can't I ever say anything, anywhere, without spies tattling on me?"

"I've warned you since day one that you are a public figure and that you should be courteous to everyone, especially those–" she waited for Tammy to fill in the blank.

"Who deserve it the least," she reluctantly said.

"What happened?"

"Dr. Dipanda asked Mouna to give a presentation on human trafficking to our Criminal Law class. She called me up so the students could ask questions, and this one jerk, as Aminatou would put it, the mostest rudest person in Equatorial Africa, said, so, if you're a whore, and a murderer, and this dude married you anyway, you must be really great in bed. And I said that it was none of his goddam business and that his mind was in the gutter and that it must take Viagra and a hand pump to get him going."

"Do you think that was a courteous reply befitting a wife of the Minister of Foreign Affairs?"

"I guess not."

"Are you proud of yourself?"

Tammy was suddenly thrust into a rare foul mood. Damn it, she couldn't even turn around without someone reporting to Aïssatou. Sudari has breathed in. Sudari has breathed out. It was getting hard to take. "Not really. He deserved far worse. I've been trying ever since to come up with an even better zinger for the idiot."

"Do you realize that you insulted the son of Tabe Tataw, the director of the Central Bank, one of Yerima's best friends?"

"I could care less. He was extremely rude. And for heaven's sake, Aïssatou, what do you want me to say? If I'd said yes, there'd have been another headline, Wife of MFA says she's great in bed."

"You should have simply said, I will not dignify that with a response."

"Oh right, then the headline would read, Wife of MFA doesn't *deny* that she's great in bed."

"Sudari, did you follow my directive to be courteous to everyone?"

"No ma'am."

"And did you respect your own vow, framed on your living room wall, that you would always behave in such a way as to bring Yerima honor?"

That cut Tammy to the quick. She gasped, and bowed her head.

"All right. I'm giving you a mid-level restriction for two weeks. I'm taking you off Yerima's schedule and I'm confining you to the women's house with the exception of school and work. The following rules apply. You will, for the duration, address me as ma'am and Yerima as sir. You will not stop on your way home for any reason, and Charles knows that I'll dismiss him if he doesn't bring you straight here. No visitors from outside the compound. No allowance. You may respond to a sum-mons to go to the main house – and you must be there in less than five minutes – but otherwise, you are not to leave the women's house. And if you violate any of these rules, I will extend the restriction. Furthermore, in your next criminal law class you will stand up and apologize to Ebai in front of everybody."

Tammy's mouth fell open. "Good grief! All I did was–"

"Are you capable of being a wife of the Minister of Foreign Affairs, Sudari? Can you handle this? You're only twenty-four years old. You're a very mature twenty-four, but in certain respects, you still have a lot of growing up to do."

"Ma'am, I survived five years of horrible servitude. I suvived a psychopathic master. I survived almost being boiled to death. I can handle two weeks of not being allowed to breathe. So yes, I can most definitely handle being wife of the MFA."

Aïssatou looked at her long and hard. Quietly. Coldly. Uh-oh, Tammy thought, I've really done it now. When she looked at the schedule in the kitchen next morning, she discovered that her restriction wasn't for two weeks, but for six. She went back to her apartment, buried her face in Cleo's fur, and wept.

Amsi put her arm around Tammy's shoulders. "Listen, darling, we've all been there. Aïssatou cut you a lot of slack at Yerima's insistence, but it's been a year now, and the special treatment is history. They've even had fights because she thought he was being way too lenient with you. But don't feel bad. The first two years that JoAnn was here, she probably spent half her time on restriction, and that was when Yerima was still Director of International Cooperation at the Ministry of Animal Husbandry. Now that he's MFA, Aïssatou's even more obsessed about protecting his image. We're not anonymous. Every single thing we do is subject to scrutiny, criticism."

"Tell me about it," Tammy said. "And it's unbelievable. Her damned spies are everywhere."

"They're not spies, Dari, just people. Yaounde is nothing but a huge village, and Aïssatou knows practically everybody. Sometimes it takes thirty minutes for her to find something out, sometimes it takes a week, but sooner or later, she'll know. That's just how this place works. And listen, darling, think of Aïssatou as an extension of Yerima. Whatever she does, it's out of intense, intense loyalty to him. Yes, she's very strict, but she's also very fair.

"You do not – and I repeat do not – want that woman mad at you. She's very good-hearted, and would never go out of her way to be mean, but if she's convinced that you're hurting Yerima's career, you know, an observation here, a comment there, and before you know it, you're history. Yerima trusts her judgment more than he trusts his own, and I'm not kidding. I'm glad that you apologized to her. That's huge."

"But she didn't change the schedule, and when I told Yerima, he flat-out refused to get involved. He said he wasn't about ready to undercut her authority by second-guessing her or countermanding her."

"To be honest, if you were in her shoes, you'd appreciate that policy a lot. Wait a few days until you've calmed down. Offer to help her with something. It'll work out, believe me. Did you apologize to Ebai?"

"Yes. He said his mother almost killed him too. We hugged. It's okay."

"Meanwhile, you can use the time to put the finishing touches on your manuscript. It's really good, Sudari. It doesn't preach, but it doesn't pull any punches. It just says look, this was my life. People can see for themselves how miserable it was. I love it."

"It's been hard, especially with all these stupid power outages. I swear, if there's one more this week, I'll positively scream."

Tammy hugged Amsi and started down the hall. Before she had taken three steps, the lights flickered and went out. She turned around, opened Amsi's door, and said "Do you happen to have a primal scream room that I can borrow for a few minutes?"

"The bunker, darling, the bunker."

The emergency lights came on and Tammy returned to her apartment, Amsi's silvery laughter echoing down the hallway after her.

Four days later, Tammy knocked gingerly on Aïssatou's door and Fatimatou admitted her. The senior wife concluded her phone conversation. "Good evening, Sudari, what can I do for you?"

"I've just come to apologize again, ma'am, for disobeying you, and embarrassing Yerima. I've been feeling really rotten and somehow, I'd like to make it up to you. Is there a big project or something that I can help you with to try to make things right? I'd really like to show you how sorry I am."

"I'm not going to change the schedule, if that's what this is about."

"I understand, ma'am, and no, that's not what I'm after. All I want to do is show you that I'm really sorry."

"Project, you say? Well, come to think of it, there's one that I've been meaning to get to ever since I was appointed to the bench, and in seven years, I just haven't had the time. You're good at organizing papers, right?"

"Yes ma'am."

"And you don't mind big projects?"

"Not at all, ma'am. I love them, in fact."

"I'll have Gabriel pick you up from school tomorrow and bring you to my office."

Next day she reported to Aïssatou in her chambers. "All right, my dear. You said you weren't afraid of a big job, so here it is." Aïssatou opened the door to a storeroom under the stairs. Dossiers were stacked every which way, covered in dust. "That's just part of what I inherited. Look over here." She opened a door marked Archives and Tammy saw a similar mess, this time on a much grander scale. Tammy went weak in the knees.

227

"Are you still on? As they say in Ewondo, everything is *azam zam zám*. Or in Bassá, *yubda-yubda*. In Fulfulde, not quite as much fun. A junk heap is *jiddere*, and to throw things into disorder is *villugo*."

"Or in English, a hell of a mess." She winced. "Yes ma'am. This is unbelievable. Your predecessor should be shot. Why on earth didn't you ask me to help you with this before? How do you want them?"

"I thought so too, until I found out he was valiantly handling the workload of three people. Now there are two of us, and we still can't keep up. Sorted by year, then by case number. All properly labeled. Are you scolding me, by the way?"

"Sort of, ma'am. I spent months with very little on my schedule, and I had no idea that I could have been helping you with this. I mean no disrespect, but as far as I know, we're both on the same team, and I can't conceive of letting you have all this piled up without my even knowing. Where can I find a broom, ma'am? And a dust cloth? And a table?"

"I'm temporarily turning the small conference room over to you. How would you like to proceed?"

"Let me start with the big room, ma'am. Is there someone who can help me move all the files out? Then I can clean, and bit by bit, move them back in."

For the first time in a week, Aïssatou smiled at Tammy. "How do you eat an elephant?" she asked.

"Yerima told me that one. I love it, ma'am. One bite at a time."

Two gendarmes moved the files, but they could only clear two shelves before the conference room had reached capacity. A *planton* was detailed to give the shelves a thorough scrub. Soon everyone was coughing and waving off clouds of dust.

1987. 1991. 1992. 1999. The piles started growing.

"Ma'am? Are there boxes? They're all going to slide apart again."

"I can get us some that copy paper comes in. They're ugly, though."

"My mother's an interior decorator, and she has a trick. Can we get hold of some wallpaper, ma'am? Even mismatched sample rolls? I'll cover them, and they'll look great."

"They'll also look suspiciously like a woman had something to do with it."

Tammy laughed. "And I need labels and a marking pen, ma'am."

It took almost two weeks, working several hours a day, to get the files in order. "Ma'am?" Tammy said. "Would you like to see?"

"Give me a second to check my messages. Are you finished?"

"I think so, ma'am. You can use the storage room under the stairs for something else; I got everything into the Archives with room to spare."

Spotless. Everything labeled in Tammy's neat writing. Most of the boxes were covered in blue-and-gray stripes, but a few were in navy-and-green plaid.

229

Aïssatou checked, and sure enough, everything was in perfect order.

"Very good job, my dear. I'll ask Gabriel to take you home."

An hour later Tammy got a text message from Yerima. "Great job, babe. But now she can't wait until you misbehave again. Have you ever had a look at her closet?"

"At the Ranch," said Six Zeta, "they had what they called an infirmary, but it was just a stall where they dumped you if you were too disgusting to work. They didn't treat you. If you got better all by yourself, okay, or if you didn't, too bad. I was there for days. Somehow they managed to get nine people into one stall. They'd hose it down once a day, but the rest of the time, we were lying in vomit and pee and shit. It was just horrible."

"They had signs up everywhere: Prisoners must be restrained, silenced, and secured in place at all times. And they meant it. When you were off-duty at the stall they took the masks off your head and took the pacifier out, but you were tethered and couldn't even stand up. And you were always so exhausted you'd immediately fall asleep.

"Your hands were always cuffed in front of you, with an extra ring that was easy to slide over poles on the hitching post or on the rocking horse, or to the hook that held your arms up when they ran you through the shower – more like a car wash, really.

"I'm so lucky that Prince Ibrahim rescued me. I still have screaming nightmares about that place."

One morning Tammy uncharacteristically arrived at the commissariat twenty minutes late. She got herself a cup of coffee, sat down at the computer, and picked up the first report. The office began to sway.

"Are you all right, sweetie?" Mouna asked.

"I just, I just, um, need to lie down."

"You're as white as an aspirin."

As she spoke, Tammy collapsed onto the floor.

"I'm taking you to the emergency room. Marie, help me get her into the car. And Martin, turn on the siren." She whipped out her cell phone. *"Zut!* Voice mail. I swear, it's all I ever get when I call that man. Yerima, I'm on my way to the hospital with Sudari. She just passed out in the office. Call me as soon as you get this message."

"We just found out that she's pregnant," he told her a few minutes later. "The OB-GYN hospital? Or Hôpital Central? I'm in Bamenda with a Swiss delegation and can't get back until late tonight, but I'll alert the house. I sure hope this isn't another miscarriage. She took the first one real hard."

But it was. She was given an emergency D&C and was feeling mightily sorry for herself when Aïssatou came to see her in the VIP wing at Hôpital Central.

"I feel like a failure," she said. "I want to have a baby so bad."

231

"You're just twenty-four, and things are getting better, you know. The first pregnancy only lasted a few days, but this one held on for two months. It'll take a while for your system to recover from all the stuff they did to you, but you'll get there. My sister will stay here with you tonight. You'll be all right, my dear. Just relax and keep trying, and before you know it we'll have another little one tearing up the *saré*."

"That's what Yerima said too, but I still feel miserable. It's so nice of you to come, Aïssatou, and thank you, Sita, for staying. I'm so depressed that having somebody here really helps." A nurse gave her a sedative, and she sobbed herself quietly to sleep.

"So, what's happening with your foundation?" Amsi asked Tammy, refilling her glass of pineapple soda.

"I've been so involved with the task force, I sort of put it on the back burner. Maître Anagho has drawn up the papers and has submitted them to all twenty thousand places they need to go. It's a heck of a lot more complicated than I ever imagined, but we'll get there. I've been to check on things a few times, but the people haven't done what they were supposed to do."

"Everything's complicated here; unfortunately, we inherited the French system of bureaucracy. And, are you still that naïve, darling? They see a foundation endowed with millions of dollars and they think they deserve a little piece of it." Tammy wilted. "Let Dr. Anagho handle it, because he knows how and how much. Fortunately, you're not in a big hurry, or the price goes way up."

"But they're always so nice."

"Often, darling, the nicest ones are the most insidious. Are you familiar with the Carrefour des Trois Voleurs here in town?"

"Intersection of the Three Thieves? Sure, every last taxi driver can take you straight there."

"Luxury apartment buildings on three of the four corners, each belonging to a former Cabinet Minister who enriched himself while he was in office. Okay? What Yerima criticizes Antoine for the most is how badly he let things get out of control. He's finally cracking down, and a lot of people – very surprised people – are going to jail. They just felt entitled to help themselves to whatever they could take, and for a long time, Antoine closed his eyes to what was going on."

"Amsi, to tell the truth, sometimes I wonder about Yerima. How did he end up with so much money?"

"Don't worry; he came by it honestly. I've seen how he's struggled over the years, and how things are finally coming together for him. First, he inherited a good bit, especially land. Plus, he's never held a position that he could really milk, even if he wanted to, and of course, he just doesn't think that way. And most importantly, Dari, darling, he's the most disciplined person I ever met. He makes money, he builds a house, and that's where he gets most of his income. That's why we're so strict with the budget; he expects us to be every bit as disciplined as he is. I'm his Minister of Finance, remember? I know these things, and you don't need to worry."

"That's a big relief." Tammy sighed.

"Can I ask you a question?" Amsi said tentatively.

"Of course, silly, anything."

"Why did you decide to come here instead of going back to the U.S.? I mean, you had a very supportive family, you were sure to have a comfortable life in a highly advanced society, and you knew your way around. Why did you choose to come to a middle-income country where you had never been before and accept being the fourth wife in a polygamous household? I know you love Yerima, but that doesn't explain everything."

Tammy smiled. "When Yerima rescued me he took me into his house and took such good care of me. He tracked my father down and Daddy came to stay with us for several weeks. Yerima and I talked and talked. Daddy and I talked and talked. He kept telling me that I was under no obligation to marry Yerima just because he'd rescued me, and in fact, Yerima told me the same thing.

"Yerima is one of a handful of people on this planet who knows what I lived through. You and Maïmouna and a few other people sort of know, but Yerima really, truly knows. He lived it with me. He dried my tears when I'd tell him how terrified I was of Ibrahim. He knew how much Taymoor meant to me and how devastated I was when his plans to buy me out of slavery and marry me didn't work out.

"He watched aghast as my friends at The Office were auctioned off to perverts and sickos, and while some of the executives didn't follow the rules and burned the girls with cigarettes, and then even though it wasn't

234

their fault they were transferred to clubs lower on the food chain because they weren't 'prime meat' anymore. He knew all that, and loved me anyway. Yerima lived with me in my servitude and was the rock that I clung to for my sanity.

"One day there was a fire at The Office and Toril and Monika and I managed to slip out. By some sort of miracle, I saw Yerima's limo, and the driver let us get in. Yerima took Toril to the Norwegian Embassy, and Monika to the German Embassy. Now, Yerima already had four wives, but we had wanted to be together, and we had been talking about my coming here as his servant, tutoring the children and such. And I started thinking, why accept voluntary servitude, even with Yerima, if I could have a normal life somewhere else? So I asked him to take me to the American Embassy. He blew up and said that I'd just been manipulating him the whole time, that the first chance I had I was ready to dump him even after all the promises I'd made. So instead of taking me to his house, or to the Embassy, he took me back to The Office."

"So that's what happened. I knew you too had a big fight but never knew what it was about."

"It was awful. Not only was I back at The Office, but Yerima stopped asking for me, Heineken had left for Colorado, Taymoor had given up, and I hardly ever saw Zima, my best friend. It was just work work work, seventeen hours a day, and I was so lonely and miserable and depressed I didn't know what to do. The executives were just horrible. I'd be proud of myself for not coming apart at the seams during one dreadful assignment, and then be sent off to another that was even worse.

"Not one single bright spot in my life, just bending over or down on my knees again and again. I thought of Yerima practically every minute, and how stupid I'd been. I went over and over and over it. That's when I decided that if Almighty God would be gracious enough to give me a second chance with him, I wouldn't mess up.

"Amsi, I was so desperate for any semblance of affection that I even let myself become fond of Ibrahim, and let me tell you, that's desperation. So when Yerima rescued me, I was fully prepared to become his servant. I wasn't sure that I could function in the real world – it's a scary place, you know, especially if you've been completely cut off from it during key formative years of your life – and it seemed to be a very reasonable temporary solution, like a halfway house. Then, Alizée left and he offered me marriage instead.

"I had never dreamed of being his wife, and I couldn't get over my good fortune. Yes, Cameroon is different. Yes, I'm number four. But Yerima makes it all worthwhile, and furthermore, I'm so happy working with Maïmouna on the Task Force, I'd happily live in a dog house just to do the work that we're doing. It's so gratifying, and I feel needed as a human being with experience in these matters, and not just a piece of female meat to be toyed with and discarded."

"But don't you think your family could have helped you too?"

"Of course, but not the same way. I love my family. I miss my family. They've been wonderful and understanding and supportive, but they only have a sketchy

236

idea of what I went through. Besides, there's no guarantee that everybody else in America would have been so nice when they found out about my background. And yes, I love America and miss America, and it's strange being number four, but I've found my place in life, and it's here. Does that make sense to you now?"

Amsaou smiled affectionately. "A lot more sense."

"Meanwhile Mouna keeps finding groups she wants me to talk to, and I'm getting quite a schedule of speaking engagements. Which, of course, I've had to put on hold until my restriction's over." She made a face. "Nine more days."

"I hate speaking in front of a group. I just hate it."

"I did too, to start with, I'd be a bundle of nerves, but after a few minutes the topic would just take over and I wouldn't care anymore. Almost every time, someone comes up to me afterwards and tells me another story. And the task force is getting a lot of help from the public. Leads, especially. And we know of one case where someone was trying to kidnap a girl and people stepped in and intervened because they'd been sensitized to what was going on. That's huge. And every month, Gérard publishes another article on the subject. I've been able to feed him a lot of information, and he's dug up a good bit on his own. Word is getting out, and people are starting to listen. I'm dedicating the foundation to Nenzima and Marisa, by the way."

"I remember that Nenzima was your friend who helped you murder Dr. Hassan, but remind me about Marisa?"

237

"She was the one who the brutes on the boat suffocated when they gagged her with insulation foam."

"How horrible!"

"I've finally tracked down her parents in Mälmo. Her father is a high-school chemistry teacher and her mother works at a florist. Now I have to figure out how to tell them."

"Isn't Yerima going to Copenhagen next month? Maybe he could call them from there."

"I think it'd be better if I tell them myself, but it's hard. She was so beautiful, and just sixteen. It's been more than six years since she disappeared. I can only imagine what they've been going through. I mean, my own mother suffered a nervous breakdown, and she knew I was still alive. Marisa just…disappeared. I don't know how to tell them. Call? Write? It just seems so cold."

"They need to know. If I were you, I'd write, then follow up with a phone call."

"She died, Amsi. Sixteen. And they just dumped her body overboard like garbage. What parent wants to hear that, no matter how you tell them?"

They sat quietly for a long time.

"Aïssatou says she wants to read your manuscript. To censor it, I guess."

"Yes, of course, she wants to make sure that Yerima comes across as the good guy. But actually, she's always been really interested in what I went through. You've been terrific, by the way, with all your suggestions; they've been extremely helpful. Aïssatou and I have had some long conversations, especially about Sheikh Saud, whom she finds fascinating, and Prince Ibrahim, whom she finds terrifying. She doesn't need to worry; Yerima is the hero, no two ways about it."

"Ibrahim seems like one scary guy, but you say he's even more handsome than Yerima? Wow. And it sounds like he loves you."

"He does, in his own weird, controlling, possessive way. He had a very lonely, unhappy childhood and nobody ever taught him how to love. His father was always in meetings and his mother only cared about Paris and Palm Beach, so he was dumped on servants, and they weren't allowed to discipline him, so he's totally spoiled. When he was twelve, they got him an Italian nanny named Lucia, who is the only person who ever loved him unconditionally. But he got drunk one day when he was seventeen and accidentally killed her. That's what messed him up so bad. He's obsessed with everything Italian – Italian chefs, perfume, all because of Lucia. I feel sorry for the man, I honestly do, because he's so screwed up. Sometimes I feel very tender toward him, and we really do connect on a physical level, but frankly, I hope I never see him again."

"Are you scared?"

"Yes. Yes, I am. I try not to be, but I know the man. I know that for the past few months, I've been watched. Nobody's done anything, but it's getting to be really spooky. There's this little knot of fear that's always in the pit of my stomach."

Dear Mr. and Mrs. Björklund:

This is positively the most painful letter I have written in my entire life, and I'm sure that for six years you have dreaded receiving it, but I knew that you'd like to know what happened to Marisa.

My name is Tamara Lynne "Sudari" Abdoulaye, and I'm from Bethesda, Maryland, right outside Washington, D.C. When I was visiting friends in Marseilles I was abducted and put on a boat with destination the Persian Gulf, where I was sold into the harem of an 81-year-old sheikh. Marisa was on the same boat, and even though I only knew her for two days, I fell in love with her. So sweet and good-hearted, and so beautiful. She told me that she had applied for a part-time job as a swimsuit model, but it was a trap. We were both brutally raped and beaten, and she was crying. To make her be quiet, they gagged her with insulation foam. They used too much, and she died of asphyxiation. They threw her body overboard shortly before we entered the Suez Canal. This took place, by my best guess, on July 6, 2005.

The sheikh had special-ordered a beautiful buxom Swede, and Marisa was intended for him, but when she died, they substituted me. I am neither buxom nor Swedish, and when he discovered that I wasn't the girl he'd ordered, he was so furious that he immediately sold me elsewhere. I am able to tell you, though, that his harem was thoroughly depressing: the previous girl had become so despondent that she smothered her own baby. So I hope you can take small comfort in the fact that Marisa was spared an extremely agonizing life.

I spent more than five years in slavery and was often envious of her, because let me tell you, I lived through hell. I was very lucky to be rescued by a beautiful man who is now my husband; he is from Cameroon, which explains the pretty stamps on this letter. I am devoting my life to combatting human trafficking; I have created a foundation and I thought you'd like to know that I have dedicated it to Marisa's memory.

I wish I had happier news to share with you, but I knew that you would want to know.

Much love and heartfelt condolences,
Tammy

"Baby," Marie-Claire told Yerima, "there's a call on line six from a Mr. Taymoor. He says he has an important message about somebody named Tamara Lynne."

"Holy shit," said Yerima, "Put him right through, doll. Tamara Lynne is Sudari's American name and she used to know a Taymoor. Abdoulaye here."

"Hello, sir, my name is Taymoor and I just wanted to alert you to something. I used to know Tamara Lynne at The Office; in fact, I put in a bid to buy her, but her owner kept renewing her lease and I don't think he ever even looked at it."

"Yes yes, she often spoke to me of you, sir, and how nice you were, and how much you meant to her. How on earth did you ever track me down?"

"Not hard, with the Internet, sir. What was hard was getting through your assistant. I said Tamara Lynne was your wife, but she knew some other name for her, so she was extremely suspicious. Like a mother lion!"

"She's very protective of me. And by the way, Tamara Lynne's Cameroonian name is Sudari, which means jewel. What can I do for you, sir?"

"A beautiful name for a beautiful lady, sir. Just between the two of us, I'm still very much in love with her. But the reason I'm calling. I'm an architect, sir, and a few months ago Prince Ibrahim commissioned me to design a harem for a special girl. At first, I thought nothing of it, but the more he tells me, the more I'm convinced that it's for her. Maybe you'd know, sir, is she the one who made him pass out?"

"Yes sir, she did."

"That clinches it. She's the one. She never did that for me, though."

"It took her ages to do it for me. It was getting to be a sore spot around here." They shared some good-natured chuckles. "Tell me about what you're doing, sir."

"It's going to be spectacular, with waterfalls and palm trees and tropical flowers and benches where she can sit and read, because I remember how much she loves to read. But I'd heard that you'd bought her from the Rodeo and married her, and I was so happy for her that someone, even if it couldn't be me, had been able to wrest her away from that pervert. Can you believe that those sweet hands slit Dr. Hassan's neck? I don't think I'll ever get over that. Anyway, the last thing I want is to see her back under Ibrahim's control, but that's definitely what he has in mind. And I just thought you should know, sir, so that you can take precautions."

"Mr. Taymoor, sir, this is one of the nicest and most selfless gestures I've seen in my entire life. We have in fact had a few indications that he wants her back, but so far nothing this concrete. Question please, sir. When will the harem be ready?"

"A few more weeks. Extremely tight security, by the way, completely enclosed, only one underground entrance deep in the estate, door electronically controlled. I'm very worried about her. Do you mind my asking, sir, how is she doing?"

"She's doing fine, Mr. Taymoor. The President appointed her to serve on his special Task Force on Human Trafficking, and she's been very busy, and very happy, doing that."

"Wow! Please extend my warmest regards to her and please, Mr. Abdoulaye, take good care of her. She deserves a wonderful life with a good man like you, not a mental case like Ibrahim."

"Thank you so much for your call. I'll pass along the message and I'm sure she'll be touched that you were so thoughtful."

Holy shit, he thought as he hung up. Holy, holy shit.

"I told you, he's the nicest person I ever met," Tammy reminded Yerima. "You kept making fun of him because he was so nice – you even almost turned it into a four-letter word – but the man is extremely, extremely nice. The Bible talks about people who are pure of heart, and he's the only person I know who genuinely fits that description. He doesn't have an evil bone in his body, not one. Don't forget, I was seriously in love with him until I met you, and then of course you blew every man I'd ever known completely out of the water."

"But did you listen, babe? Ibrahim is building a harem for *you*. This is no longer a matter of speculation; he's planning to take you back."

"Yerima, there's no way on earth that we can take enough precautions, and I absolutely refuse to go into hiding and destroy my life."

"Then it's almost certain that you'll be saying 'Yes master' again. I'm trying my best to keep you from falling back into his clutches."

"I know, I know. But short of locking me in a vault, I don't know how to prevent him from getting his way."

"Hmm, lock you in a vault. Now there's an idea," he said, eyes twinkling. "But do be careful."

They worked out a set of signals that she could use if she found herself in immediate danger, and he told her that, with the President's full approval, he'd established several plans of action.

"We're doing our best to keep him away from you, but if he grabs you, we'll try to keep him from getting you out of the country. And as a last resort, if he succeeds, one way or another, we're going to get you back. But please, don't ever put yourself in a position where you're vulnerable. No more taxis. Wait inside until you see Charles; if you need, go out and wave at him, and go back inside until he's right in front of you. When vendors bring things to the house to sell, evaporate. Don't hang around after class; go straight to the car. It only takes a few seconds of inattention, and you're wearing an inventory anklet again. Promise?"

"Excuse me, darling, you think I want to go back through all that crap again? After all your heroics to set me free? Don't worry, Yerima, I'll be extremely careful."

"And if the unthinkable happens, do what you and Zima did with Dr. Hassan. Be nice to him. If you get snotty, he'll probably wind up killing you, and I'd rather know that you were alive – even with him. Make him relax, think you've capitulated. And if he ever lets you see an email from Saud, look at the first letter of each word and put them together for a secret message from me."

"It's not going to happen."

"Ibrahim? Don't underestimate the man. If he wants something, he takes it. And babe, look out, he wants you."

That night, alone in her own bed, Tammy dreamed of Taymoor. They were back at The Office, and he showered her with kindness in that place devoid of kindness. He spoke to her lovingly in that place devoid of love. He was tender with her in that place devoid of tenderness, looked at her instead of through her, called her Tamara Lynne instead of Beauteous Gluteus. She basked in his attentions, reveled in his gentleness, soaked up his humanity.

When she awoke she realized that she was moist with desire. Fortunately, she thought to herself, he's nearly five thousand miles away. But the dream rattled her. She loved Yerima profoundly, but she realized that she wasn't completely over Taymoor.

Dear Tammy,

Thank you so much for your kind letter. Yes, we dreaded getting it, because now all hope that she is still alive is gone, but we thank you from the bottom of our hearts for telling us what happened. We hugged and cried, hugged and cried. Life has never been the same without our darling Risa and we grieve for her profoundly.

Best of luck with your foundation. We are enclosing a small check that we hope will help you spare other girls from such misery.

If you are ever in Sweden you must visit us. We would very much like to meet you and thank you in person.

Much love
Sonja and Boris Björklund

P.S. Our son Bjorn enjoys stamps and was thrilled to add the beautiful ones on your letter to his collection.

Prince Ibrahim surveyed the construction of the new Giardino delle Cascate, Garden of the Waterfalls, now nearing completion, and it met with his enthusiastic approval. Taymoor had done a brilliant job. Four stories high, completely enclosed. Perfectly air-conditioned. A lush garden with coconut palms and tropical flowers, just like Tahiti. A ten-meter multi-tiered waterfall delight-fully splashing down moss-covered rocks, just like Tahiti. Secondary falls at four other locations. A glass-walled elevated bedroom, sheer genius. A small stream, with arched bridges, meandering around the perimeter, and benches offering perfect spots for relaxation nestled strategically throughout.

She will love it, absolutely love it, he told himself with a smile. The macaws and swans would be arriving soon. All it needed was Mukhmala herself, and Habib was taking care of that. She was going to absolutely love it. They would make each other faint from passion again and again, and they would be so happy. She was going to absolutely love it.

Tammy had just found out for sure she was two months pregnant, and was in high spirits. The due date wasn't ideal, October 8, which would really complicate her second year of school, but she figured she'd cross that bridge when she got to it. And, of course, she still had to do well on her final exams, which were fast approaching.

She almost wept, she was so happy. She was married to the sexiest, most incredible man on the planet, and at long last she was going to give him a child, and life was wonderful.

A fresh selection of children's books had arrived, so Tammy was at the bookstore. Ditto would love this book on astronomy, she thought, and little Michael would flip over the dinosaur picture book. Oumoul, the budding vet, would adore the volume on dogs, and the novel where the young heroine gained a good dose of self-confidence would be a perfect choice for Samira.

"Did you find everything you needed, Sudari?" Christine asked.

"These are just perfect. The kids get so excited, and that means a lot to me. They haven't yet caught onto the fact that I'm turning them into hopeless bibliophiles like their Néné Sudari."

They laughed as Christine rang up the sale.

Whew. For once, she hadn't gone over budget. Aïssatou had warned her that if she did one more time, she'd be placed on restriction for an entire month.

"Why don't you bring them in some time and let them pick out their own books?"

"Nine kids? Uh, Christine, nice of you, but your shop might not survive. Maybe I'll try them one or two at a time. And soon, um, possibly ten?" She gave Christine a sly wink.

"Oh, really? Now, that's wonderful news. Congratulations!"

"Well, I'm trying not to get too excited, because I've had some medical issues, but I hope that this time, it'll work out. Thanks so much, Christine, for having such beautiful books."

"No problem. My sales of children's books have gone through the roof, thanks to you. Oh, and by the way, I've sold 46 of the boys' football books and 14 of Bintou's book about the mouse."

They hugged. "They'll be thrilled. See you in a couple weeks, no doubt."

"Stay well, Sudari. And I really mean that."

Tammy gathered up her precious package and went outside, where Charles should be waiting. Oh, right, he'd gone to get gas. A crippled beggar approached on calloused knees and Tammy gave him a handful of coins. *"Alhamdulillah,"* he said, thanks be to God. His spot was right outside the bookstore, so they saw each other often.

"Have you had a decent day?" she asked him.

"Not too bad, madame. More books for the kids?"

"Of course. By the way, my prayers have been answered. I'm going to have a baby."

He cheered. "I've always told you, madame, *ça va vient, ça va vient."* It will coming, it will coming. His heart was in the right place, even if his grammar needed a little work.

"Okay, Mohammadou, see you next time." She was ready to go back inside when she saw the Mercedes less than half a block away.

She paid no attention to three laughing men walking together down the sidewalk.

Until they surrounded her.

Until one of them pressed something hard and cold to her back.

"Madame Abdoulaye, I strongly suggest that you cooperate. Otherwise, we have strict orders to kill you."

No one found anything unusual about the party of four in close formation as they made their way to a navy blue Mercedes idling nearby. Two of them got into the back seat, one on each side of her, and the other into the front passenger seat. "You know where to go," the one in the front said to the driver.

"Excuse me, sirs," she said. "I'm supposed to meet my husband in five minutes, and he'll be very concerned if

I don't arrive on time." It wasn't true, but she had to call him. Had to.

They took her handbag, found her cell phone, and turned it off. "No calls," they said. One pulled out a syringe. "Now, madame, you're going to take a nice long nap."

"Excellency?" said Charles breathlessly. "I just saw Madame Sudari get into a Mercedes with three men. I went to get gas, sir, I was only gone a few minutes, and was just seconds away from picking her up. Seconds."

"It's okay, it's okay, Charles, it's not your fault. Follow them."

"I have been. It looks like they're going to the airport, Excellency."

Yerima spun into action, trying his best to stay calm. "Hello, sugar. Sorry, I have an emergency, and I need to speak to the President right away."

"Hold on, doll-baby, he's just finishing up a meeting. Let me go get him for you."

"Antoine? They got her. We strongly suspect that they're headed to the airport and his private jet."

"Damn. Damn. I know you hoped he was out of her hair. Damn."

They discussed the scenarios that they had previously established. Antoine said he'd alert National Security, and Yerima said he'd tell Immigration to be on the look-out at all airports and border crossings. They knew they only had minutes to act, or she'd be out of their reach. And if he ever got her back to his harem, it would be virtually impossible to get her out. He groaned. He was furious, but knew that poor Sudari must be scared out of her mind. He tried to send reassuring thoughts her way.

A very nervous Prince Ibrahim was monitoring events from his study.

Captain Suleyman said, "Your Highness, we've been cleared, but it'll probably be thirty or forty minutes before we can take off. They're trying to reclaim the runway; dozens of baboons have taken it over, and they can be really vicious. Then there's a corporate jet and several commercial flights ahead of us. Par for the course for aviation in Africa, Your Highness," he added with a chuckle. "Years ago they finally put up a tall fence, which keeps the antelopes and goats out, but the baboons just climb right over it. Hardly slows them down at all."

"We can't afford delays, Captain. You have some precious cargo on board and you need to get out of that airspace as quickly as possible."

"I'll try to explain that to the baboons, Your Highness. I'm on the Internet trying to find someone who speaks baboon right now."

"I can probably help," Ibrahim said wrily. "I happen to have a number of them on my payroll."

The pilot laughed. "Once, Your Highness, I was trying to fly out of rural Kenya, and a pride of lions had moved in under the wings to get into the shade. There was also a slight delay. Like, two hours, until the lions finally decided to move on. Nobody was about ready to shoo them away."

Ibrahim was too tense to be amused. At least, the delay was due to wild animals, something natural, and not a broken-down vehicle or something that could have been that damned professor's own doing. It was risky, mounting an operation there on his home territory. He was Minister of Foreign Affairs, his cousin was the President, another cousin head of National Security; a lifelong friend, Commandant of the Air Force, good friends or cousins almost everywhere else. But in thirty or forty minutes, baboons willing, Mukhmala would be on her way back to where she rightfully belonged. Even the damned professor, with all his connections, would have a hard time mobilizing everything in that brief window.

Minutes dragged by. One bottle of prosecco had already bit the dust, and another was well under way.

"The baboons have been cleared, Your Highness. We're fifth in the queue."

Fifth. So much could still go wrong. Ibrahim fidgeted. Fretted. Took another soothing swig.

Mouna had just finished a meeting downtown when word arrived. She and the Commissaire of Immigration both jumped into action. But he couldn't find the jet on the network. "A private jet belonging to an Arab prince," she prompted him. "How many of them with HZ tail numbers can there possibly be? Block it. Please, block it, Ako. That plane just can't take off."

"I can't find it, Mouna," was the frantic reply. "No trace of the damned thing."

"It's got to be there somewhere. We only have a few minutes."

"I understand, but it's not in the system. There's absolutely no trace of it. And I can't block it if I can't find it."

She repeated the tail number. "Maybe a couple figures were transposed, so easy to do. Please check again. Or just search for HZ."

"Oh wait oh wait oh wait. Here it is. You were right. Got it! And I've just issued an emergency order to stop its departure."

Maïmouna exhaled.

"Fourth in the queue, Your Highness. In fifteen or twenty minutes max, we're gone."

So annoying, thought Ibrahim. Why didn't they have more runways? And a better-staffed tower? Twenty minutes was an eternity.

At the airport, the head of the immigration office was holding his head in exasperation. A two-year-old child needed an emergency medical evacuation, but he was on his mother's passport, and the mother couldn't travel, which meant that legally the little boy didn't have a passport, and the father was frantic, but laws were laws, and he'd explained things twenty-five times and the father still didn't want to understand, and it was taking forever, and the lines were getting longer, and this was the kind of situation that everybody just hated because it didn't seem fair, and it wasn't, but laws were laws. Out of the corner of his eye he saw a red alert on the computer, but he was still dealing with the distraught father, who had the impression that he was just trying to make things unnecessarily complicated to be able to extract a bribe – not an unexpected reaction – but in this case, most assuredly not true.

The Camair-Co flight thundered into the sky.

He finally had a chance to look at the red alert.

What? The wife of Minister Abdoulaye kidnapped? On that plane? Oh my God! "Traffic control? Just got emergency instructions from the very top – repeat, the very top – to block departure of the private jet. Undeclared passenger."

"Roger. We have revoked clearance and ordered it to stand by."

The Air France flight took off.

"Second, Your Highness. They've revoked clearance and ordered us to stand by, but you know what? I'm going to take off anyway. There's not much they can do to stop me." Captain Suleyman taxied into the on-deck position. When the Turkish Airlines jet was safely in the air, he blithely ignored the orders from the tower and moved unchallenged into the take-off slot.

Ibrahim thought he was going to be sick to his stomach. *Subhan Allah!* Good heavens, what was taking so long?

"Oh God. Some nerve! Obstruct the runway, it's the only option. Georges, quick, get onto that *piste*. Keep that goddam jet from taking off."

Georges floored it.

But it took off three or four seconds before he could get there.

The two commissaires got the Commandant of the Air Force on the line. "We understand that it departed despite all our best efforts. Can we intercept it, Bakary?" asked Commissaire Maïmouna.

"Not as easy as you think," said Colonel Njoya. "They're flying due south, the quickest way out of Cameroonian airspace. It's only 92 nautical miles to the border with Gabon – 172 kilometers – which gives us ten, maybe fifteen minutes. I issued orders the moment I knew she'd been kidnapped, but this is a peaceful country, and we don't keep Air Force jets fully fueled with pilots sitting in the cockpits waiting to scramble. Yerima and I have been friends for thirty years. I've met Sudari and know her story. I've been in the Air Force for twenty-two years, and been Commandant for four, and this is the first time we've ever had a situation like this. We are not, may I gently remind you, a military super-power. Even the President himself makes fun of our 'Armed Farces.' We're there on the joke list next to 'Posts and Telecomplications' and the 'Genmerderie Nationale.' I'm doing everything I can, believe me, but I frankly doubt that we have enough time to pull it off."

"Is that the flight plan they filed?"

"It sure is. Moreover, we have to–"

"I don't care what you have to do, Bakary. Just do it. My cousin's wife, my dear friend, is on that plane, kidnapped, destined for a psycho's harem, and we've got to rescue her."

"Bring that puppy back," the Commandant told the two pilots as they prepared to take off.

"A vos ordres, mon colonel!"

The first managed to get off the ground two minutes and eighteen seconds after Ibrahim's plane had left, and the second, forty-seven seconds later. They did their level best, but the jet simply had too much of a head start, and they couldn't catch up. "Too late, sir," was the reply. "It's gone. Over Gabonese airspace now. Very sorry, sir."

Mouna made a frustrated call to Yerima, who in turn called the President. "The bastard succeeded. Do I have your authorization to shoot off a stiff diplomatic note?"

"Yerima, I know how upset you are, but I'm not prepared to turn this essentially personal matter into an inter-national incident. You can call Dominic and tell him the story, but it has to be Yerima talking to Dominic, not MFA to ambassador. Understand?"

"Yeah, you're right, I guess. What a scumball. And what a bummer."

He flopped into his chair and sat for the longest time, deep in thought. Hmm, he thought, suddenly brightening, it'd be nearly impossible to spring Sudari from the harem; Taymoor was clear that Ibrahim had taken enormous security precautions. Yerima treated himself to a sly smile. "Sudari, babe, Ibrahim isn't going to get away with this. I've just figured out how I'm going to make him give you back."

A very somber Tammy was seated in the office of Mr. Rasheed, Director of Administration of Prince Ibrahim's estate.

"At nine o'clock every morning you will be escorted here, where you will return the jewels and gown of the day before so I can get them back into the vault. Thereafter you will report to the sports center, where a personal trainer will give you instruction for one hour. You will come back to this office, and I will issue the gown and jewels that your master has selected for the day. This is when you will also order your meals. Lunch will be served at one and dinner at seven-thirty. You will be escorted back to Il Giardino delle Cascate where an attendant will assist you with your bath. Another will do your hair and make-up. Then you may do as you please."

"I most respectfully wish to point out that I have no master, sir. I was emancipated. And married."

"Prince Ibrahim has asked me to remind you that the sentence of death imposed on you was never carried out and it would be a very simple matter to transfer you back to the Rodeo. If that is what you choose – and it will indeed be your choice – he will ensure that, instead of the normal five to twelve hours, the process of execution will be extended over at least one week. During that week you will be fed your own body parts, such as your eyeballs and fingers. And finally, conscious, and feet first, you will be fed to an anaconda. Mukhmala, you know His Highness. How far will defiance get you?"

"Nowhere, sir. He'd crush me like a scorpion. But I want it to be very clear that I'm here over my strongest objections."

"He went to a lot of trouble to take you back into his possession. He doesn't want to take stern measures against you, but he will if he needs to." Mr. Rasheed pulled a notebook from his drawer. "For example, how would you like to write ten thousand affirmations of submission in Arabic, and ten thousand more in English?"

Tammy's mouth dropped open.

"Or, do a petit point of the affirmation two meters wide and eighty centimeters long? Or, he knows how much you dislike certain training equipment, most particularly, the BJ simulator – you remember it, I'm sure. You could be spending hours a day strapped to that machine." He flipped the page. "There's lots more, as you can see. Have you ever been in a standing cage? I understand it's not very comfortable. Oh, and recently, he's been having recalcitrants hot-iron branded. He does it on the sole of your foot so as not to mar your appearance."

Tammy put her hand on her forehead and tried to keep from disintegrating.

"Have you decided to cooperate?"

She bowed her head. "I promised my husband that I would stay alive, so that one day I may be reunited with him, sir. I will cooperate."

"You are forbidden to mention the man you've been living with, or anything about him, or where you were. One more word about him, or one more tear, and I have orders to have you devocalized at once. Prince Ibrahim never sold you. He has simply taken his property back into his rightful possession. All right. Now. You will kneel, and in a firm voice you will recite the affirmation of submission, referring to His Highness as your rightful master and to yourself as his lawful slave."

"Yes sir." She knelt, righting herself when a dizzy spell almost made her keel over. She gulped. Not even a squeak would come out.

"Well?"

"I'm trying, sir. It's hard. Very, very hard." She collected herself. Anyway, it was just temporary, until Yerima could find a solution. Just temporary. "Prince Ibrahim is my rightful master, and I…" She panted with effort. "And I am his lawful slave." She rested for a moment and tried to paste herself back together. She was momentarily transported back to The Office, when she was still truly a slave. No longer, but she had to pretend that she was. "He rules me completely and absolutely, and I must obey whatever he commands immediately, fully, and willingly."

"Again, this time without stopping."

She managed, the fourth try, with much difficulty, to do it to his satisfaction. She had just mouthed the words. Ibrahim was never going to succeed with his plans, but she had to play along, give Yerima time.

"Come with me, please. A few formalities at Induction, then a thorough physical."

The new ID bracelet soldered around her ankle was a diamond tennis bracelet. Diamonds or not, it indicated that once again, she was inventoried property.

She was also issued a beautiful bracelet that covered the back of her left hand with half-carat diamonds, one for each word in the revised affirmation of submission. A four-carat diamond represented the word master, and a wooden bead, slave. A ring slipped around her middle finger held it in place and a diamond-studded bracelet circled her wrist. It was stunning – a good twenty-five carats of shimmering stones.

But every time she saw her hand, hundreds of times a day, it would remind her of her condition – her temporary condition! – and, even more painfully, that her wedding rings had been taken away. Finally, Mr. Rasheed brought out the strangest contraption that Tammy had ever seen. "This is called a *burqah*," he said. "It's an honor to wear this; it identifies you as His Highness' favorite. First, a beautiful gold-embroidered headscarf. Then it fits over your face, like this."

It was made of leather, hung with overlapping disks of gold, and studded with more diamonds. A strap about a half-inch wide covered her eyebrows, and another went down the center of her nose. Two wing-shaped pieces covered the end of her nose and extended across her lower cheeks. Another strap went under her chin. He pulled it snug and padlocked it in place.

"A *burqah*, sir? I thought they were long cloaks." It felt very strange, and moving her jaw to speak had suddenly become an awkward effort.

"This one is special; it's from Eastern Arabia. They used to be rather common – my grandmother wore one – but nowadays, most women wear conventional veils."

Past the door marked Women Only, Dr. Lolowah was warm, smiling. "*Ahlan wa-sahlan*, welcome, welcome." She pointed to the *burqah*. "Oh, you're the famous Mukhmala. He gave us a tour of your harem the other day. I wanted to move in myself, it's so spectacular. And I've never seen diamonds like these on anyone here. You're a very lucky girl."

Tammy made a face.

"Ticker okay, lungs fine. Blood pressure elevated – have you been under stress?"

"Something like that, doctor."

The doctor ignored her. "We just want to make sure that you haven't picked up any strange tropical diseases. What? Pregnant?"

"Two months, yes ma'am. I'm married."

"Fortunately, the angel has not yet given the fetus the breath of life. I'll schedule you for surgery first thing in the morning."

Yes, I live in incredible luxury, but I'm not the least bit interested in diamond necklaces and designer gowns, and I hate the very idea of having my own slaves, even though I like Amina and Ayesha and they're very helpful. I'm as lonely as can be, and frustrated, and resentful, and to top everything off, I'm missing every last one of my final exams, and it's my own stupid fault because I stayed outside talking to Mohamadou too long. Yerima said it would only take a few seconds, and sure enough, that's what happened. All I want to do is go *home,* but I'm here, and I'm trying to make the best of it.

Ibrahim told me that he wanted to give me a beautiful little piece of Tahiti, but he's actually made me hauntingly homesick for Cameroon. Squawking parrots wake me up in the morning. The waterfalls remind me of the tour I took with my family, and the coconut palms and tropical flowers look exactly like the ones I left behind in Yaounde. This place is absolutely breathtaking. Ibrahim had a stunning vision, and, of course, Taymoor is an architectural genius.

I asked for a kitty, and to my amazement, Prince Ibrahim agreed, but he is utterly clueless about how to do anything – anything! – in an ordinary way, so he gave me a panther cub named Rafiki (Swahili for buddy). Ibrahim can't stand cats of any description because you can't boss them around, but Rafiki and I understand each other. He thinks about the Serengeti, and I think about the beautiful rolling hills of Yaounde, and we both know perfectly well that we don't belong in a harem. He purrs at me like a motorcycle, and licks me with his vegetable-grater tongue, and I scratch his broad head that he lays in my lap. He's essentially the only friend I have, my only confidant. And vice-versa.

I'm not getting along very well with Ibrahim. After Yerima and I had our fight, I'd been so lonely and depressed that out of desperation, I let myself become very fond of Ibrahim and gave myself to him willingly, but now I have absolutely no desire for him. He knows that I'm holding back, and it's really getting to him.

He has ordered me to make him faint at least once a month, but it requires intense commitment from both partners, and he can dream on, at least as far as I'm concerned. I don't know what I'm going to do, because the only time it happened is when we played one of Yerima's games, and guess what, I don't feel one bit like playing games. Normally, in the ten minutes or so it takes for me to be delivered to his bedchamber, despite my own best intentions and Yerima's good advice, the resentment builds and I arrive obedient but bitter, submissive but nothing more than dutiful.

I wasn't surprised when Ibrahim finally ran out of patience. "We're going to put this girl in the black room," he told Palermo, "until she remembers why she's here. Set the timer for one hour, around the clock, and set the machine on 85 percent."

The room was so cramped, Palermo couldn't even stand up straight. He attached me to a stainless steel table and put my legs in the stirrups. Then he strapped on a vibrator – I remembered it from my bondage therapy course at The Office – and closed the door. Total darkness, not a sound. The vibrator came on, and every time things were getting really nice, the damned thing shut off. And it did this every hour around the clock, day after day. I thought I was going to go berserk. I'm not sure how long I spent that way. Days.

When I was finally taken back to Ibrahim, he was as cold as cold could be. He knew my body so well, and was so expert, that he could make me grow positively frantic with desire – and then leave me hanging. After two days or so of toying with me like that, he finally asked point-blank, "Are you finished with your stupid foot-dragging now? I know what you're capable of, and you're not producing. But you will. I guarantee that you will. Now come over here and give me a BJ. If I like it, I will let you enjoy being female again. If I don't, back you go to the black room for another week. And we will continue like that until your attitudes and your performance are what I know they can be."

He had me. He knew he had me. And of course I caved in. After all, I reassured myself, it wouldn't be for long. Yerima promised that he'd get me back, and I knew that one way or another, he'd come through.

Ibrahim lets me read a weekly email from Sheikh Saud, so I see Yerima's coded messages, but it can only be two or three words at a time, and I live in terror that Ibrahim will figure things out and cut that avenue off too. Helps keep me sane, but just barely. I'm not allowed to answer them, so I haven't been able to tell him that Ibrahim aborted my pregnancy. It's just too painful. Although, he probably figured it out.

I keep telling myself that I'll only be here a short while, but sometimes, frankly, I think I'm kidding myself. Like I did with Dr. Hassan, I program my sanity to last one more day, one more hour. I count heavily on the fact that Yerima's doing everything he can, but honestly, he doesn't have many options. This place is a fortress. A beautiful, beautiful fortress – ten times more beautiful than the Rainbow – but a fortress nevertheless. Short of a commando operation, I don't know what he can possibly do. And that's extremely depressing.

And I miss Yerima so very much! I wake up in the morning to the sound of wild parrots and expect to look out the window at the mango tree, and sigh when I realize that I'm not in Yaounde. I miss his mischievous sense of humor, his commanding presence, his ability to talk intelligently about almost anything. The way he winks at me and sends my heart racing. The way he touches my nose and I grab his finger and kiss it. The household business meetings. Teaching the kids. Cleo and Titi. Lord, I even miss JoAnn.

But it doesn't do me a bit of good to be homesick. Like my mom used to say, "don't waste your time crying." I think about Yerima a million times a day, but I need to be realistic.

Ibrahim lets me order up to five books a week from the American Cultural Center, subject to Mr. Rasheed's approval, and I clutch at these books as if my life depends on them. In reality, it does. The first time, I polished all five of them off in two days and then had nothing to do, so now I make sure I ration my reading time. The other day I was reading Maya Angelou's *I Know Why a Caged Bird Sings* on my favorite bench near the east waterfall – I just love hearing the way it gently splashes its way down – and I noticed a small folded piece of paper almost concealed under a rock. I knew it couldn't possibly be trash, and I'm always cognizant of twenty-six security cameras, so I was careful to be very discreet when I picked it up and unfolded it, hiding it behind my book. It said simply, "TL, love always, T."

My heart nearly burst, I was so touched. Damn, I realized, I'm still in love with Taymoor. I began keeping an eye out and found four more tiny messages. *Keep smiling. My sweet, sweet Kiwi. Never lose hope. So beautiful, so sweet.*

Made me want to cry. What a kind and beautiful man.

Never lose hope. Damn. I'd come precariously close.

One morning, Palermo was escorting me from Mr. Rasheed's office to the sports center, and we passed Milano with a girl crawling on her hands and knees in the other direction.

"What on earth?" I asked.

Palermo shook his head. "Princess Mirsada is a sadistic tyrant," he said. "Everybody hates her. They're scared to death of Prince Ibrahim, but they absolutely hate his wife's guts. That was her most recent maid. They never last more than a few days, she's so impossible. She didn't move fast enough when Her Highness told her to do something, and she's being taken for a flogging. A ten-kilo weight has been attached to her neck, and another to each ankle, so she has to keep her head down and crawl everywhere. That woman will have you flogged if you breathe wrong. The other day, a maid didn't put the right amount of sugar in her tea, and she put her in the tumbler."

"Tumbler?"

"It's like a barrel, but instead of smooth insides, there are thick pegs and wooden fists and other things sticking out. They turn it on and it keeps throwing you against them, and after fifteen minutes, you feel like you've been run over by a freight train. Everybody hates her. She's so arrogant, and has a hair-trigger temper. Impossible woman. Impossible."

"I don't know," Tammy commented, rolling her eyes, "the wrong amount of sugar sounds like a capital crime to me."

"Always a huge sigh of relief around here when she goes to Zurich to visit her, ahem, sister. We're convinced that her so-called sister is really Prince Mohammed, but Ibrahim doesn't seem to care, so why should we? I don't think those two have shared the same bed since Prince Daood was born."

"They're cousins, right?"

"Of course."

Thanks to modern technology, even if Ibrahim is in Aruba or Tahiti, he can give me orders by remote control. "Lay down your book," he'll tell me, "go to the bench by the south waterfall, and sit there with your hands folded and your head bowed until I give you further orders." Or, "Take off your gown, but not your jewels. I've decided that you will go without clothing today." Or, "Lie prostrate beside the fish pond until the chime sounds."

He hasn't changed one bit. He still loves being in complete control.

Did I mention how much I miss Yerima? It's downright painful.

The other night I was sound asleep, dreaming of Yerima. Suddenly I awoke to sweet kisses, gentle caresses, expert stroking. I realized too late that it was Prince Ibrahim. He told me later that it was the only time in his life he'd ever come to a girl rather than having her brought to him. My body remembered all the wonderful times we'd had together and before I knew it, I'd given myself to him completely. He made beautiful, beautiful love to me, as only a man who truly loves a woman can do, and I clung to him with the desire that only a woman who truly loves a man can know. When he left, happier than I'd seen him since he took me back, I broke down in tears. For the first time I felt like I'd been unfaithful to my husband. Because I had wanted Ibrahim, wanted him desperately, and I'd given myself to him unreservedly. Yerima told me to make Ibrahim happy. I did. And now I'm more miserable than ever.

Ibrahim blew into his new villa in Aruba, followed by the chauffeur and valet who were laden almost comically with baggage. Nigel had done a fabulous job.

It was only eighteen rooms, but had a magnificent master suite, a sturdy fence, a huge wine cellar, and a secret under-ground room where livestock could be held with complete discretion awaiting shipment. Nigel had also arranged for temporary household staff through a highly recommended local company.

The major-domo, polished and professional in a morning coat, was over in the far corner, giving instructions to the two black-and-white uniformed housekeepers. Henrik, the white-coated chef, called the sous-chef into the kitchen so he could show him where to store the huge delivery of meats, produce, and staples in the small but well thought-out commercial kitchen.

"There's lots more stuff in the limo," Ibrahim said, addressing Kenneth, the valet. "First thing is for you to fire up the Jacuzzi, then unpack. Where is the chef? I need to speak to him about dinner tonight. Major-domo? Come here. I want to instruct you about how I like things. What is your name, please?"

The major-domo turned around and faced Ibrahim. "My name," he said quietly, "is Abdoulaye."

CHAPTER TEN

Yerima enjoyed the look of stunned shock on Ibrahim's face. "Welcome to Aruba, Your Highness. We've prepared a memorable stay for you."

The staff closed around him and before Ibrahim knew what was happening, Kenneth had clipped handcuffs onto him.

"This is absolutely outrageous," said Ibrahim.

"Kidnapping? Outrageous? Really, Your Highness? Hmm. Shall we show His Highness to his accommodations?"

They took the elevator to the basement and opened the door to the wine cellar. Yerima pushed a button and the back wall slowly pivoted, revealing an underground chamber. He turned on the light and activated the air conditioning.

"Do come in, Your Highness. Oh, Kenneth, he won't need his cell phone or his computer. He also won't need his clothing. Here's a hospital gown that His Highness can wear while he recuperates from a serious and very puzzling illness."

They chained Ibrahim solidly to a metal bed. "Kenneth, put the bedpan under him. Good. Now, Your Highness, please be sure to let us know if you need anything. In a few days, or a few weeks, depending on your mood, we can talk about something that you borrowed from me. Have a pleasant afternoon." He turned out the light, locked the door, and left Ibrahim all alone.

Ibrahim's phone rang, and Kenneth answered. Nigel. "Yes, sir, he's arrived safely, but I'm sorry to say, he's taken quite ill, sir. The doctors are baffled. He's resting quietly and we have orders not to disturb him. Yes, sir, of course, I'll be glad to call you back tomorrow with an update. Very weak, dizzy, almost incoherent. Certainly, sir. My pleasure, sir."

"Nice job," said Yerima. "Nigel's the one person we need to keep guessing. Make sure the master suite looks lived in. Run the bathtub. Use the soap. Move his things in, you get the idea. And if anybody shows up at the door looking for him, we've taken him to the doctor for more tests. Be nice. Invite them in. Let them look around."

"Sir? One suggestion, sir. Why don't we just put him in the master suite? Nigel knows about that room; he's the one who bought this place. And if we say he's sick, really act like he's sick. Put IVs in both arms, use those leather medical restraints. Give him a catheter and a shit-bag. Stick a food tube down his throat. Fill him so full of laxatives he doesn't dare move his ass a goddam centimeter. Get a nurse to sit there and look devoted. A couple bodyguards to, uh, protect him."

Yerima took a second look at Kenneth. Extremely short hair, muscular build, not a trace of subservience. "You're no valet, are you? Military?"

"And you're no major-domo, sir. I looked you up. An honor to meet you, sir. And yes sir, former SEAL, U.S. Navy. My fiancée was killed when they tried to kidnap her four years ago when we were in Jamaica, and it made me so mad I've been working for Abubakr ever since."

"I like your ideas. Does Abubakr have a doctor and nurse we can trust?"

"Of course, sir. Let me get them over here." Abubakr, who had devoted his life to combatting human trafficking and helping its victims, had set up a front company that supplied the household staff.

The transfer was made.

"Bastard," said Ibrahim.

"How long you spend like this depends entirely on your willingness to return something to me."

"Bastard," repeated Ibrahim.

"Well, it seems that the prime rib won't be delivered to this room, then, Your Highness. I hope you enjoy your pureed salt-free baked potato."

The smiling male nurse put the feeding tube down his throat and patted him affectionately.

Just in time, in fact. Nigel sent his colleague Dirk to check on things, and sure enough, there he was, as sick as sick could be, but being dotingly cared for by household and medical personnel. The staffing company was doing an excellent, excellent job.

Whew.

"You haven't ever done this before, have you, sir?"

"No, Kenneth, I haven't. Is it obvious?"

"Yes sir."

Yerima laughed. Maybe he could learn a thing or two.

"I like the fact that you're polite, sir, very good. And you're tough. But I sense that you're afraid of him."

"You know, Kenneth, you might be right. I know this man. He can be a monster. And do you know why we're doing this?"

"No sir."

"Long story, but a brief version goes like this. My wife was a victim of human trafficking and spent five years in slavery, and for three of those years, she belonged to him. Complicated stuff happened, and I bought her, emancipated her, and married her. Then he decided he wanted her back, and kidnapped her. She's now back in his harem. I wanted in the worst way to rescue her, but it was impossible, so the only other option was to grab him. Maybe in a week or two he'll decide to be reasonable."

"And you still manage to be polite to him, sir? When he stole your wife?"

"Of course, according to him, I stole his favorite slave. Kenneth, to tell the truth, this is one of the hardest things I've ever done."

"Don't worry, sir. We'll fix him for sure. He's not going to get away with this."

"Your wine cellar is amazing, Ibrahim," Yerima said. "I had no idea there were so many different chiantis and proseccos."

"So is this *steack au poivre*, Abdoulaye. Henrik is a fine chef. About the wine, Nigel knows what I like."

272

Ibrahim was sitting on the side of the bed, no longer under restraint, but there were four armed guards in the villa, including two who were always in the same room with him.

"So, let's talk about the girl. I want her back, and you want to keep her. In your own way I think you love her as much as I do, and I respect that. I respect that very much. So what are we going to do?"

"You bought her under false pretenses. She was supposed to be executed for murder, and you didn't carry out the sentence."

"But I bought her. She became my property fair and square, and I could do whatever I wanted. I chose to emancipate her, and of her own free will, she agreed to marry me. She's my wife, Ibrahim, not my slave. And you have no right to go kidnapping another man's wife."

"I never sold her. I released her for execution, not emancipation. She's rightfully my property, Abdoulaye, and I plan to keep her. Deal with it."

"She's my wife, Ibrahim, and I'm not about ready to give her up. Deal with it."

They were silent for a few minutes.

"Tell you what, Ibrahim, why don't we let her decide for herself?"

"Because you think she's going to choose you."

"I don't know. I really don't know. She has strong feelings for you, and you can maintain her in a lifestyle that I can't begin to touch. I really don't know. What mere man can *ever* predict what a woman will do?"

They laughed.

"I have an idea, sir," said Kenneth. "Let me make a phone call. Mr. Nigel, sir? Kenneth. We need your help with something, sir. His Highness keeps asking us for something called Mukhmala. We can't figure out what this is or how to find it. We know it means velvet, so we thought maybe it was wine, but nobody's heard of it and we don't know what to do. Oh, it's a girl! Now a lot of things are making sense. Is there any way you could get her here, sir? I think having her around would help his morale. Yes, sir, he's doing a good bit better, sir, eating solid food and sitting up sometimes, but he's still not himself. Yesterday he wanted a shave, which is always a good sign. All right, sir, thank you very much, sir, let us know when we should send the limo to pick her up." He hung up. "She'll be here tomorrow afternoon."

"How the hell can she travel with no passport?" Yerima asked.

Ibrahim shrugged. "We have passports."

"Erika Jungkind" arrived and was taken directly to Ibrahim.

"Master," she said, and prostrated.

"My sweet Mukhmala, I have a big surprise for you. Tell him to come in."

A familiar footfall. She looked up sharply. "Yerima!"

"Sudari." His voice trembled. "Stand up, babe." She rose. "Ibrahim and I have been talking. We both love you very much, and we know that you love both of us. I want you to stay with me, and he wants you to stay with him, but only one of us can have you. So we've decided to let you choose; it's the only fair thing to do."

She thought for a moment, looking first at the rich prince who owned her, then at the one she loved. "Prince Ibrahim, dear master, if you will emancipate me, and marry me, I choose you."

Yerima winced. She gave him half a wink, and he relaxed.

"But – but – I can't do that. Your family background is simply, uh, not appropriate. A good family, but in no way aristocratic. I even checked your Dutch relatives all the way back to 1700 and I'm sorry, butchers and farmers are simply not appropriate. I'm very sorry, but I cannot marry you."

"Then please, dear master, allow me to return to my husband." She lay prostrate before him and kissed his feet. Dozens and dozens of times.

"She chose me, Abdoulaye," he said victoriously.

"She certainly did."

"Mukhmala, rise, my dear, and go to your husband."

She had given him the satisfaction of letting him order her to do what she wanted to do in the first place.

Abdoulaye put his arms around her and they shared a long kiss, working as best they could around the bothersome *burqah*.

"Of course," added Ibrahim, "this means I'll have to have her killed. If I can't have her, you can't have her. You never dreamed I'd have her kidnapped, but I succeeded, and that's a lot harder than having her killed. So enjoy her while you can, Abdoulaye, it's not going to last long."

Yerima's arms fell away. "You really mean that, don't you, you scumball?"

"I don't play around, especially with something that rightfully belongs to me." He took an arrogant sip of prosecco.

"Sudari, come out here, babe, we need to talk." She followed him onto the verandah. "He'll kill you for sure." His lips quivered. "Go with him, babe. Your life is far more important to me than anything else. I love you more than I ever imagined that I could love anybody, and I won't have you stupidly throw your life away."

"But Yerima…"

"You could make a good life with him. I know you don't love him the same way you love me, but please know that you have my blessing, my permission, my insistence, that you make him happy. It's the only way to keep you alive, and when I think about you every minute of every hour for the rest of my life I want to know that you're alive, and living in luxury, and that you're not unhappy. Please tell me that you'll go with him."

"Yerima, I love you so much. I want to be with you. I gave my life to you, not to him."

"But if you stay with me, you'll be dead in a few weeks. You know this man. He'll do it. Even if you took up residence in the bunker, he'd find a way. Go with him, Sudari, it's the only solution. I'm not exactly wild about it either, but it's the only thing to do.

Somehow, some way, I'll get you back. Chin up. We'll figure out something."

She was sobbing. "Damn it all, I guess you're right. Why do bullies always win? I don't want to do this, but I know you're right."

They returned to the master suite. "All right, Ibrahim, you win, she's decided to go with you. But you must put in writing that if anything ever happens to you, she will be returned to me at once."

"Fair enough. I knew you'd be reasonable. All right, Mukhmala. Welcome back. You may pay your respects to Abdoulaye." In his own handwriting, he gave Abdoulaye the note that he had requested.

"Thank you, master." She fell on the floor and clasped her husband's feet. "Yerima, I will always love you with my whole heart. And please tell the children how much I love them."

"God bless you, Sudari, I will miss you every minute. Now go take good care, very good care, of this prince called Ibrahim." She stood, and he held her in his arms one last time.

On the verandah he called Antoine. "I'll be back at work on Monday," he said sadly. "No, things didn't work out the way I wanted, but she'll be safe, and that's all that really matters."

As he hung up His Excellency Yerima Abdoulaye, doctor of veterinary science, prince of the proud Fulani people, Minister of Foreign Affairs, wiped a bitter tear of defeat from his cheek.

Yerima had a brilliant idea – really brilliant, in fact! – but the more I think about it, the more I realize that nothing is going to work with Ibrahim. Nothing. Yerima must feel horrible about letting me down, and of course, I'm devastated, but there's no way I can be mad at him. Yerima tried his best, but you can't win against Ibrahim, no matter what. And now I need to get a grip on myself and face up to the unpleasant fact that I'm going to be stuck here for as long as Ibrahim damned well pleases.

It's really touching, all the trouble and expense he went to. The harem alone must have cost several million dollars, and the gowns and jewels, millions more. He decided that they would make me happy, and that's all there is to it. I mean, I don't exactly mind wearing fabulous designer gowns, but they're not me at all. Today I have on a slinky gold lamé YSL. Yesterday it was a stunning black-and-silver brocade Armani. They're not at all like the frilly fairy-princess gowns at the Rainbow; most of these are form-fitting, with unbelievably rich cloth. But they're really not for me, they're for him. The jewels are amazing, but they're to decorate me for him. A nice watch and a pendant or two, that's really all I want. And every time they put an $800,000 emerald-and-diamond necklace on me, all I think of is, they took my wedding rings away.

I read Saud's weekly email, and saw a cryptic message from Yerima: "mom not well." My heart went straight to my toes and I burst into tears. He wouldn't dream of sending me an email, "mom dead," but I knew that that's what he meant.

She wouldn't want me to "waste my time crying," as she always said, so I swallowed my tears and put on a brave smile. She had suffered from my enslavement almost as much as I did, I thought bitterly, and those monsters had killed her just as assuredly as they had killed Marisa. Just when she was getting better I wound up with Ibrahim again, and I'm sure she just gave up.

How do you properly grieve for someone you can never replace? Someone who was always there, smiling, counseling, encouraging. How do you grieve for the mother who gave you life, suckled you, sportingly cleaned up the peas that you spat on the floor? How can you possibly grieve for the person who molded you, gave you values by being a living example, and always expected the best from you?

I'd been close to Grandmother Caldwell and had never hurt so bad in my life when she died, but this was far worse. I felt empty, rudderless, numb.

And the worst part was, I dared not show that I was grieving, or Ibrahim would want to know why, and ask how I knew…

I spent a long time the other morning in prayer, begging God not just for strength and the ability to keep a semblance of sanity, but for some serious guidance. *Try love,* I heard again and again, but that wasn't the least bit what I wanted to hear. *Try love. Go the second mile. Remember the story of Joseph.*

I sighed. That's the trouble with asking God for advice; you keep getting answers you don't want. But I did start reflecting on the story of Joseph, which I hadn't thought about in a long time, and I realized that I could now relate to it in a whole different way. Let's face it: he was a spoiled brat, which is why his brothers hated him so much. When he put on his fancy robe that morning, I'm sure it never once crossed his mind that he'd go to sleep that night as a slave. Joseph must have been terrified when he was shipped off to Egypt. He must have been hotly resentful about how unfair it all was, and totally rebellious.

How long did it take him to figure things out? The Bible gives no clue. Two years? But he did, and that's what counts. I can just imagine how one morning he told himself, Shit, if I'm going to be a slave, I'm going to be the best goddam slave I can possibly be. Somehow, he found the guts to wrestle his attitudes into line, and did such a good job – even though he no doubt hated where he was and what he was doing – that he became major-domo of Potiphar's huge estate, and later, in super-power Egypt, second only to the Pharaoh himself. Talk about making the best of a rotten deal!

Maybe he got whipped, and it set him to thinking. I remembered how I'd been paddled right after I got to Sheikh Saud's, and what a diabolically effective disciplinary technique it was. As I lay there unable to move, day after day, all I could do was think, and I realized that all the rules I'd grown up with, all the rules I'd ever known, had become totally irrelevant; all that mattered was what my master wanted. And the day I applied my mother's maxim, actively loving my master instead of simply obeying him, is the day my relationship with Saud turned around.

Lord knows, I didn't want to love Ibrahim, or try very hard to please him. However, all hope for any other

280

solution had evaporated, so it was time to resign myself to reality.

I caught myself. No, damn it, not resign myself. No, damn it, not accept it. Do what Joseph did, and embrace it.

Damn. When everything else fails, try love.

I thought about Joseph all morning, how he not only managed to keep his dignity and self-respect, but also earned the respect of his master. I'd always thought it was a cool story, especially since he could finally say nyah-nyah-nyah to his brothers, but it was only now that I really appreciated the mental struggle he must have gone through.

Maybe I was a bird in a magnificent cage with waterfalls and palm trees, but dammit, I decided, I was going to sing!

I took a deep breath. I smiled at Ibrahim. I flirted with him. I caressed him. I spontaneously kissed his feet. Ironic, how losing all hope became a turning point. Before, I figured I could get away with being just a little reserved because I wasn't going to be with him very long, but now, with all hope of rescue gone, I got the message that I really had to behave myself. It's helping. It's helping a lot, in fact. He's more relaxed, more playful. But he's ticked that I still haven't succeeded in making him faint.

I just got word from Sheikh Saud that Amberine died. I cried and cried. Sometimes it's so hard to understand the will of God.

I'm the prisoner of a man with staggering wealth, a man who loves me profoundly, in his own strange way. And

I'm trying my best, my very best, to find ways to make Ibrahim happy and to be happy myself.

It's just so unbelievably complicated.

One morning, after Tammy had been in Il Giardino delle Cascate for a total of nearly four months, Milano was escorting her from the sports center to Mr. Rasheed's office when a eunuch intercepted them. Something about him looked familiar, but his turban was way too big and obscured half his face.

"Change of orders," he said, "I'll be escorting her from here. You are to return to Admin."

That voice! She bowed her head to hide her excitement.

When Milano turned the corner, she breathed his name. "Taymoor!"

He winked. "Once I knew that this harem was intended for you, I built a few things into it that I somehow neglected to mention to Ibrahim." He grinned impishly, took a remote control from his pocket, and a wall panel slid silently open. They stepped inside a dimly lit passageway and the panel closed again. "Hurry, my sweet," he said, "We need to be all the way outside the gate before they realize something's amiss." He took a veil and *abaaya* from a box in the passageway. She rapidly put them on over her gym suit, and pointed to her bracelet. "Gloves! Where did I put the gloves? Oh, here they are. Hurry, hurry."

He grabbed her hand and they ran, discarding pieces of uniform as they advanced. He stumbled, caught himself, pulled on his long white *thobe,* secured a headpiece in place, and with a touch of a button, another wall panel opened behind a partition in the huge underground garage. "My car's right over here. Quick, quick." The chauffeur opened the back door of the limo for her and she slid in next to another black-cloaked figure. Taymoor grabbed the other woman – actually, an inflatable dum-my – and let the air out. "Same number of passengers exiting as entering," he said with a sly grin. "They always check."

"Head straight for the airport, but use back roads," he told the driver as he took his place next to Tammy. "Captain Didier? We'll be there in thirty or forty minutes, and will need to depart immediately," he said into the telephone in excellent French.

"Je ne me rendais pas compte que tu parlais français," Tammy said. I didn't realize that you spoke French.

"I didn't know you did, either. Didn't I ever tell you? I studied at the Ecole Nationale Supérieure d'Architecture in Paris La Villette."

They laughed.

The guards at the gate saluted the familiar figure of the Prince's personal architect, and Taymoor waved acknowledgment.

"Taymoor Taymoor Taymoor," she said, shaking her head in disbelief.

"Tamara Lynne, my sweet. I want in the worst way to put my arms around you, but we'll have time for that in a little while. I've got to get you out of the kingdom as fast as humanly possible."

"I didn't realize you liked opera, either," Tammy said as he slid in a CD and music filled the car.

"I don't, really, but I ran across this the other day and just had to have it. It's Mozart, and it's called *Abduction from the Seraglio.*"

Tammy threw back her head and laughed so hard she was gasping for breath. Wow, she thought, I haven't laughed, really laughed, in months.

Forty-five minutes later they boarded a private jet. "I'm not as rich as Ibrahim; I chartered it. But it'll get us where we need to go. Have you ever been to the Riviera, my sweet? I have a villa there and I figure we could both use a vacation. First, though, let's get you out of all this black stuff. All right, Captain Didier, let's go." He turned to Tammy. "Finally, you're here with me. It's been several years, but I think I can remember where we left off." He led her into the elegant bedroom. "You're even more beautiful than I remembered, and I'm so happy to see you I could just explode." He held his head.

"Something wrong, dear Taymoor?"

"Killer headache – first time in my life I've ever committed grand theft – but I have a wicked, wicked idea about how to make it go away." He grinned.

Soon she was wearing nothing but the bracelet, the *burqah*, and the anklet. She snuggled in beside him and held on happily while he covered her from head to toe in melting kisses.

"How on earth…?" she began.

"Not now, my sweet, I'm busy."

The intercom crackled. "Third in line for take-off, sir."

His phone rang. "Oh, this is my head of security. Yes, Ali?" He laughed giddily. "Like clockwork. We're almost ready for take-off; I'll let you know when we've cleared the airspace. Thanks." He chuckled. "Can you believe? The prince's favorite slave has vanished into thin air. They're completely flummoxed. And they can run camera feeds all day long and not see a thing. For some strange reason, the camera in that part of the hallway is a dummy."

She laughed. "You're a sneaky, wicked devil indeed, Taymoor."

"And I'm about to do some wicked, wicked things to my favorite girl. How do you get that stupid *burqah* off, anyway? It really looks strange. And worse, it makes you hard to kiss."

"It's padlocked on, my dear dear dear Taymoor. They take it off twice a week to shampoo my hair and give me a facial, and whenever they take me to him, but the rest of the time, there it is. I'd also like to get these other things off."

"I want to leave them on until I officially emancipate you. And I have no plans to do that right away. I've never had my own slave girl before, and it occurs to me that it might just be a lot of fun."

"You must be one of the only wealthy men on the Gulf who doesn't own dozens, sir."

"Well, I have, I don't know, fifteen or twenty domestics – gardeners, housekeepers, and the like. But my own *jaria?* No. I always thought that was too decadent, too self-indulgent. But if that *jaria* happens to be my sweet Tamara Lynne, then maybe it's okay."

"Next in line for take-off, sir."

They hardly noticed when the jet gained speed and roared into the air. Ignored Captain Didier when he told them that they were safely over the Red Sea. Still busy when he announced that they were over the Sinai. Barely coherent when they started over the Mediterranean. And fast asleep in each other's arms when they landed.

"Don't you dare disturb them," the chuckling captain told Jean-Yves, who was standing outside the bedroom in a tuxedo, wildly gesticulating in despair. "You saw the way they were looking at each other. They've already started their honeymoon. Besides, they're paying us by the hour."

"They didn't even have lunch. Top-of-the-line Veuve on ice, and they didn't touch it." He shook his head. "This isn't a honeymoon, Captain, it's a heist. She's wearing a slave bracelet. And an anklet with a medallion on it; that's usually an inventory number and the seal of her owner. And judging from the diamonds, her owner isn't a parking-lot attendant, that's for sure. Not him, though, or he'd have his own jet."

"What's that weird thing on her face?"

"*S'pas*, dunno, Captain, never saw anything like that. I work this route a lot, and you wouldn't believe some of the stuff I've seen, but that's a new one on me."

At some point Taymoor came to, and realized that they were no longer moving. "My sweet, we've landed. Wake up, wake up, my sweet."

There was a discreet knock at the door. Taymoor slipped into a robe and cracked it open.

286

"May I serve you lunch, sir?" asked Jean-Yves. "I'm terribly sorry, sir, I'll need to reheat everything, and I fear that the quality has deteriorated."

"Give us five minutes," said Taymoor. "And don't worry. I was enjoying a sumptuous, sumptuous feast." He winked and shut the door. "I brought you a dress," he said, "I hope you like it." A black *fustaan*, embroidered in red and gold.

His phone rang. "Sorry, Ali, I was, um, busy. Yes, we've landed safely." He turned to Tammy. "I missed sixteen calls from him. He was positively panicked."

"Oh my. Whatever were you doing?" she teased. "It's simply beautiful, Taymoor," she said, slipping the dress over her head. "Beautiful. I saw your little notes, by the way. So nice of you."

He stood back and admired her. "I own you now, you know. I think you should call me sir."

"Yes indeed, dear sir. Instead of the scariest master on the planet, I now belong to the nicest." She smiled, playing along.

"My sweet, beautiful Tamara Lynne. I missed you so much."

Jean-Yves was refilling Tammy's glass with Veuve Clicquot when the immigration officer arrived and saluted. "Passports, please, *mes sieur et dame?"*

Taymoor dug out his own and handed it over. "I have a villa here, and we'll be spending several weeks in the area."

"Madame?"

"Madame doesn't have papers. You see, sir, I rescued her from slavery this very morning. She belonged to a psychopath. Show him your bracelets, my sweet."

"The medallion on the anklet says that I am inventory number 1, Giardino delle Cascate, with the seal of Prince Ibrahim. This Eastern Arabian *burqah* on my face identifies me as his favorite. I'm one – was one – of about a hundred and fifty women that he owns. And each of the diamonds on this bracelet represents a word of the affirmation of submission that he often required me to recite."

"*Sacre bleu!* Good heavens! We see that sometimes. You do plan to regularize things with your Consulate as soon as possible, Madame? You are American? Please give me all your particulars, just so I have them on record."

"Yes sir. Yes sir, of course."

"If you don't mind my asking, sir, how did you go about this rescue?"

"I don't dare divulge any details yet, sir, because she's still in grave danger. It's a wonderful story, though. She was rescued once before by an African ambassador, but the Prince had her kidnapped again and returned to his possession. He's absolutely obsessed with her, which is why we need to be so careful. He'll track us down here eventually, but by then, we'll be somewhere else. You see, sir, she made him faint."

"Faint? Well, in that case, madame, I will need to take you into custody." They all laughed. "I can see why any man would find such a beautiful lady captivating," he said with a bow, "and why she has so many admirers.

288

"*Bon séjour*." Have a nice stay. He turned to leave. "Prince Ibrahim, you say?"

"Yes sir."

"Very good-looking man? Black hair–?" He drew a streak with his hand.

"He's the one."

"Be careful. He has a villa here too, and his people are everywhere. If I were you, sir, I'd take her to America. She won't be safe here."

Taymoor sighed. "We'll figure that out soon enough. I do have a penthouse in Manhattan and a villa in Malibu. Thank you for your kind advice, sir."

"Good luck, madame."

Jean-Yves shot a told-you-so grin at Captain Didier and poured the last drop of champagne into Tammy's glass. "Congratulations on your freedom, madame."

"I just hope that this time, it's forever. Thank you so much for your kind wishes."

"Is the limo here?" asked Taymoor.

"Yes sir, whenever you're ready."

Taymoor apologized for the modesty of his Tuscan-style villa, but it was one of the most beautiful houses Tammy had ever seen. Elegant but understated, just like Taymoor himself. He took her straight to the master suite. "Take off your dress, and kneel before your new master. Stand up. Turn around. Kneel down." He laughed. "Stand up. Oh, this is too much fun."

Tammy smiled. He was having a ball. The dear, dear man deserved it.

He laughed. "I've never had my own *jaria* before, never. Now get in bed, and stay there until I specifically give you further orders."

He began to disrobe, and lost his balance. He caught himself on the foot of the bed just in time.

"Are you all right, sir?"

"I've just got another colossal headache, that's all. What I need is a nice hot shower."

"No sir. What you need is for your very own *jaria* to give you a beautiful bath, then a relaxing massage. Guaranteed to relieve even the worst headache."

He beamed at her, his hazel eyes full of love. "Would you do that for me?" He grinned. "I like this. I may just plan to get headaches on a regular basis."

"With great pleasure, sir."

She didn't move.

"Well?"

"I'm not allowed to leave the bed until specifically ordered, sir."

He laughed. "This is really, really fun. I'm not used to this at all, but I think I'll catch on fast. I just need to decide where I can keep you where that psycho won't find you. I imagine that it'll be about a week before they figure out what happened, and then, you know, my sweet, we'll both be in serious trouble."

Tammy closed her eyes. "The Rodeo for sure, for both of us, sir. He'll hunt us down to the ends of the earth."

Taymoor became pensive. While she was toweling him dry he suddenly said, "What about a tragic accident? That's really the only solution, you know."

Tammy's mouth fell open. Was her new master, the nicest man on the planet, the only man she knew without a single evil bone in his body, now contemplating murder?

CHAPTER ELEVEN

Next day, when they rose after completing the *salat* –
Taymoor insisted that they say all five prayers a day
together – she sensed that he wanted to ask her
something. "Sir? What may I do for you, sir?"

He sat on the bed and played with her hair. "I don't
even know how to ask you, my sweet."

"Whatever it is, the answer is yes. I love you, Taymoor.
I've never stopped loving you. And now I have to do
whatever you wish. But more than that, I *want* to do
whatever you wish."

"It's something I've, uh, wanted to do for, uh, a long
time, but I just never…"

"It's all right, sir. The answer is yes."

"You don't even know what I'm going to ask."

"I know that you love me. I trust you. The answer, sir,
is yes."

He hesitated yet. Finally he closed his eyes and blurted,
"Would it be all right if I tied you up?"

"Of course, sir."

"I'm not talking about chains – I'd never dream of
putting chains on my sweet Tamara Lynne – just, uh,
something, uh, to remind you that you're, uh, under my
authority and that I don't want you to go…? What? It's
okay? Really?"

"Of course, sir. I'm used to it. One time Ibrahim kept me chained to the bed and blindfolded for eight straight days."

"Eight days?"

"Yes sir. He let me eat four meals and once lick his plate. He said he wanted me to be hungry for his body. And he didn't want me to even know what day of the week it was or whether it was night or day; he wanted me to focus strictly on pleasuring him."

"Blindfolded. Hmm. You wouldn't mind?"

"Sir, I know that you respect me, and that you love me, and that you just want to have a little fun. It's all right, sir, believe me. You of all people deserve some fun."

"You know, my sweet, if you keep spoiling me like this, I may never get around to emancipating you."

It wasn't the first time he'd said that, and it was starting to make her nervous. She quickly reminded herself that life with Taymoor, even as his *jaria*, would still be a huge improvement over Il Giardino. He wasn't nearly in the same league as Yerima and Ibrahim as far as the bedroom was concerned, but with her unobtrusive coaching at The Office he'd gone from a boring four to a respectable seven or so. He was a kind-hearted person, and he'd take good care of her. And he'd rescued her from Ibrahim, so he deserved being spoiled.

He saw her look of disappointment. "My sweet, there are other issues as well. The instant that I emancipate you, we're committing adultery, and I have enough on my conscience as it is. Furthermore, I don't know if Ibrahim succeeded in annulling your marriage; according to my nephew, who used to be on Ibrahim's staff, his lawyers were working on that. So it's not just that I'm being selfish – although it's that too, of course."

She remembered at The Office, he'd been so concerned about adultery that he always made sure he was covered by a *zawaj al-mutaa,* or temporary marriage. She made a face as his words sank in. Anulling her marriage. Damn!

Taymoor opened the closet door and began surveying the contents.

"May I suggest that you use socks, sir?"

He grinned, and tied her wrists to the bedposts. "Is that comfortable?"

"Yes sir, it's fine."

Then he tied a sock around her eyes. "Can you see anything?"

"Just a little bit of light, sir."

"Hmm." He folded up another one and slipped it under the blindfold covering one eye, then did the same with another. "How about now?"

"Nothing at all, sir."

"Oooh, this is amazing. I had no idea – I mean, I kind of suspected – oh wow, this is doing things to me. How do you feel, my sweet?"

"Very comfortable, sir."

"But, I mean…"

"Oh. Completely under your loving authority, dear sir."

"Oh, yes. This is doing things to me. This is really doing things to me." He took her in his arms and made love to her like he had never done before.

Damn, she thought, after she'd come for the third time, he's just promoted himself to an eight. Maybe even an eight-point-five.

"Did you like it?" he asked as he untied her and removed her blindfold.

Dear man, he was still unsure of himself, still afraid that he'd humiliated her. She didn't say a word, just covered him in kisses.

As they lay there in the warm afterglow, his arm across her chest, a look of profound melancholy crossed his face.

"What's the matter, sir?"

He sighed. "I just lost a bid for doing a big hotel. I'd really wanted that job. I thought I'd submitted a great concept, too. Five hexagonal towers of varying heights…"

She wasn't the least bit fooled. "And, sir?"

Another sigh. "I'm dealing with some other stuff right now that isn't quite as much fun –" he kissed her forehead – "as having you for my very own. You know, my sweet, I try to lead a highly principled life. Two years ago, I won a bid to design a bank. The bank is built and people are happy. Dazzled, in fact. But I just discovered that my nephew did some things he shouldn't have done, and I shouldn't have won the job, and now I'm feeling rotten. I need to make restitution, and it's a big mess. Among other things. I'll tell you everything, of course, my sweet, but not right this minute."

She knew better than to press him. Nevertheless, several times she noticed that he was uncharacteristically uncommunicative. He was always popping pills, and there were times that he looked old to her, even though he was only fifty-eight. Most of the time, though, he was just like she'd remembered, smiling and considerate. And having the time of his life, playing lord and master.

One day he went into a different room to take a phone call and left her tied to the bedposts. A maid let herself in and began dusting. She caught an image of Tammy in the mirror and shrieked, duster flying.

"Monsieur likes me like this," Tammy explained.

"But of course," the maid replied. "That's not, I mean... What is that thing on your face, madame? I never saw anything like that before."

Tammy remembered, Oh right, this is France. "It's called an Eastern Arabian *burqah*. An old-fashioned veil. I used to belong to a prince and it marked me as his favorite slave."

"Slave?"

"Monsieur rescued me."

"Slave. You hear sometimes, you know, things. So it's true."

"Very, very true."

"Are you okay, madame? May I clean?"

"Of course. And thank you."

"We need to move," Taymoor told her a few days later. "Ibrahim has found the secret passageway, put two and two together, and he's scouring every nook and cranny, looking for us. I thought it would take a week, and it took nine days, but really, we need to move."

"How do you know, sir? And where will we go?"

He grinned sheepishly. "The security system I installed in Cascate? Two sets of monitors – one in his offices, and one in mine. Ibrahim was so irate that he fired his Director of Administration, fired his Director of Security, had Milano flogged, and threw a bottle of chianti that smashed a forty-thousand-dollar Chinese vase. The two directors thought it was prudent to relocate at once. Rasheed, from what I hear, is in Rio, and Abdurahman in Winnipeg."

Tammy smiled. "That was downright sneaky, sir."

"Wasn't it, now?" He shook his head. "Somehow I get the strange feeling that now I might not get the contract to redo Ibrahim's sports complex." They laughed. "I could watch you anytime I wanted, sitting on the bench reading, or talking to the panther, or shackled to the bridge, or eating lunch, or getting out of the bath. I tried to forget about you when he kept renewing your lease, but I couldn't. Building that harem where another man could keep you almost drove me insane. I'd sit at the monitor and watch you, so beautiful, so lonely, so melancholy, and my heart ached for you. And then I'd watch as Milano or Palermo would take you to him, and it got to the point that I just couldn't stand it any longer. You weren't the least bit afraid of that panther, were you?"

"He was the only friend I had, sir. And vice-versa. Actually, Rafiki was a lot less scary than Ibrahim."

"Another thing, my sweet. You knew that he always read your emails, but one message struck him as odd, and he had it checked for codes."

Tammy gasped.

"He was furious. He was going to take a red-hot branding iron to the sole of your foot."

She shrank back, horrified.

"I had to get you out of there. Fast. And he had decided to keep you chained to his bed until you made him faint again."

She held her head in her hands. "Taymoor, sir, how can I ever thank you, sir? Oh God."

"Make me faint too. I'm serious. Ever since I heard you did that for Ibrahim, I was jealous. I wanted it too. Exactly what did you do? I want to know. I want to know exactly."

"It was one of Yerima's games, sir. I would pretend to be disobedient, and he would need to correct my behavior, and impose a mild punishment, usually lying prostrate in the position of contrition. My body knew it was in for a real treat, so the twenty-eight minutes I'd lie on the floor would get my juices flowing and be practically ready to rape him. Then he would summon me, and I'd refuse to go. He'd come after me, and I'd resist him. We'd struggle. But of course, Yerima is way stronger than me, and it wouldn't take long for him to overcome me. Conquer me. It would always really turn both of us on, and amazing things followed."

"I asked you about Ibrahim, not Yerima." Taymoor was thoroughly annoyed. "You talk about him way too much."

"Yes sir, I'm getting there, sir. It's complicated, sir. When I confronted Ibrahim about his drinking, he blew sky-high, and imposed all kinds of corrective measures on me, one of which inadvertently put me in the position of contrition. He demanded to know why his punishment was having absolutely the opposite effect of what he intended, so I told him about the game. He thought it sounded like lots of fun, so we tried it, and we both ended up passing out."

"Both of you? At the same time?"

"Yes sir."

Taymoor cocked his head to one side and smiled. "I've never had women resist me, though."

"How could they, sir? You're a beautiful person and a very attractive man."

"Would you like to play that game with me sometime?"

"Whatever is your pleasure, sir."

"You like it, right?"

"Yes sir. Sir?"

"Yes, my sweet?"

"For it to work, sir, I will need to be very defiant, and you will need to be very aggressive. Otherwise, it's a lot of fun, sir, but not intense enough to make us faint."

He grinned. "All right, I'm filing all this away for future reference. But back to our move. We're going to stay at a friend's château for a few days. I don't dare take you to any of my own properties, because it would be too easy for Ibrahim to find us. And I don't want to cross any more borders. That guy the other day was nice, but a lot of immigration people would have a fit. It'd also attract a lot of attention, and that's the last thing we want. I'm working on a more permanent solution, but I need to make sure that we'll both be safe. We have a saying, a chameleon doesn't leave his tree until he's sure of another one. It's very complicated. Have you ever been to Martinique, by the way?"

"No sir. Yerima's been there several times, though."

A small slap. "How many times do I have to tell you? His name comes up way too often. I want you to stop talking about him. I want you to stop thinking about him. You belong to me. That was a warning. Next time, it will be considerably more than that."

She was stunned. Careful, she reminded herself, he hasn't emancipated you yet. And she recalled, several years before, he warned her that if she disobeyed him he'd occasionally beat her as the Koran prescribed. "Yes sir. Sorry sir."

Taymoor escorted Tammy in a borrowed coat and long black wig straight to the *chambre du seigneur* of the château, not even allowing her to stop and exclaim over the exquisite period furnishings and paintings. He wasn't in a very good mood when he told her to strip and wait for him in bed. When he returned an hour or two later, he clearly had something up his sleeve. He kept laughing to himself in a secretive way, casting enigmatic smiles at her. His phone kept ringing, and he'd go out of earshot to take the calls. Several times she overheard something about Paris, but could never put it in context.

"I went to the toy store. Me! Look what I got us." He pulled out velvet-covered restraints, an embroidered leather blindfold, and a pair of falsies. "I want you to wear these all the time. You were away the day the angel issued womanly bosoms, weren't you, my sweet? Oh, you look fabulous. You're turning me into a maniac, my sweet. Me! I'm beginning to understand why Ibrahim is so obsessed with you. I just never, I mean, this isn't the image I thought, I mean, I never really thought of myself like this. But it's too much fun. Me! I never knew. I need to go back out again and I want you to stay right here and wait for me. Do you think you can find your way to the bathroom if I blindfold you?" She nodded. "All right. I'm not going to tie you down, because I don't want any accidents on a borrowed bed. But let me put this on you, and I also found some earplugs. They're amazing; you wouldn't hear a nuclear explosion. Are you comfort-able?" No reply. Oh, of course! He released one. "Are you comfortable?" She nodded. "How do you feel?"

"A little bit scared, sir."

"And?"

"Totally subdued, sir. I've never done this before. It feels like I've had a major sedative; I'm almost incapacitated."

"Good. Maybe I'll be gone fifteen minutes; maybe it'll be three hours. But when I come back, I want to see you exactly like this, legs wide open, just waiting for your master to return. Focus on all the fun we'll have when I get back."

"May I cover, sir? It's really cold."

"All right. It is a bit drafty in here, isn't it? When they built this place in 1724 they neglected to put in central heating. But I want to know that under those covers, my sweet *jaria* is ready to receive her master." He put the earplug back in.

The earplugs had a far more profound effect on her than she'd imagined; she felt completely cut off, completely isolated, completely at Taymoor's mercy. Almost imperceptibly, her female places decided that they were enjoying the experience.

She dozed off and awoke again. Oops, not in the required position. She lay there minute after minute, marveling at the transformation in Taymoor. He'd always been a kind and considerate lover, but he was turning into a tiger. She was far away, remembering their sweet encounters at The Office, when she felt something on the bed. In a flash, the tiger was upon her. She was ready. She wrapped herself around him, hungry, needy. He found his release, but caught his passion, built it back, and let her have her own. She lay there exhausted. Happy. And amazed.

A few minutes later he removed the blindfold and earplugs and lay his arm affectionately across her. "Committing grand theft is absolutely the best thing I ever did in my life," he said.

"You rescued me from a scary psychopath, sir."

"And all you did was get your sweet revenge on Dr. Hassan." They laughed.

They spent days playing with each other, trying out ideas in a book he'd bought. He got excited about almost every page, but there was virtually nothing in it that Tammy didn't already know.

"Sometimes I forget that you used to be a whore. They really trained you well, didn't they?"

Without thinking, she said, "No sir. Yerima could have written that book."

"All right, that does it. The second time in two days that you talked about him." He slapped her – hard. Her mouth fell open. *Taymoor?* "Get down on your knees over there by the pillar. No, with your back to it." He brought her hands behind it and the new restraints held them in place. "From here on, you will call me master. And every time I ring this little bell, I want you to say, 'I now belong only to my master Taymoor.' Understand?"

"Yes sir."

Another muscular slap.

"I mean, yes master. Sorry, master. Very sorry, master." She looked up at the stranger standing over her. He was starting to like this master stuff way, way too much. And to think that she'd encouraged him. She sighed.

"Are you comfortable?"

"No, master."

"Good. How do you feel?"

"Completely under your authority, master."

"Not my loving authority?"

"Not this time, master."

He smiled slightly, secretively, as he sat on the bed working on his laptop. Every few minutes he'd ring the bell. The first time, disapproving, he made her say it three times.

She grew more and more frustrated with her body, which was betraying her. As she knelt there, becoming increasingly nervous about the monster she felt responsible for creating, her longings for him became more and more insistent. After twenty minutes she was stewing; after thirty, squirming; after forty, panting.

Taymoor kept doing his email and, except for periodically ringing the bell, paid no attention to her whatsoever.

At fifty-one minutes, according to the ornate clock on the wall, he sighed, set the computer down, and pulled put something else: a paddle, one side covered with coarse grit, and the other, with small metal studs.

"Now for the rest of your correction. I want you to bend over this settee. This time, it will be twenty-five strokes. And I'm warning you, if I hear that man's name again, it will be fifty."

Tammy couldn't believe either her eyes or her ears. Twenty-five strokes? With *that?* He had to be out of his mind.

He untied her. "All right now, bend over."

"No sir," she said, shuddering. Never had anyone, not even Ibrahim, used something on her as horrible as that.

He came after her, furious. "Now it's thirty strokes."

"You're not going to use that thing on me, sir."

"And I told you already, you must call me master!"

The *chambre du seigneur* was huge, and for a few minutes she had no trouble dodging him. He was more and more enraged. "Now, damn it, you're getting thirty-five. You must do what I say! You disobeyed me, and now, believe me, I'm going to teach you a lesson." He finally cornered her, got her in a hammerlock, and thrust her angrily onto the bed. In a flash he was on her. Sobbing in fear, she fought for everything she was worth.

Taymoor was on fire, but she battled back. No way! Against her will, soon she was swept away in the maelstrom. At length, at long length, she surrendered, found his quickening rhythm, and together they soared into the blinding sun.

She was the first to regain consciousness. The blurry mass lying heavily but blissfully upon her gradually reconstituted itself into her master. He opened his eyes, looking completely lost. Then it hit him.

"Mush maa uul," he breathed, Holy Toledo. "It worked! It worked! Now my life is complete."

Tammy had had longer to recover, and had already rebooted her brain so that it was more or less functioning again. "Master, you are a low-down, good-for-nothing, devious, sneaky devil," she said.

He howled with delight. "You should've seen the look on your face. You were so pissed, and so scared. But it worked, even better than I'd hoped." He went off into more gales of laughter.

"I never knew you could be so underhanded, master."

"Just my little twist on the game. I'm not used to being aggressive. So I thought it would be fun if I could make you really resist me. Not pretend to, but really, genuinely resist me. It worked! And I'm sorry that I slapped you, but I had to make you believe I'd use that paddle."

She reminded him how sneaky he was when she sat at his feet to give him a pedicure. She said it again when she scrubbed his back, and when she fed him *poireaux gratinés,* and when she tied his shoes. Each time, he threw back his head and roared. He was proud that they'd both passed out. He was proud that he'd completely fooled her. And he was proud of being a newly minted very sexy man.

But she couldn't help but notice: now he'd stopped talking entirely about emancipating her.

Every few days, they'd move. Lots of people owed him big favors, so he had no trouble borrowing villas or *châteaux* or limos to keep Ibrahim's henchmen guessing.

"Just being extra careful," he said. "Walk a month, but don't jump." She knitted her brow, confused. "It just means, don't take any unnecessary risks."

One afternoon, Taymoor barked at her. "Tamara Lynne, stop thrashing around! You're driving me nuts. Plus, I notice that you are ignoring my orders about the position you should assume. No chocolate truffle for you tonight. And if you keep disobeying me, I'm going to get one of those spreader bars I saw at the toy store so you'll be obliged to keep your legs the way I want them. The lady there said that they can be very uncomfortable."

"Very sorry, master. No truffle? You are a cruel and heartless master indeed." She sighed again. "Yes, I'm familiar with about a dozen different kinds, and some of them are horrible. Master, please, master, I'd really appreciate having something to do."

He smiled. "You are doing exactly what Allah created you to do, and doing exactly what your master wants. There is no reason for me to give you anything else to do." She sighed. "I heard that. You know, my sweet, some masters would have you flogged for exhibiting reluctance." He glanced at the clock. "Actually, it's time to pray. Do your ablutions, cover yourself properly, and report back to me."

She washed as prescribed, put on her dress, and covered her head with a *shershif*. She hadn't told him that she'd gone back to being a Christian, and it made him happy to see her doing the *salat*, so she went along with it. She stood next to him, but a couple of feet back, first, to show respect, and second, as he put it, so he wouldn't think "unprayerful thoughts" when he saw her bending over during the prayer routine. Then, as usual, off with the dress, and back into bed.

It had been nearly four weeks, and the fun of letting Taymoor play lord and master had entirely worn off. Now, more than anything, she was colossally bored. Could she help him with his paperwork? No thank you, and besides, she might stumble across something that would ruin the surprise. Could she please read the paper or watch the news? There was no need to. She was busy bathing him and feeding him for about an hour a day, and they'd make love for an hour or two, but the rest of the time, she had nothing to do but lie in bed hour after hour staring at four walls. The good part about moving every few days was that the four walls changed; today, they were champagne and gold, the other day, ultra-modern red leather and black silk, and before that, pale blue and ivory.

She loved Taymoor, she truly did, and she was extremely grateful that he had rescued her. Yerima had cautioned her that she'd fallen in love with him mostly because he had been nice to her in a place where kindness was in very short supply, and that if she married him, she'd be nothing more than his blonde-haired pet. He'd warned her that, as nice as he was, Taymoor saw women strictly as servants to men and would do nothing to stimulate her intellectual growth. How she missed Yerima, with their intense discussions on world affairs, the shared excitement of discovering a wonderful book, the thrill of –

"Tamara Lynne!"

"Bis-khidma, ya agati?" How may I serve you, master? She tried her best to sound upbeat.

"I have told you repeatedly to stop thinking about him." Without meaning to, she sighed yet again. "Did you hear me?"

"Yes, master."

"Will you obey me?"

"I'm trying, master."

"Try harder."

She wasn't allowed to change position, but she turned her face away, hoping he wouldn't see the tears that were welling in her eyes.

He stared at her for a long time. He sighed sadly, and at length went into another room to make a phone call. "For two reasons, I've decided on a change of plan," she heard before he went completely out of earshot.

A few days later, she asked if she could throw the damned paddle away, but he said, "Why? Maybe I'll hang it on the bedroom wall. Just to remind you that I own you, and if you don't behave, well, it'll be right there handy."

"You are a sneaky devil indeed, master."

"You are going to be so surprised," he said. "This is the most fun I've had since I decided to build that secret passage. Tamara Lynne, I've never had a vacation like this in my life. It has been the happiest I've ever, ever been."

"It makes me very happy to hear that, dear master."

"You are going to be so surprised."

She sighed. It could be worse: at least she'd belong to a man who'd just promoted himself to a ten.

Prince Ibrahim felt invigorated after his rice-and-sand massage. It sounded strange, but felt so good he had it every time he was in Tahiti. Smelling faintly of coconut oil, he climbed into the back seat of the four-wheel drive. "Arava, we're going to Tautira. How long will it take?"

"About twenty, thirty minutes, Your Highness. Spectacularly beautiful drive, and not far, but dangerous. Really rugged terrain, you know. High cliffs, deep ravines, sharp turns. The limo would've been a big problem."

"Everything in Tahiti is spectacularly beautiful, especially the girls."

A new broker, Temana Boisvert, said he had eight of the most beautiful girls on the island eager to meet him. Ibrahim gave him a call. "We're on our way, Temana. Exactly where is your house again? Here, explain it to my driver." When Arava gave him back his phone, he grinned. "Did you understand?"

"Yes, Your Highness. I know the place. It's a beautiful little house, right outside town. Tautira is a small place, Your Highness, only a couple of paved streets. Not hard to find your way around."

Ibrahim settled back and started getting caught up on phone calls. A pharmaceutical firm in Japan had approached him about a reliable and less costly supply of manganese ascorbate, so he placed a call to Johannesburg. Then to Macapa. Progress. Plus, both his English and his rusty Portuguese were getting workouts.

Time to check on another front. "Habib? Update?" He listened for about thirty seconds before he blew up. "You now have twelve days left. Twelve days, you hear me? I want both of those two-faced snotballs hauled before me in cages. Don't you dare tell me that. Your job is to find him and bring him to me. I don't care if he's gone to the moon, you find him! This wasn't just a capricious act; it was carefully thought out and fiendishly executed.

"Yes, he stole her, but she was under no obligation to go with him. I want to give serious thought to how they're going to pay for this, and keeping them in cages until I decide will keep them in a properly penitent state of mind. Twelve more days, or you'll regret it." Another call. "Nigel? Keep an eye on Habib. One excuse after another why he can't find that *maakira* (scheming) architect and Mukhmala. He may try to fly the coop. What? Yes, on my way to Tautira to check out some pretty volunteers. Talk to you later."

Arava tried to ignore the ugly threats he'd overheard and struggled to maintain control as they mounted a steep rutted road. They jounced. They jostled. They lurched. At one point the vehicle even slid a few meters back downhill on the road, slickened from a morning rain. He tried a different approach, and this time, made it up the grade.

Ibrahim held on for dear life. "I think I'm going to lose my lunch."

A moment's pause. "Uh, me too, Your Highness."

They laughed heartily.

"Almost there, Your Highness, almost there."

Finally, they pulled up next to a modest white bungalow almost buried in bougainvillea blossoms. A strikingly handsome forty-something man in a red hibiscus-print shirt came racing down the stairs. "*Manava! Manava!* Welcome, welcome. Your Highness, I'm Temana, so nice to meet you, Your Highness. And it's such an honor, such an honor, for you to come all the way out here. You know, opportunities are so limited, and the girls became very excited when I told them about you."

"Eight of them, you say? I'm very *nayiq,* very fussy, you know." Even if just two or three of them were acceptable, the excursion would be worthwhile. Usually, due to security considerations, he insisted that girls be brought to him. Plus, of course, it was more befitting his rank. This trip hadn't been very successful, though, so he was bending the rules. And in any case, volunteers were a whole different story. He'd sell them on living in luxurious estates, excellent food and medical care, a glamorous lifestyle surrounded by handsome princes like himself (heh heh) and oil tycoons. It almost always worked.

"I think you'll like what you see. Come right this way, Your Highness. May I have the honor of serving you a cool drink, Your Highness? My wife makes amazing hibiscus lemonade."

"No thank you, maybe later. I'm eager to see these girls."

They went through the living room, ceiling fan whirring, a macaw repeating, *Manava, manava!* Of course, even the parrot spoke Tahitian. He chuckled. A broadly smiling Temana opened another door and ushered him in.

Ibrahim froze.

Instead of eight pretty girls, there were eight young men.

Arab men.

Two of them, with guns. Pointed at him.

They stared at each other in mutual disbelief for a long moment.

"We're sons of the pilot," two said.

"The pool contractor," said two others.

"The physics professor," said three.

"The oil executive," said the last one.

It was Temana's turn. "You had my daughters kidnapped, both the sixteen-year-old and the fourteen-year-old. I've been waiting for this moment for nineteen long months."

"We just want to get this over with," said Talal. We promised Temana we wouldn't mess up his house."

"We can negotiate. We can talk. Surely there's something you fine young men–"

"No," they said with finality. "We wish we could do to you what you did to our fathers, but fortunately for you, we're not monsters."

They slipped handcuffs on him, took his telephone, frisked him to make sure he didn't have a second one, and bundled a white-faced Ibrahim unceremoniously out the door.

Taymoor had told her again and again that it was going to be a huge surprise. Nevertheless, Tammy was dumbfounded when he blindfolded her, plugged her ears, made sure the falsies were in place, and gave her a strong sedative that put her completely under. She strongly suspected that all this was a ploy to make her think he was taking her to Martinique, whereas he was actually going to keep her in the house he'd built for her several years before. She smiled to herself. What a dear, dear man. His love for her was so touching, so pure, so selfless. She'd pretend to be really surprised; he deserved nothing less. And actually, she would be. She'd never seen the house. He'd shown her pictures of it, but it'd been several years, so it really would be a big surprise.

When he removed her earplugs, she heard unmistakable thunder and the drum of heavy rain. She was now thoroughly, thoroughly confused. What? Martinique? Well...

"All right, my sweet, come along. Hold this gentleman's arm. We'll have your blindfold off in just a few moments."

What the assembly saw emerge through the door was a man in traditional Arab garb and a large-breasted woman, several paces behind, covered from head to toe in black.

"All right. Stand right there."

Taymoor took a microphone and addressed the assembly in French. French? Things were getting stranger and stranger. How could he keep her in Martinique when he lived half a world away? Unless he'd decided to move as far away from Ibrahim as possible, but even so, he'd track them down and destroy them. And Martinique was alarmingly close to Aruba... Nothing was making sense. Nothing.

"Ladies and gentlemen, thank you for coming today. My name is Taymoor, and I'm an architect. I understand that a member of your own household had once been a victim of human trafficking, so I thought perhaps you would enjoy helping to celebrate an emancipation. This girl once belonged to a very strange

314

and troubled master, but I fell in love with her and stole her for my very own. Now I wish to emancipate her, and want all of you to share in this joyful moment."

Murmurs. A few chuckles.

"Kneel." She was guided into place. *"Quand tu te mets à pied, tu ne seras plus une esclave, tu ne seras plus mon esclave, tu seras une femme complètement affranchie et libre.* When you rise to your feet, you will no longer be a slave, you will no longer be my slave, you will be a fully emancipated and free woman." He let this sink in. "All right, my sweet, rise."

She stood. Applause, even a few cheers.

"Let me continue," said Taymoor. "Please remove your gloves." Gasps rippled through the crowd as the diamond bracelet was revealed. "Now, you may remove your *abaaya.*" The black cloak came off and they saw a heavily veiled woman in a black *fustaan.* "Take off your veil." Her hair was wrapped in black cloth, she was still blindfolded, and the *burqah* was still in place.

"Let me have the honor, my sweet, of removing your blindfold."

"Néné Sudari!" screamed Cathy, racing across the floor.

Tammy's eyes locked with a tall man in a white damask gandoura. Tranfixed, she took a step toward him.

Taymoor was weeping openly now. "Tamara Lynne, my sweet, my very sweet Tamara Lynne, may I have the honor of escorting you to your husband?"

He took her arm, but before they'd taken three steps, she was enveloped in clouds of white damask and spun

315

around and around. Taymoor laughed, and continued lamely, "Your wife, dear sir. And your husband, dear lady."

"Néné Sudari, why are you wearing that funny thing on your face?" Cathy wanted to know. "And why did you go away? And I have a new baby sister. She cries all the time, and I told my mommy it was because you went away. And Abi didn't know if you were ever coming back. And – and – Bintou pulled Cleo's tail and Cleo scratched her. Bad. And I fell down and hurt my knee, see? And–"

A big hug. "Sweetie, I'll tell you everything, but not right this minute, okay? I'm so happy to see you!"

The applause and cheers would not stop.

Yerima finally took the microphone. "I'm rarely speechless, as most of you know," he began, "but I'm so moved by this incredible act of generosity that I honestly don't know how to begin to thank you, Mr. Taymoor. Sudari always told me what a nice person you were, but nice doesn't begin to describe the selfless love that you have demonstrated here today." He clasped Taymoor and they shared a long and heartfelt embrace.

"I have one more ceremony I would like to perform, if that's all right?" Taymoor shifted his weight, and nearly fell over.

"All you all right, sir?" Dixon asked. "Would you like to sit down?"

"No, but perhaps you could lend me a cane?"

Yerima whispered to Kadry, who returned moments later with a red-and-black beaded cane – the handle, the head of an elephant, and the shaft, the elephant's trunk.

"Stunning! May I proceed?"

"Certainly. And the cane is yours to keep."

"I brought tools to be able to remove the vestiges of servitude that she is wearing. Would you like to do the honors, Excellency?"

"All done!" said Yerima. He held out his hand. "May I present to you, ladies and gentlemen, Madame Sudari Abdoulaye."

Tammy bowed, to wild applause. Yerima handed her the microphone. "Taymoor, you are the kindest, most generous person I have ever met and I consider it a high honor to call you my dear friend. But you're also extremely sneaky. You had me thinking that you were taking me to the house that you had built for me, but instead you brought me here. No words can describe the despair that I felt when I found myself once again as the possession of such an unbalanced and controlling master. And no words today can describe the gratitude and love I feel for you. Thank you, dear Taymoor."

"What the hell?" a thoroughly confused Yerima asked Taymoor, who was grinning from ear to ear.

"I'll explain everything tomorrow. Now, from what I understand, we're going to have a party." Taymoor gave a high-five to Chef Emmanuel, and within minutes, the room was filled with food, champagne, and high-energy dancing.

"You knew about this?" Yerima asked the chef. "All these preparations right under my nose and I didn't suspect a thing?"

He grinned. "So did Dixon and Marie-Claire. We've been planning this for more than two weeks. But oh my, Madame Aïssatou was starting to ask some really bothersome questions."

"You devious, underhanded, wonderful people! Bonuses for all of you."

Amsi grabbed the mike and to the tune of "Hello Dolly," started singing, to appreciative laughter, "Hello Dari, well hello Dari, it's so nice to have you back where you belong…"

Next day, over a heavenly concoction of chicken, vegetables, and plantains called *poulet DG,* Taymoor was finally prevailed upon to elaborate. "There were two reasons I knew I had to act. One, as I already told Tamara Lynne, is that Ibrahim was planning to have the sole of her foot hot-iron branded because he discovered that she was receiving coded messages." Yerima blanched, and Taymoor paused. "The second is far more important, but first, I thought you'd find this news article of interest." He pulled a folded paper from his pocket.

> *Sahib sumuw il-malaki,* His Royal Highness Prince Fulaan Ibrahim bin Abdullah bin Saud, 50, tragically fell to his death Tuesday afternoon during a sightseeing excursion in Tahiti. Temana Boisvert, chief of police of Tautira, the closest town, said that the crevice into which His Highness fell was so deep, and so inaccessible, that it took rescuers more than sixteen hours to reach him, and the prince could

not be revived. "His Highness loved Tahiti, came here often, and we are all saddened by his untimely passing." The death has been ruled accidental.

His Highness, one of the most prominent metals traders in the world, leaves a grieving widow and two grown sons. He was known for his generous gifts to charities helping widows and orphans, as well as his opulent lifestyle. May peace and blessing be upon him.

Tammy burst into tears. "It's really true, isn't it? I loved him, I hated him, I was scared to death of him. But he was such a big part of my life, and now he's gone. Oh, Yerima."

He held her close. "You don't have to worry about him any longer, babe."

"Taymoor...?"

"No, my sweet, as it turns out, I didn't need to. Sons of men he'd destroyed took care of that."

"I think I just understood something," said Yerima. "He wasn't really going to hot-iron brand you; I bet that was just his version of Taymoor's ugly paddle."

They laughed.

"Well, in any case, I made sure that the branding iron was well hidden under a stack of towels in a rarely used part of the sports center. They'll find it in a year or two."

Tammy decided she could finally ask what she'd been worried about. "Taymoor, my dear friend, how is your health?"

He shrugged. "I'm seeing doctors and they're giving me pills. Expensive pills. But I'm still getting headaches. I'm going to see a different specialist when I get back." Tammy and Yerima exchanged glances; they both sensed that he'd left something unsaid. He cleared his throat. "Now for the second reason. I had originally planned to keep you with me in a condo in Paris, which I bought under a German friend's name. When I wear a suit, I can be quite convincingly German, you know." He pointed to his light brown hair and grinned. "My grandmother was Scottish, by the way.

"Anyhow, very good security in the building, but neither you nor I would have been able to set foot outside without running serious risks. At least, ahem, before the accidental fall. The build-out was about three-quarters done. I was planning to work from there; these days, with the Internet, it really doesn't matter where you're physically located. And I have an Egyptian friend who could be my twin, and he was going to lend me his passport so I could come and go with no trace of my name on official records. Everything was going along just fine.

"I have just spent the five happiest weeks of my life with you. I tried my best, but my sweet Tamara Lynne, I never really owned you. And you were such a good sport, trying your best to belong to me, but you didn't succeed either. In spite of your own good intentions and in spite of orders from your wicked master, you kept thinking about this man, kept talking about him." He smiled fondly and shook his head. "Several times I caught you weeping, and it just broke my heart, so I had to change my plans. There's another minor reason, too, that you will understand in due course. Abdoulaye, my friend, you don't own this woman, and you never will.

But there's only one place on earth where she belongs, and it's by your side."

Four days later, when they accompanied Taymoor to the foot of the stairs of the jet, umbrellas practically useless against the wind-swept rain, Tammy gave Taymoor a huge hug. "Dear, dear Taymoor, I can't begin to thank you for everything – rescuing me, restoring me to my husband, the nice check. Your life has been filled with acts of kindness – unbelievable kindness – and you just keep piling on more."

"You have made my life complete, and made me a very happy man. Abdoulaye, take good care of my sweet Tamara Lynne. And Tamara Lynne, take good care of your husband. May God keep you from all harm."

They embraced, and Tammy and Yerima stood arm in arm until the plane thundered into the sky. "It's been a wild ride," said Yerima. "I was afraid that you were gone forever, but here you are, safely back in my arms."

"And this time, believe me, my love, my hero, my darling, I'm not going *anywhere.*"

EPILOGUE

Tammy and Yerima used some of the money that Taymoor had given her, as well as part of the proceeds from sale of the *burqah* and bracelets, to take their long-delayed honeymoon. They spent a week in Washington, where Tammy delightedly showed him her favorite haunts – and where she wept bitterly at the place her inconsolable mother had been buried two months earlier. The remainder of the money went into a trust fund for all of the children.

They spent three days in Colorado with Heineken and Angie and their crazy menagerie, two days in Aubagne with Pierre and Clotilde, and several days laughing non-stop in Hamburg with Yerima's nutty brother Tidjani and his German wife Katrijn. They went to Switzerland to present their condolences in person to a grieving Sheikh Farook at the family chalet in Gstaad. They bought a new set of wedding rings in Antwerp. They had an emotional dinner with Marisa's parents in Mälmo, and stopped in Bergen and had a laughter-filled lunch with Toril. In Tahiti, Temana showed them to the place where Ibrahim died.

And they finally made a long-overdue visit to a certain horse ranch in northern Cameroon. Yerima also took her to the fascinating Kapsiki rocks – petrified volcanic cores that now project like towering pillars from the earth. At last she met the *lamido* Daoudou, and they saw elephants and lions and giraffes in the wild in the Waza Game Preserve. "Now I feel like I'm officially in Africa," she said.

Tammy got special permission from the dean to take her first-year exams way off-schedule, and was ranked second in her class, right after her erstwhile antagonist, Ebai Tataw. "By far the most original excuse for missing finals anybody's come up with yet," the dean observed with a huge grin. The task force gave her a standing ovation to welcome her back, and once again, she has a steady stream of speaking engagements.

The foundation is finally up and running. The first project is to build a safe house/boarding school for girls in the heavily Muslim North, where the need is most acute. Several conservative imams loudly denounced the school as un-Islamic, and for several months, the project was in serious jeopardy. Fortunately, Yerima knew exactly which strings to pull, and convinced his brother the *lamido* to come out in strong support. This was amazing, since traditional rulers usually preserve tradition regardless, and are rarely on the cutting edge of social change. Soon after, several others followed suit, and the imams fell silent. Construction is now underway, and Amsi is helping her line up teachers and counselors. "I told you he could charm a starving crocodile," Amsi said to Tammy. "And Daoudou, believe me, is a starving crocodile. Highly, highly traditional. Don't ask me how Yerima pulled that one off, but he did."

Tammy has bought her own car and hired her own driver. With this major bone of contention off the table, she and JoAnn have been able to establish a polite, if not terribly warm, relationship.

Sheikh Saud broke the sad news to them that four months and two days after Taymoor left Yaounde, he died peacefully in his sleep from a massive brain tumor. "If there's ever anybody who'll go straight to heaven, it'll be that dear man," she said, burying her face in Yerima's chest.

"So that's why he brought you here," he said. "He knew. He knew. That's why there was a change of plan. It was no less kind of him, however. At this point, I don't care what the reason was. I'm just so thrilled to have my brave and beautiful Sudari back."

Antoine was handily reelected, and Yerima is now Deputy Prime Minister, which, to everyone's surprise, translates into a marginally less demanding schedule. But the happiest news of all is that Tammy is six months pregnant with a little boy they will name Saoudou, in honor of their dear friend Sheikh Saud. After a scare early on, the pregnancy is progressing normally.

"I'm so grateful to be back with my husband," Tammy says, patting her swelling stomach fondly, tears of joy welling in her eyes. "At long last I'm going to be a mother, and I'm so happy to be able to give Yerima a son.

"I thought I appreciated my freedom first time I was rescued, but now, every single day is unbelievably precious. There are times when frustrations accumulate, but I thank God for them, because they mean that I'm living in the real world, where good people can get brain tumors, necrophiliacs can make tons of money, and life is far from fair. But give me such problems any day of the week, rather than the suffocating, stultifying life of a harem."

Many of Prince Ibrahim's girls wept when they heard the news. Some cheered. Most simply shrugged.

Sheikha al-Jauhara threw the biggest and most lavish party she'd ever thrown; people gushed about it for weeks. Prince Daood, Ibrahim's favorite cousin, broke down in tears, as did Sheikh Saud, Ibrahim's lifelong friend.

Princess Mirsada, Ibrahim's widow, knew that tragedy would befall him. "I warned him from day one that that American slave was bad news," she told her elder son, Prince Saud. "That fall was no accident, and one way or another, she was behind it. The very first day I found out about her, I had the overwhelming feeling that she would be nothing but trouble. But would he listen to me? Of course not. And look where it got him. Did that man ever listen to anybody? And just look at the result."

It took more than three weeks to sell off the contents of Prince Ibrahim's *hareem*. Prince Daood bought the Rainbow, the only one to be sold intact. No one else had the same vision – or the same budget – as Prince Ibrahim himself, so the girls were sold piecemeal. The two in Arrivederci Ragazza were spared and sold at a discount, and Rafiki went to a private collector.

The fountain in Il Giardino Posteriore is silent now, and the courtyard is empty. Ivy has taken over the harem walls, and cobwebs are appearing under the carved settees in the salon. It hasn't occurred to anyone to empty the stale tea in the samovar, and it's covered with mold. The garden is overgrown, scorpions are everywhere, and the refectory is filled only with echoes. Mournful wailings are sometimes heard from a fig tree, and on moonlit nights, ghostly figures have been seen clustered around the fountain.

The splashing water has been turned off in Il Giardino delle Cascate. The parrots and swans have disappeared – nobody's sure what happened to them – and the tropical plants are starting to turn brown.

Sometimes the curtains in the elevated glass-walled bedchamber move all by themselves, and they say that it can be none other than Prince Ibrahim, searching, still searching, for his beloved Mukhmala.

Printed in Great Britain
by Amazon